D1360298

THE SAME MOON

The Same Moon

A Memoir

Sarah Coomber

A Camphor Press book

Published by Camphor Press Ltd
83 Ducie Street, Manchester, M1 2JQ
United Kingdom

www.camphorpress.com

Cover art by Andria Villanueva.

ISBN   978-1-78869-205-2 (paperback)
         978-1-78869-206-9 (hardcover)

The moral right of the author has been asserted.

Set in 11 pt Linux Libertine

The Same Moon is a work of nonfiction. To protect the privacy of others, certain names and attributes have been changed. The author is grateful to the editors of the following journals and newspapers for publishing, mostly in different form, pieces of this book: the *Christian Science Monitor, Memoir Journal, Cha: An Asian Literary Journal,* the *Japan Times,* the *Star Tribune, The Font: A Literary Journal for Language Teachers, The Light: An Alumni Publication of Youth for Understanding,* and the *Minnesota Daily.*

On Truth and Memory

THE story I tell in *The Same Moon* is as close to true as I can write it, given the limitations of my memory, perceptions, and ability.

I have been writing this story since I first visited Japan at age sixteen, when I recorded many of my experiences in a journal. I continued to journal when I returned for a visit at age twenty-one, during the two years I spent teaching there in my mid-twenties, and on subsequent visits.

I used those journal entries as the basis of two graduate school projects — one a series of essays that was part of my master's degree in mass communication/print journalism at the University of Minnesota and one a lengthier work for my master of fine arts/nonfiction degree at Eastern Washington University.

Along the way, essays emerged, some of which have been published in the *Christian Science Monitor*, the *Japan Times*, the *Star Tribune*, *Cha: An Asian Literary Journal*, *Memoir Journal*, the *Font: A Literary Journal for Language Teachers*, and the *Light: An Alumni Publication of Youth For Understanding*.

I recognize that memories are essentially snapshots of an experience, and that every time we return to an old memory, it's like taking a snapshot of a snapshot. They get blurrier and blurrier as we remember memories of a memory. While I might focus on one area of the image and stop noticing the bigger picture, another person in the snapshot might see it quite differently, having looked at it fewer times or focused on other parts of the picture. Other people might have lost these snapshots altogether.

So let me be clear: *The Same Moon* is my story, and I take full responsibility for any errors, misperceptions, or faulty memories that have influenced it. I also accept responsibility for the decisions that led to these events taking place — the bad and the good.

Because it is my story — and not necessarily the story of others who appear in it — I have changed the names and identifying attributes of a couple of the people who walked this journey with me. Those changes have not altered the story itself or the truths it contains.

To my husband, Jon Suomala, and son, Daniel, who have given me the time, space, and encouragement to tell this part of my story; to my parents, Jim and Eleanor Coomber, and Brother Matthew, for introducing me to the arts of writing, diplomacy, and compassion; and to the Maedas — Koichi, Ryoko, Chieko (Otōsan, Okāsan, and Obāchan), Miho, and Yukie — who welcomed me like a third daughter into their family: I love and thank you all.

To the good people of Shuho-cho, who gave me refuge, tolerated my moxie, and challenged me to see just about everything in a new way, I offer my deep gratitude.

When I look up into the night sky and see the shining moon, it comforts me to know that all of these people I hold dear enjoy its same soft glow.

Contents

THE SAME MOON

1

Moonstruck

RYOTA gave me the moon the summer I turned seventeen.

I had just repacked my suitcases when I heard his voice in the entryway of the home where I had spent the previous two months. I hurried downstairs, my host family gathered, and we all shed our slippers, stepped into our shoes, and meandered through a labyrinth of stone-and-plaster-walled streets to the neighborhood *udon* shop. There we shared our last supper together, slurping long fat noodles out of steaming bowls of broth, Ryota and my family visiting in their vexing language, I struggling not to weep for missing all of them already, imagining myself running away, disappearing for a few days so my flight would leave without me and I could remain in their quiet city by the Sea of Japan.

Later, ambling home, Ryota and I lagged behind my family. He reached for my hand and held it. This was our second time. The other, captured weeks earlier in a photo taken by my same-age host sister, Miho, had occurred before Ryota's baseball practice. In it, he wears his crisp white uniform and I am in a blue T-shirt and blue-and-white-print skirt, what the high school principal allowed me to wear in lieu of the traditional sailor-style school uniform they would have had to special order to fit my five-foot, seven-inch frame. Ryota's left hand linked with my right, we flashed shy grins and made Vs — peace signs — with our free fingers, I wondering by what miracle I was clasping the hand of the most beautiful boy at Hagi High School. The last time I had held hands had been two years earlier in the back of a bus rolling across the dark North Dakota prairie.

I had been something of a dateless wonder at my little Lutheran high school, the sum of my own carefully cultivated reputation plus a gender-skewed grade — sixteen boys to twenty-nine girls. A budding perfectionist, I gunned for honors — valedictorian, piano performance awards, scholarships, and any other prize that would prove my academic and musical prowess. I also sought out volunteer opportunities to demonstrate my very goodness — Sunday school teacher, hotline answerer for latchkey children, Key Club president. I looked askance at the class clowns, those I saw as wasting valuable time. By the time I realized there was more to life than an impressive college entrance application, anyone I might have wanted to date was already enmeshed with a girlfriend. And those girls would not have released their prom escorts without a fight.

Arriving in Japan, I recognized that aiming for any type of perfection would be foolish, as I had to all but start over in the life-skills department, learning how to eat with chopsticks, how to use an Asian toilet, and how to manage a new language. Suddenly I had no reputation, no tests to take, and no piano to practice, but I did have lots of time on my hands.

And sheen. As the first international exchange student at Hagi High School, everyone knew me immediately. One of few foreigners who visited or had even heard of the little city of Hagi in those pre-Internet days, I was an object of curiosity: my blue eyes, my brown hair, my fair skin, my height (at five foot seven, I was taller than nearly all of the girls), my ability to drive a car back home, my cultural connection to American music and movies. It did not matter that I was less well versed in American pop culture than most American teenage girls, not to mention the pop-culture-savvy Miho, who was a cheerleader and fashion aficionado, because in Hagi I *embodied* American pop culture, triggering memories of Hollywood teen movies. When I went to the beach and met younger schoolgirls, they told me I was sexy in my swimsuit. With my modest chest and sturdy legs, I knew this was sexiness by association.

By some miracle, though, I was, for the second time, holding the hand of the handsome baseball player who had decided to spend the evening with me. And he was in no apparent rush to go home. Ryota and I lingered in the dark shadows of centuries-old stone walls in my adopted neighborhood as my host family walked ahead and disappeared around the corner. High above us, stars glistened in crystal constellations, like mobiles stilled by the falling summer night.

"*Mite — Hokuto Shichisei,*" he pointed to the sky.

"The Big Dipper? I see it," I replied, scanning for another formation, something, anything, that would prolong the delicious moment that had my heart spinning in my chest, but my knowledge of the stars was scant.

Then Ryota pointed at the slim crescent glowing above us. "*The moon,*" he said, alternating between Japanese and English. "*It is the same, here and in America. We can think of one another when it shines down on us, you in America, me in Japan.*"

It was the most romantic thing I had ever heard, on the big screen or off. I nodded yes, I would think of him every time I saw the moon. Untouchable though it was, it was the perfect souvenir of this moment, this boy, this summer on the other side of the world, of this place where I had learned that I was more than a studying and practicing machine, where I had learned that people could accept me even if I wasn't perfect. It was a place I found myself feeling almost more at home than I did ... at home.

Our evening did not end with a kiss — but so what? I had not yet been kissed by any boy, and I had heard a rumor that kissing was not such a big deal in Japan. Besides, he had held my hand and given me the moon. It was enough.

* * *

Ryota's moon followed me for years, trailing me through my senior year of high school, off to college, onto a study abroad program in India, through graduation, back to my parents' house, and into my marriage. Six years after Ryota gave me the moon, I was a graduate student in a journalism program that proved far more theory-heavy — OK, duller — than I had expected and was living in St. Paul, Minnesota, with my new husband, who, like me, had grown up on the northern Great Plains. Having dropped out of college, he was working nights and weekends at a restaurant, and whenever he found a couple of free days, he scheduled multi-day Dungeons & Dragons game-a-thons with his buddies. I attended one or two, playing the part of supportive young wife, getting to know my spouse's friends and hobbies, but inevitably I would last only an hour or two before the grisly techniques they conjured for injuring and killing one another's characters would disgust me, and I would beg off, hoping my husband would feel similarly and join me so we could do something more interesting, like going home to our old one-bedroom apartment, or heading out cross-country skiing, or to a movie or grocery shopping. *Anything* else.

But it seemed he always chose them, or his video game-playing best friend who had moved in downstairs from us. Or his work buddies, guys and girls, their late-night shifts bleeding ever later into what he told me were ice cream runs and poker games, while I lay awake in our bed waiting to hear the sound of our car rolling to a stop in the parking lot beneath our bedroom window.

I came to resent the time he spent with work colleagues and gaming friends over time with me, gaming over family visits, multiple-day game-a-thons after which he returned home to me exhausted and sick. This was not the rosy-cheeked, *plein-air* couplehood of hiking, camping, skiing, and travel I had envisioned. Before we married, every future had seemed possible, including my dream to return to Japan, to live there long enough to experience all four seasons. I had imagined myself teaching and traveling with my husband, who surely would learn to love that country and culture as much as I did. After we married though, when I brought up Japan, he had one question: "What would I do there?" I was unable to give him a satisfactory answer.

A few months post-wedding, I dug out a special photograph. In it, my mother and I and a Japanese family stood before a vermilion shrine festooned with banners of purple and white. Shot on New Year's Day three years earlier, the image exuded a feeling of carefree travels abroad.

Ostensibly.

But I had not chosen that photograph so I could gaze at my mother or my host family. I had placed it on the bookshelf in the corner of the dusty, white-walled living room I shared with my husband because in it, smiling next to me, stood handsome Ryota.

* * *

When I left for Japan for that summer after my junior year of high school, I had not expected it to become anything more than the place I spent a high school summer, a geographical fling. But the sense of wholeness I encountered there as I shed my customary competencies was something I craved more of. I would never have described it this way then, but my time there was a chance to reenter a childlike state, being led around by Miho and her younger sister, Yukie, being cared for by their accepting parents and grandmother, and having little responsibility but to go along with the family's schedule. It was a beautiful break. Even my name, altered by the pronunciation of my hosts and new friends, contributed to my sense of newness: I was *Sah-lah*.

When I returned to the bustle of senior year — preparing for a solo piano recital, and applying to colleges and scholarship programs — the only way I could tap back into that feeling was by writing letters. I started copying characters from my Japanese–English dictionary into stilted notes, Japanese words forced into English grammatical structures, in which I tried to convey to my schoolgirl friends, to my host family, and, yes, for a while, to Ryota, that I would never forget them. And they wrote back the same.

Over the next couple of years, emissaries from that world appeared in mine, Miho visiting my home in Minnesota twice that next year while spending her senior year of high school in Nebraska, and a girl from her neighborhood arriving to spend spring break with me during my freshman year at college.

I tried to tap into Japan in other ways too, taking courses in Japanese language, and Asian art and literature, and by working with other Japanophiles and native speakers at a summer camp in Minnesota, where I learned more about Japan than I taught.

But none of it could recreate the feeling of being there. As I prepared to embark on a biology program in India for the fall semester of my senior year of college, almost passing Japan en route, it seemed silly not to change my return ticket to include a stop there. More confident in the Japanese language by then, I anticipated having real conversations with my host family, especially my host parents and grandmother, who spoke little or no English. My mother would meet me in Hagi for the second half of my stay, for New Year's, her first trip abroad in thirty years, a surprise gift from my father. I could hardly wait to introduce her to my other family, my other world. I had no plans to see Ryota. We had been out of touch for years.

Everything went according to plan. After four months in India, I arrived in Hagi and found that unlike during my seventeenth summer, when I had understood only the outlines of Japanese behaviors and customs, when my lack of language had forced me to fit much of what I encountered into pre-existing boxes in my mind, this time, at age twenty-one, the language and gestures that swirled about me made some sense. It was as if on my first visit I had experienced Japan in black-and-white — this I understand, that I do not — my memories metaphorically resembling early woodblock prints, people and places recorded in black ink on white paper. On this, my second visit, I was able to add hints of color to old memories and new encounters. I spent less time observing Japan through my peripheral vision, trying to figure out how to be, than looking at it head-on, figuring out what to do. And I loved what I saw and heard: my host family was as delightful as they had been when most of our communication had depended on charades, and I stepped right back into my role of ingénue explorer. Life is easy when people don't expect very much from you.

One night not long after settling back into their home, I awoke with a start. I had dreamed of an encounter with Ryota. He and I were sitting, talking, and he slowly put his arm around my shoulders, pulling me close. *How strange*, I thought.

The next day, at my host parents' suggestion, I made a courtesy call to the high school I had attended during my summer exchange. In the teachers' room, after the initial pleasantries, the teachers changed topics. "*Will you be seeing Ishida-kun?*" they asked, using Ryota's family name. I was surprised and a little embarrassed that they even knew of our brief high school relationship, but of course we had met at the school, where I had been escorted to dozens of English classes, the teachers requiring each student to ask me a question in English.

I had met hundreds of students in all, many of whom were paralyzed at the thought of speaking English to a foreigner, while others were disconcertingly brash in their fledgling use of a second language. Propped up at the front of these classrooms, I was asked umpteen times about my favorite sport, my hobbies, my family, and whether I had "a lover," a word that in their mouths sounded more like "rubber" — what?! — or "robber" — hmm? While the girls played it fairly straight, the boys were more imaginative, sometimes looking up key words in their Japanese–English dictionaries and adapting the stock English phrases they found:

"You are the most beautiful I ever saw. What are you doing Sunday? Will you go eat sushi with me?"

"My name is Morita. Will you change your name from Coomber to Morita?"

"My grandmother says Americans eat Japanese. Have you ever tried Japanese? You can try me. My body is very nice."

About the time I thought I could not bear being trotted out before yet another class, an attractive senior boy stood up to take his shot at speaking English with me. As he looked at me and offered a genuine-seeming smile, I hoped our interaction would not take an unfortunate turn.

"What type of boy do you like?" he asked.

I stood before our forty peers speechless, my face growing warm, "blushing up," as my new friends would say. All I could do was shrug my shoulders and tell him I did not know. I waited for the punch line.

A shy smile played across his face as he proceeded to tell me in an earnest voice the type of girl he liked: one who is warm-hearted, whose eyes always shine, and who likes to clean things. "Because cleaning objects enables us to purify ourselves," interjected his young unmarried teacher, offering a nutshell explanation of what I would later understand described a Shinto tenet of purity. The teacher seemed drawn into the moment. "Does Sarah match this description?" she asked him.

"Yes," he smiled.

And that is how Ryota entered my girlish heart.

"*No*," I told the teachers, "*we haven't been in touch in nearly four years.*"

A couple of hours later, my host parents' telephone rang, and my smirking younger sister Yukie handed me the receiver.

"*Sah-lah?*"

* * *

A few days later, on Christmas Eve, Ryota returned home from his university near Tokyo, some five hundred miles away, and appeared in the *genkan* of my host family's home. Wearing the navy suit coat of his university baseball team, he smiled and bowed to my host mother before reacting with a start to see me shuffling up behind her in my standard-issue house slippers. He was even more attractive than before, his shoulders broadened, his face matured. A man.

In our first visit he told me everything (or so it seemed) that had happened to him since our farewell outside my host family's gate, and then he asked, "*What did you do, after you left Japan?*" and settled in to listen. Our conversations were still a hodgepodge of English and Japanese, but we understood each other well. And we became inseparable, meeting for morning jogs along the beach, touring tea houses and shrines, eating at side-street noodle and coffee shops, he always holding the door for me, walking on the rocky side of the path, and picking up the check. He took me to his favorite spot by the Sea of Japan, which by coincidence overlooked the point I had chosen as mine. He took me Christmas shopping and bought me a valentine-red sweater, brought me to his home, introduced me to his surprised mother, and played ballads for me on the piano while I looked at old photos of him and drawings he had made as a young boy. He took me upstairs to his bedroom, where he showed me the stack of letters I had written and photographs I had sent, all kept safe in a little drawer. When he delivered me back to my host family's home, I stopped before opening the squeaky iron gate to their garden and asked if I could give him a hug. He, at long last, leaned in to kiss me.

There could have been no more perfect Christmas Eve, my return to Japan everything I had wanted and more than I had dared dream.

When my mother arrived, I introduced her to Japan, to my host family, and to Ryota as we carried on our fast-forward dating, he joining us on a visit to the vermilion shrine at Tsuwano, where we celebrated New Year's Day, and where some stranger took a photo that captured for me a feeling of sheer happiness, a photo that I would gaze on two years later from a place near despair.

* * *

Ryota had pledged to visit me in the States when he got the money, and I had promised to return to him in Japan. We kept in touch for a time, but like our parting in high school, after a few letters, a couple of phone calls, we let each other go. The last letter I recall receiving, his neat, slightly leftward-slanting Japanese characters covering two pages of thin blue paper, spoke of his everyday life, of wrapping up university studies, taking tests, playing baseball, and going on a trip with his team to Kamakura, where he slept in a house made of snow. He relayed the sadness his mother felt when I left Hagi and said that she often asked about me, wondering if I had written him, or if he had written me. "*When the busyness of university ends,*" he wrote, "*I will visit you in Minnesota.*"

Meanwhile, I applied for an English-teaching job near his university, but nothing came of it (I was a biology major, after all), and I have forgotten whether I told Ryota of my efforts to get back to him. What I do know is that months passed. Contact, and then hope, faded.

Meanwhile, in the States, an economic recession settled in around us, and my friends and I got practical: we made plans to move home with our parents, to marry young men with prospects, to embark on short-term jobs, to shelter in the protection of graduate school — or some combination of the four.

I watched my college post office box with hawk-like intensity for another blue letter from Japan. At the same time I began hedging my bets, moving on, dating other men.

No one else offered me the moon.

* * *

What kind of newlywed life is this? I wondered. Several of my friends and classmates had also married over the previous year, and I was sure none of them had photos of old beaux hidden in plain sight. None of them pined for romantic paths not chosen ... did they? They all seemed so happy. Maybe things would get better for us too.

But I was crying nearly every day, so much that years later, when my mother looked back at photos taken during that time, she did not recognize her own daughter's puffy, sad face. The situation felt untenable, but I had been raised a good Lutheran girl. I had prided myself on staying pure — mostly anyway — until marriage. I had promised till-death-do-us-part in front of a couple hundred family members and friends. Now I could imagine no acceptable escape clause.

Still, a phrase echoed in my mind, "unequally yoked, unequally yoked," words from some long-forgotten sermon. I imagined my husband and me, two oxen harnessed to a cart, straining in opposite directions, never getting anywhere. Although at the time I was not certain it came from the Bible, I knew the point of the saying was that we were *not* to be unequally yoked. But it seemed I was, joined to a husband with whom I did not see eye to eye. *Is this to be my fate*, I wondered, *pouring so much energy into bickering that I will have no energy to chase my dreams?* I began shutting down, curling in around myself, trying to protect my heart, my thoughts, whatever was left of me. I had no energy to hear about other people's problems — or their joys. *This cannot truly be God's plan for my life, can it?*

I certainly did not dare tell anyone of my fears, one of the greatest of which was the possibility that I would have to admit that I had made a very big mistake, a very public mistake, an undoable mistake. Perhaps, I feared, an unforgivable mistake, my life ruined.

Only twenty-three years old when I set Ryota's photograph on the shelf, I compared that dreamy time in Hagi with my acrimonious marriage. How could it be that despite our lack of a shared faith or culture, despite our short time spent together, I had felt closer to Ryota than to my American husband? I found comfort in reliving our New Year's Day in Japan and the even longer-ago night during my high school stay when we were just kids, holding hands and breathing the night air.

And I recalled a moment when I might have left the trajectory that had taken me down my path to apparent ruin. Around the time I had gotten engaged, Ryota telephoned me at my parents' home in Minnesota. He was — wonder of wonders! — in the States, in California, traveling with his baseball team. Hearing his voice rocked me, filled me, but at the time I was too shy to tell him that I would whip out my shiny new credit card and buy a plane ticket and cross half the country the very next day, whatever the cost, if only he would ask. Reality revealed itself in that place where dreams meet resources, where possibility meets pride. After a brief conversation, we had said goodbye. And I was left to wonder, *What if I had made that trip to California? What if I had made my way back to Japan instead of to the altar?*

With Ryota's photo on our shelf, Japan glimmering on the edge of my mind, I began chasing the hope of wholeness I had twice found in that other world whose memories and possibilities were keeping me from falling completely apart. Before long I was imagining an escape to a place that was almost as far away as I could run, that place with an added attraction: the unresolved matter of the moon.

My husband never mentioned the photo of Ryota I had hidden in plain sight, or the holder to which I transferred my keys, a gold circle chained to a round, lacquered-wood doll, her hair blacker than a new-moon sky and kimono painted bittersweet. Ryota had given it to me at the time of our happy New Year's Day. Pairs of those dolls, called *Ouchi ningyō*, symbolize harmonious couples. Carrying the one lonely doll felt right.

I knew it was too late to retrace old paths. I was a married woman and had no idea whether Ryota was a married man. Besides, everyone knows that a short-term love, especially one limited by time and geography, is little more than a fairytale. And how many princes and princesses argue about money or get hung up on surprise bad habits? A love so constrained is like a weather pattern, easy to recognize but impossible to conjure. And certainly long-term reality can never be as fair.

But Ryota had given me the moon and left on me an unforgettable impression: with him I had felt as well matched and complete as the little clams the Japanese eat each March in Girls' Day soup, the perfectly fitting bivalve shells said to represent well-married couples.

I wondered what it would take to feel that whole and happy again.

2

Leaving

TEN months after we wed, I left my husband.

The end came one evening when a fight over dinner escalated into a fight over us and everything we had been and everything we were becoming to each other. Our anger and sadness swelled, seeping from the kitchen into the living room, expanding through the living room into the hallway, overflowing into our bedroom, our closet, our bathroom, filling our apartment with wretchedness until it was as if something popped.

Lying side by side exhausted on our perpetually unmade bed, we fell into a melancholy peace. It was over. Our hopes that we could find a way to complement each other, to live, as promised, till death parted us, died.

In retrospect, our mutual mourning had begun long before, but now each of us would go it alone. I would spend years raking through the wreckage of my heart for clues to how I could have made such a colossal mistake, while knowing the truest truth was that I had known better all along: that despite our romantic beginning playing star-crossed lovers on a community theater stage, we had few commonalities to sustain us.

Somehow I got our futon and desk moved to another old apartment several St. Paul neighborhoods away, where I could close the door to my many-windowed second-floor bedroom and pretend I lived in a solitary tree house set in the branches of a thriving old maple tree whose deep-green leaves turned brilliant yellow that autumn, filling my room with sunshiny light even on sad gray days. From this refuge I slogged through work, a second year of studies, and the paperwork for a divorce. On a serious austerity plan, I gave over our car, purchased on my own good credit, to him of the better-paying job and spent hours riding city bus-route loop-di-loos, trying to get from Point A to Point B in time for work and class. I went through pounds of onions and garlic, beans and rice — my roommate, returning home to our aromatic apartment, crinkling her nose and complaining about the smell of my "third-world food."

Some Sundays I walked to nearby churches, trying to find my way back to God and, I hoped, to forgiveness, of me and by me. I had never intentionally left my faith, but as I struggled in that marriage, finding a church had been the least of my worries. I was always the engine pushing these forays, which became one more thing to disagree about. In my new neighborhood, alone, I began seeking God in high-ceilinged edifices of brick and stone, sitting on hard pews in half-empty sanctuaries, listening to well-trained choirs sing familiar hymns. Struggling to emerge from my personal tailspin, I found going through the motions of liturgy, standing up, sitting down, kneeling, was not enough. I recalled fervent gatherings of praise and pleading in Mexico while on a college mission trip, where hands were raised, hands were held, and worship of song and dance had felt as necessary as work, as satisfying as a meal. The traditional Minnesota-style worship I was finding did not nourish my sad soul.

I began finding my joy in Sunday-morning walks instead, wondering why I was Christian, why Protestant, why Lutheran, and decided it was all happenstance, an accident of birth that leads each of us to the faith we embrace, that spirituality is simply a mirrored ball — I pictured a disco ball — that reflects God, vaguely, in different ways to different people. Whichever part of the ball we focus on becomes familiar, whether it means following Christianity, Hinduism, Buddhism, or another faith. God is God is God. Our human perspective matters little. And a walk might be enough. That is what I told myself anyway.

Faith was not the only thing becoming arbitrary for me. I also doubted my career path. I had turned my focus from biology during my semester in India, where one morning I had transitioned directly from deep sleep to sitting upright in my bunk, certain that I was meant to write, not to spend my days toiling in a lab or traipsing through the woods collecting leaf samples. I had entered journalism school in an effort to shore up my writing credentials, but as I dealt with marital problems I quickly grew lethargic, uninspired to design a thesis or to compete with the program's true believers, classmates who had been born with ink in their veins, always on the hunt for the next hot story.

I had different dreams. As my second year of graduate school and my year of marital separation ground on, my goal was to vanish, to escape the embarrassment I felt over my poor judgment in love, to forget the ten-attendant wedding and DJ dance-reception that had ushered my husband and me into a marriage that had not taken root.

I wanted a real-life do-over.

* * *

During my senior year of high school I had adopted a happy place. Whenever I became nervous or overwhelmed, I would close my eyes and, just like that, be back in the Sea of Japan, floating relaxed near Hagi's white-sand beach, the summer sun warming my face, cool waves gently rocking my body, no responsibility in the world but to get back to my host family's home in time for dinner.

While my host sisters mostly avoided the beach and the sun's skin-darkening rays, I could not get enough of it, bicycling there on free days to lie in the hot sand until it was time to cool off with a swim to the jetty. Some days I relaxed alone; other days I made new friends. It did not matter to me, as long as I was near the sea.

By the time I returned to Minnesota, I knew that beach, Kikugahama, well enough to imagine it fully, to see the turquoise water, to smell the briny air, to hear the waves crashing and lapping at the shore, and I clung to it as I prepared for my senior piano recital, selected a college, and applied for scholarships. No challenge was so monumental that a mental visit to Kikugahama would not get me through it.

Going through a divorce at age twenty-four came close, though, because every time I opened my eyes, my problems persisted. Kikugahama could dissipate nervousness but not erase bad choices. I wished I could go beyond my visualizations and return to that dream world. And I began to wonder, *Why not?*

I applied to teach English in Japan, requesting Hagi for my placement, Hagi, so far off the beaten track that even if my husband changed his mind and wanted to track me down, he would have to make an enormous effort to do so. If you imagine Japan's four main islands as a person reclining in a chair, the city of Hagi would be perched just above a knobby kneecap on the Sea of Japan side, near the southwestern tip of Japan's largest island, Honshu. Unlike the east side of the island, which bustles with bullet trains racing up and down the country's spine, connecting smaller outposts with the metropolises of Kyoto, Osaka, and Tokyo, the west side is slower paced and requires extra time and effort to reach, on local trains, buses, and cars.

Hagi, with its palm trees, bright flowers, and beaches licked by the sea is visually exquisite, in part due to its long reign as a castle town, although the castle, completed by the Mori clan in 1604, was burned down in 1874 to demonstrate allegiance to imperial rule. Centuries later, the ponderous stone foundations and broad carp-filled moat remain, this absent edifice casting a long shadow over nearby neighborhoods, mazes of centuries-old walled streets that disorient those who do not belong. Tucked in among these old streets are studios, where potters continue to mold distinctive *Hagi-yaki* cups, vases, and bowls — considered by tea ceremony masters as Japan's second-best ceramic ware — in the manner introduced here by two Korean ceramicists in the late 1500s. Shrines, temples, and stately houses of long-gone samurai and merchants remain, overlooking contemplative gardens of stones, trees, moss, and water, and obedient pines and wizened orange trees scent the air, the left-behind subjects of an abandoned feudal domain.

Hagi would be the perfect escape from a tattered life.

But when I received my acceptance letter, the offer was to teach in a place called Shuho-cho. Like Hagi, it was located in Yamaguchi Prefecture, but where in Yamaguchi was unclear. Even if it had been possible in 1994 to find Shuho-cho on the Internet, I had no idea how, so I hopped on my bicycle and rode to the library of a nearby college. There I found a map of southwestern Japan and eagerly scanned the area labeled "Yamaguchi."

I saw no Shuho-cho.

I started again, moving my eyes more slowly back and forth, a little alarmed. Did it really exist? Did it have a different *yomikata*?

After all, *kanji*, the Japanese characters adopted from China, can be read in multiple ways. (For example, the *kanji* character for "-cho" — technically "-chō" — is 町, which can also be read "-machi," with both readings meaning "town.")

Or was Shuho-cho too small to be included even on a regional map? I went dot by dot by dot until at last I found the name "Shuho-cho" beside one of the tiniest dots, in the middle of Yamaguchi. It appeared to be near Akiyoshidō, a cave I had twice visited with my host family. (And, returning to the topic of *yomikata*, the two names share the same first character, 秋, which means "fall" and can be read either "aki" or "shū.") I could not recall a town near the cave, but it did not worry me. This Shuho-cho, regardless how small, would be less than an hour's drive from Hagi. Worst-case scenario, I would teach during the week and run away every weekend to see my host family and the sea.

Still, as the deadline to sign my contract approached, I was racked with indecision. As I considered the idea of returning to Japan, my mind worked like a record player, an automatic arm gliding over the LP until it dropped its needle into a groove that it followed round and round, and I would think the same song over and over, about how signing up for teaching English for a year would set my career, friendships, and real-world life back so far that my future would surely be doomed. But the refrain I sang in response to my brain was that I had no other plans, no pressing goals at home, and with most of my energy spent trying to hold myself together, my friendships were stagnant anyway. My future in Minnesota had become blurry, and Japan shone with the promise of a fresh start, a place where old sadness could not follow. And because I imagined myself spending a noncommittal year floating on its surface, not getting entangled in any particular activity or relationship (unless, of course, I were to reconnect with Ryota ... then all bets were off),

I would avoid future sadness too. Shuho-cho was not really a place to *go to* but a place to *leave to.*

Another thought-song my jukebox of a brain played had to do with my escape being a Jonah-like maneuver, that I would be running from God's will for me, whatever it might be. I prayed, begging for an answer, either a benediction or a better idea, from what seemed to be a very silent God. Maybe I would go, and he would just have to send the whale.

I shared my uncertainty with my Southern Baptist grandparents, the people I had most feared would disown me after the divorce, the people who instead had humbled me with grace, love, and compassion. My grandfather was dying of leukemia, and my worries seemed silly in the face of his imminent death. He offered the most obvious and clear-headed advice of anyone: "Make a decision and follow it through."

I could do that.

The afternoon he died I sat, unaware, in a hairdresser's chair getting my long, wavy hair cropped within an inch of my scalp, hoping, as young women often do, that changing my look would change my life. Maybe it did, but afterward it also seemed I had unknowingly shorn myself in preparation for mourning.

Meanwhile, Japan had blossomed in my mind into something of a dream world, a refuge, its appeal being what it was not — not my real life, not my real home — a far more powerful antidote than a haircut. I decided the disappearing act I was engineering would be a set piece in my life, a one-year extended vacation with little bearing on what would follow. I would fulfill the responsibilities of my contract. I would bring my pocket Japanese dictionary but no study aids. I would look up Ryota — or maybe let him lie. Beyond that, I would spend time with my host family and experience four seasons in Japan. I would figure out what to do with the rest of my life. And after one short year, my contract would expire and I would disappear again, this time from Japan, rejuvenated, remade, and ready to return to my real life. Could there be a tidier, more perfect plan?

I signed and returned my acceptance papers. Yes, I would wrap up my studies and classes. Yes, I would raze the memories of my short-lived marriage's haunts. Yes, I would pack up my apartment. The detritus of my real life would have to get along without me: the antique couch, an advance gift for the master's degree in mass communication/print journalism I had not yet achieved; my Canadian grandparents' chrome and gray Formica kitchen table; assorted chairs, pots and pans, sheets and towels, boxes of books and papers, all to be stacked in a storage locker; family reliably settled on the northern Plains and friends sure not to roam too far in one short year; credits toward my degree tallied and stored on some university mainframe; regrets and disappointments piled in a corner of my mind; sweet cat bunking with a trusted friend in St. Paul. All of it would await my return to the States, that day when I would press play and carry on.

3

Letters from a Dream World

Not long after I committed to a year on the Japan Exchange and Teaching — JET — Program, I received the following letter, in fairly clear English, in the mail:

Date: May 19, 1994
From: Akio Shinoda, Head, Shuho-cho Board of Education

Dear Ms. Coomber

How are your preparation for Japan progressing? We would like to help you by giving you some information about your future situation in Shuho.

We are located in the center of Yamaguchi Prefecture about 20 miles from Hagi, where you have visited before. It takes an hour from Shuho to

Hagi by bus. This area is surrounded by mountains and rice field. We have a big cave called Akiyoshido, which is the second biggest in the world and a national park called Akiyoshidai, which is karstic plateaus. Every year a large number of tourists visit our town to see these two wonderful nature. We hope you also came to see them while you were staying in Hagi. In summer, the temperetures reach 90 F and in winter they fall to 30 F. There may be snowfall in winter. This February the snow lay about 20 inches deep. The rainy season is quite long with some heavy shower. It is from May to July.

Cencerning your accomodation, you will be living in an apartment. (Please see enclosed plan and photographs). The rent is ¥15,000 per month. the apartment is supplied with a TV, VTR, bed, desk, washing machine, two-ring gas stove, refrigerator, tables, etc. Your apartment is owned by the Sumitomo Cement Company. There is a supermarket about three minutes from your apartment by foot. There is also a bus stop about three minutes away by foot. But there are not so many bus services because this is a rural area as you know.

With regards to your office, your supervisor will be Mr. Sasaki and the Head of Board of Education is Mr. Shinoda. We will help you arrange a bank account when you arrive and prepare your hanko (official stamp) and meishi (business cards). We will pay your salary on the 21th of each month ...

In average week you will spend Wednesday in the office and the rest of week at school. Your teaching situation is described as a junior high school semi-regular Assistant Language Teacher. There are two junior high school in Shuho-cho. Both schools have only 120 students, and you will visit each school once or twice a week. We would also like you to visit the elementary schools and teach community English classes. You may also be asked to get involved in local community activites. We are very much looking forward to meeting you at the beginning of August. If you have any questions, please do not hesitate to write or call us. Our office hours are from 8:30 am to 5:00 pm Monday to Friday. Good luck with your preparations for Japan.

Your sincerely,
[signed]
Akio Shinoda
Head of Shuho-cho Board of Education

The first thing I did after reading Mr. Shinoda's letter was some math. My initial concern was how I would pay my rent of ¥15,000 a month — until I realized I would be making more money and paying less rent than I ever imagined. My salary would be $36,000 a year, tax-free, and my rent would be $150 a month. I was in clover.

Mr. Shinoda's envelope included a thick pack of photographs that showed a pristine, white-walled apartment building sitting amid bright-green rice paddies under a sunshiny sky; a sparkling-clean interior and hardwood-floored hallway; a balcony overlooking the fields; three bedrooms, two of which were traditional-style with sliding-door closets and tatami mats; an off-white kitchen; a living room; a closet containing a petite pink toilet; a bathing room with a square tub; some Western-style doors, some sliding doors. *Would this be mine?* I wondered.

The photographer also had captured the surrounding neighborhood: soft, tree-covered mountains, paddies, and, dotting the landscape, traditional-style wood-and-plaster homes topped with tile roofs; a junior high school building; preschoolers pushing scooters; an unassuming one-story shopping center, its outdoor sign featuring a smiling red-haired, pig-tailed cartoon girl and the name ナッティー — "Nattie."

Other photographs documented nearly everything I could purchase at Nattie: pink cuts of meat; bags of white bread and buns; bananas, oranges and apples, cabbage, broccoli, peppers, and what I would learn was burdock root, all neatly wrapped in plastic; coolers of milk, yogurt, and butter; bottled teas and sodas; fish, packaged whole and prepared as *sashimi*; shelves of instant coffee and tea; ramen and other kinds of noodles. Displays of lipsticks and eye shadow, shelves packed helter-skelter with drugstore-type goods, racks hung with old-lady blouses and slacks, stacks of Kleenex boxes. The back of that last photo was labeled "sundries," as if I would be shopping at a frontier trading post.

I could not have conjured a better place to recover from two dreary years in St. Paul. Picture-perfect Shuho-cho appeared clean and quiet, its store well stocked, the apartment lovely. But I had a hard time believing the apartment and the life displayed in the photographs would be mine. Who ever heard of one person occupying a spacious, three-bedroom apartment in Japan? Would I have roommates? And what would my work be like?

I must have written for clarification, because I received two more letters, one written June 24, 1994, from Sasaki-*san*, my supervisor-to-be, and one written July 14, 1994, from Kashima-*kachō*, Sasaki-*san*'s supervisor. Both letters were full of encouragement and these men's hopes for an international exchange in which their students would learn English and I would learn about "Japanese cultures." Kashima-*kachō* wrote his regret about not having shared more details of my teaching assignment, adding, "But please don't worry. People are kind and students are nice to teach." Sasaki-*san* offered another tidbit: "One more thing is that there are no people who can speak English in our office. So we'd like you to teach us English."

I chose to believe Mr. Kashima but not Mr. Sasaki. All three of these letters had been written in English, and they had included a phone number, inviting me to call their office with questions. Instead of testing them with a phone call, I convinced myself that Sasaki-*san* was just being modest.

On arrival, I would wonder who wrote those letters, because it could not have been Mr. Sasaki, Mr. Kashima, or Mr. Shinoda, the latter of whose most coherent English phrase, which he laughingly trotted out with some regularity, was "Dis is a pen!" — a staple sentence from some long-ago English lesson.

Clearing out my St. Paul apartment, I packed my old life in boxes and my new life in suitcases — tossing in that pocket-sized Japanese–English dictionary. I watched the mailbox for one more envelope, which arrived just one week before I was to leave: my divorce decree. Now I was free, free to drop through the trap door I had fashioned, free to escape to the place of my dreams.

4

Welcome to Girl Land

I ARRIVED in Japan with a herd of young foreigners, thousands strong, all of us recruited to help Japanese schoolchildren learn English. We were bused en masse from Narita Airport to Tokyo's swanky Keio Plaza Hotel, where we spent our days holed up in conference rooms and banquet halls getting oriented to the goals of the JET Program — primarily to bring conversational English and Western culture into classrooms that had long been focused on teaching English grammar for the all-important university entrance exams. Our other job was to learn about Japanese culture. We were bombarded with advice: "Dress conservatively." "Expect the students to be shy." "Get involved in your community." "Encourage your co-teachers to use English in the classroom." "Learn Japanese."

At the end of each day, we were loosed from the hotel halls to hit Tokyo's crowded streets, our eyes pinwheeling, faces bobbing like helium balloons as we tried to make sense of Tokyo's blinking, buzzing streets, each lit like a collection of oversized "Lite-Brite" toys—brightly colored pegs pressed in patterns against the black, backlit screen of evening. We wandered mazes of nightclubs and pachinko parlors, restaurants and shops, young male hawkers calling and waving people through doors to who-knew-what was awaiting them, jaded-looking young women with little-girl voices handing out packs of white tissues plastic-wrapped in advertisements for phone services, electronic stores, and clubs.

I was not as lost as many of the new JETs, the majority of whom had never been to Japan before or studied its language. At least I had spent a high school summer there, and part of a college winter vacation. Plus, I had Miho.

Miho, my host sister, had long ago uprooted herself from Hagi, her little hometown by the sea, to attend university in Tokyo. By this time, she was a confidently transplanted Tokyoite, a working woman, sexy and bold in her miniskirt and long, red-tinted hair.

When she arrived at my hotel one evening after work, I was probably wearing my pink floral sundress that would have better suited the patchwork-clad Holly Hobbie doll of my childhood. We were a study in contrasts. Soon she was hauling me and a couple of my new JET colleagues off to Tokyo's flashing, clanging Roppongi district, known for its many available varieties of fun, both innocent and not-so. Miho and her friends were regulars at a club called "Friday," and she wanted to introduce me to her people there.

The dark, wood-paneled space comprising a dance floor ringed by tables was not much bigger than a good-sized basement rumpus room, but it featured a proprietor who was not so much managing the room as reigning over it. Wearing a kimono and hair in a traditional-style up-do, Mama was husky-voiced and glorious. I, jet-lagged and barely put together, was transfixed, bedazzled even, imagining myself in the presence of some fallen latter-day *geisha*.

The place soon came alive, with Mama deftly managing a pack of young, costumed male dancers who were performing a prop-filled revue of fractured fairytales. Among them was the popular Japanese story of the Tongue-cut Sparrow, in which an old hag cuts out the tongue of her husband's pet bird. In the Friday club presentation, however, the poor sparrow lost not his tongue but, well, his manhood.

I had been to bars and clubs back in Minnesota, where my friends and I danced to over-amplified rock and country music, and where on special birthdays we'd sip swimming-pool blue drinks out of plastic buckets, but this sort of lewd revue was new to me. Surely Friday was exactly the type of spot my father, raised in a particularly conservative church, one that had broken away from the more moderate American Baptist Church, would have been taught to avoid. We had laughed together at his stories of the admonitions he had heard as a young man at church — one that he had escaped at his earliest opportunity, not to bust loose as a sixties party animal, but to find a more comfortable faith in the Lutheran Church. Still, I could not help but think, if this were the night that Jesus chose to come again, would I want him to find me at Friday? Not really. But here I was — along with a couple of other JETs — as Miho's guest, Miho who had settled in with her drink, who was beaming and chitchatting with Mama, laughing at the boys' antics, applauding them, and calling out to them by name. Of course this was a cross-cultural experience. Didn't that call for some special dispensation? I decided that if, on the off chance this were to be the night of Jesus' second coming, he would understand.

A flattering, solicitous hostess, Mama perched at our table during breaks in the fairly vulgar action, keeping us well-watered, periodically calling out orders to the boy dancers, who hastened to obey. After a while, Mama disappeared briefly, and then — surprise

33

— re-entered the room bewigged and dressed as Tina Turner, then later Madonna, metamorphosing from one femme fatale into another, Miho beside me shrieking "Mama!"

As the evening wore on, Mama took a longer rest at our table, letting her face and body slouch, breaking character all the way to her voice, which suddenly dipped low, revealing her to be a well-disguised *him*. By the end of the evening he had lasered his catty, teasing manner onto my embarrassed new friend Brian, an affable fellow Minnesotan. The next year Brian would tell me of his decision to come out of the closet and I would remember his awkward, blushing face that night. Mama was no geisha — nowhere near — but a savvy entertainer, able to read his guests' thoughts like a news ticker.

The next day, I flew with several other JETs out of Tokyo's din and into Yamaguchi's Ube Airport, roughly five hundred miles to the southwest. On arrival we herded up, scanning the arrivals area for our new supervisors and colleagues. Where the other JETs each found one or two representatives there to welcome them with quiet smiles and bows, I saw a trembling white sign several feet long: "Welcome Ms. Coomber!" it shouted. When I smiled in recognition and waved at the men holding it, an enthusiastic — almost rowdy — contingent of maybe a dozen fluttered back excitedly, one of my new handlers, gray-haired and grinning, jumping up and down in his black leather loafers.

* * *

I imagine I looked garish that day in my red knit tee, flower-patterned pants, and dangly earrings as I approached the crowd of navy-suited, white-shirted men. My new posse quickly absorbed me into its fray, the other JETs fading out of sight and mind as I was greeted with bows and handshakes, relieved of my bags and piled into a caravan of cars in what resembled a friendly kidnapping. I was Shuho-cho's first-ever JET, and I imagine that for this crowd my appearance was an accomplishment. Having successfully imported their very own foreigner, they had joined a new class of towns.

Our parade wound its way over low passes and through long-tunneled mountains to Shuho-cho, the suffix "-cho" literally meaning "town," and when we arrived, I, not knowing then that "-cho" was less a descriptor than an administrative category, quickly decided that the "town" label had been used pretty loosely. Most recently I had lived in Minneapolis–St. Paul, but I had grown up in the small city of Moorhead, Minnesota, which is connected by bridges over the Red River to Fargo, North Dakota, the resulting community having a joint population of roughly one hundred thousand in the 1970s and 1980s. So I knew cities, big and small.

I also was very familiar with towns, having spent countless childhood vacations on car trips through what many consider fly-over land — "Are we there yet??" — crossing the wide-open North Dakota plains to visit one set of grandparents in Saskatchewan, and passing through the slightly narrower prairies of Minnesota and hills of Wisconsin to visit another set of grandparents in Illinois. I had gathered more data on towns as a student at a private Lutheran high school in Fargo, because we played Class B sports against schools of similar size in blink-and-you-miss-them towns throughout eastern North Dakota. In my experience, a town was a place defined by a few consistent features clustered together: a bar, a church, a post office, a café, a school, some homes, and, usually, a phalanx of grain elevators and a gas station.

In this Shuho *Town*, even if you were to substitute *shrine* for *church* and forget the grain elevators, the place felt less like a town than a rural area containing several sleepy constellations of homes, mom-and-pop shops, and a primary school each. These neighborhoods were separated by small mountains from one another and from the central administrative area of town offices, a few small restaurants, and a high school. I had a hard time believing that 7,500 residents called this *cho* home, but although it was not what I had expected, it was so different from the place and life I had fled that I loved it immediately.

That sunny arrival day, everything was fresh and new, and I was a blank slate to my handlers, having suddenly shed my identity of melancholy divorcee, of poor graduate student. I went from office to office meeting local leaders and others in a blur of polite bows, pleasantries — "*Dōzo yoroshiku onegaishimasu!*" — and tiny cups of green tea. Finally, I arrived at my apartment building with two men, Satō-*kakarichō*, a mid-level Board of Education staff member, and my immediate supervisor, Sasaki-*san*.

Similar to so many characterless apartment blocks that pepper Japan's cities and towns, the outside of this building looked like a giant white box — the dimensions of a ten-ream paper container — with windows. But after we climbed the outdoor staircase and walked along the second-floor balcony, my handlers turned a key in a pale-green metal door, and, suddenly, there I was, at home. We removed our shoes in the entryway and stepped up into an airy apartment that stretched the depth of the building from front door to back balcony, and proved to be a combination of Eastern and Western styling, sliding doors and slamming, hardwood floors and lightly textured wallpaper, tatami-matted rooms with wood-grain ceilings. It was the very apartment I had seen in the photographs, and it really was all mine.

My new home was filled with brand-new furnishings, from a black twin bed with lights on the headboard to a kitchen rug stitched with the words "joyful cooking" to an electric stapler sitting on a shiny dark-wood desk. And it was quickly apparent that almost every object for which it was possible to choose a color had been selected in pastel pink: pink toilet, pink bathroom sink, pink rugs, pink fuzzy floral blankets, pink sheets, pink jug to hold hot tea water, pink ironing board, pink hangers, pink dishwashing tub, and, if memory serves, pink vacuum cleaner.

Girl land.

Was this the impression my new employers had of young American women, that we wrapped our single lives in soft pinks like little girls? (I doubted they knew of my divorce.) Or did this reflect their experience of Japanese women? Had their wives suggested creating a pink palace? Or did it belie my supervisors' hope that my presence in their schools and their community would be as innocuous and gentle as a baby girl's?

Or perhaps this pinkness contained the complexity of that rosy color I would learn to love in *ukiyo-e*, "pictures of the floating world."

These paintings and woodblock prints emerged in seventeenth-century Japan and depicted the people and happenings of the walled-off entertainment districts known as "floating worlds." Here the ruling Tokugawa shogunate would turn a blind eye to social class — warrior, farmer, artisan, or merchant — and release visitors from class-based restrictions. In the floating world, people were allowed to live whatever life they could afford, enjoying kabuki theater, bunraku puppet theater, the company of courtesans, sumo wrestling, and other pursuits. But only in these places.

Woodblock printing emerged in the floating world as black ink on white paper and evolved in the eighteenth century to include multiple blocks, each adding a new color. Pink and green were among the earliest, their simple hues implying a full spectrum of color, a full spectrum of life.

Arriving as I was from an unhappy couple of years enduring similar colors — black, burgundy, and green — what my ex-husband and I settled on as compromise colors for items on our wedding gift registry, the pink felt like an elixir. Like the commoners in the floating world, I could adopt a new, non-divorcée identity, a fresh, pink identity in Shuho-cho. I could commit to the pink. I could own the pink.

"*Utsukushii desu,*" I told them. "It's beautiful."

My new colleagues seemed tickled, murmuring to each other as I inspected the apartment. These two guys — Sasaki-*san*, a man I took to be thirty-something, with boyish good looks, and Satō-*kakarichō*, a tall, gentle fellow I figured to be in his forties, eyes wide behind large-lensed black glasses — had been put in charge of setting up an unknown young woman's apartment, a foreigner's, no less, and they appeared relieved to see how well they had succeeded.

Sasaki-*san*'s letter had informed me that no one in his office, now our office, spoke English, and I had chosen to disbelieve him. Now, as we spent our first hours together speaking in gestures, testing out one another's vocabularies, and consulting our dictionaries, I realized he had been perfectly truthful. As Sasaki-*san* dredged the recesses of his mind for helpful English vocabulary, Satō-*kakarichō* simply blinked his wide bespectacled eyes and chuckled congenially, absolving himself of any linguistic responsibility. We stayed in the land of pleasantries.

Soon they retreated so I could unpack my suitcases into the empty drawers and closets — had anyone ever lived here? If so, they had left no trace. No detritus. No inkling of a life lived. It was impossible to envision how in the coming months I would come to fully inhabit that place, entertaining new friends around my table, preparing lesson plans, pursuing new hobbies, and filling closets with teaching materials and gifts. That afternoon, as I walked barefoot across the cool hardwood floors of my quiet, spotless apartment, I felt a sense of relief mixed with pure hopefulness. I was home but not home. It was exactly what I had been seeking.

A couple of hours later my supervisors picked me up for dinner at a restaurant that was hidden away on the upper floor of a building in the neighborhood. There we met the Board of Education leadership and sat on a tatami-mat floor before low tables, my hosts encouraging me to relax, to stretch out my legs, which I had folded beneath myself, sitting on my ankles and the tops of my feet the way I knew I should in a formal setting in Japan. A demure older woman (truly a woman and probably a grandma to some of my students), wearing a kimono, her hair pulled up, served us plates of sashimi and teriyaki-basted eel.

We drank to our new affiliation, we spoke of our hopes for the coming year, and my new colleagues looked at me meaningfully and said something that sounded like a confession of relief. "*Nihongo ga perapera desu ne!*" they exclaimed.

It sounded like a compliment, and I knew they were talking about the Japanese language — *Nihongo* — but precisely what they were saying eluded me. What was this word "*perapera*"?

I asked for clarification and watched a flurry of discussion ensue. How would they explain to the new English teacher that they had complimented her on her *perapera* (fluent) Japanese? When at last the din subsided, Mr. Shinoda, whom I would learn to call Shinoda-*kyōikuchō*, the head of the Board of Education, turned to me with his wide eyes and good-natured, toothy smile and said, "You Japanese." Pause. "Berry good!" Pause. "OK? OK!" And everyone smiled and laughed with relief.

It was the first of many such compliments that I would receive for my early language skills completely unearned, sometimes from shopkeepers or strangers on hearing my greeting, "*Ohayō gozaimasu*" — "Good morning." In this case, I had instantly proved my complimenters wrong, but they had kindly helped all of us save face.

Not much later, the unobtrusive *obāsan* who had been caring for us quietly bowed us out the door. I was back at my apartment before eight o'clock and soon sitting alone on my second-floor balcony, seeing that the contrast of Shuho-cho with Tokyo could hardly be greater. Overlooking the gravel backyard of my apartment building and the darkening rice paddies around it, the moon like the white tip of a fingernail above, I watched the occasional car chase its headlights down a nearby road. A neighbor's television set chattered, and crickets and frogs chirped in the rice paddies. Otherwise all was still. I had made it to a place of peace.

"You know," I wrote in my journal, "if I were to choose a place that could keep me out of trouble for a year, this would be it."

5

Meeting the Neighbors

THE August heat simmered relentlessly, beads of sweat budding on my forehead and running down my nose, my neck, trickling between my breasts; even my calves felt slippery. The hot spell was punctuated by typhoons cycling above us, propelling winds like a giant hair dryer, blowing my freshly washed towels and shirts, hung out to dry on the balcony, sideways. Pressure howled down the hallway of my apartment and buffeted the sliding doors that separated my bedroom from the living room, glass panes rattling in a wooden grid, until the whole door jumped its track and crashed to the hardwood floor, every pane, miraculously, intact.

When evening fell and cooler air, still hot but not frantic, washed across the hills, I savored it. That is, until I went to bed and closed up my apartment for the night, the victim of an overactive imagination. My situation seemed too perfect, and I feared, completely irrationally, that my ex-husband would appear without warning, and, when I pretended not to hear the doorbell, would somehow make his way to the sliding-glass door that led from my second-floor balcony to my bedroom. As if he would have any desire to see me again after our bad ending. As if he had any clue where I had gone. We had no friends in common.

Unfounded though this anxiety was, it is why I kept my windows and doors closed against the cooling night, turning for relief to the droning air conditioner, mounted high on my bedroom wall. After some hours of listening to its labors, I would switch it off and fight for a few hours of sweaty sleep before the sun rose, obscenely early. And if the light of the sun failed to wake me, the infernal town chimes would.

My introduction to the chimes came my first morning in Shuho-cho. Still jet lagged and excited, I was out my apartment door before 5:30. In a matter of steps, I reached a narrow asphalt road that led me through bright-green rice paddies, where various styles of dragonflies arced and dipped, red wings, blue wings and double-decker black wings vibrating in moist, sun-saturated air. Here and there farm wives in galoshes walked perky-faced, curly-tailed dogs. Roosters crowed.

The pastoral setting could hardly have been more different from the St. Paul neighborhood where I had lived the previous two years, its brick apartment buildings and stately old homes sitting cheek-by-jowl along grids of bumpy streets that carried fast-moving cars, buses and bicycles, the occasional squirrel zigzagging the gauntlet. Shuho-cho felt like paradise. Until suddenly, into my idyllic scene, an electronic rendition of "Edelweiss" came shooting across the fields, echoing among the mountains. My heart skipped. I looked at my watch. Exactly six o'clock.

The next morning I did better and slept past sunrise — until six o'clock sharp, when again the sound of "Edelweiss" rolled over my balcony and reverberated through the sliding glass door to my bedroom. An auditory assault.

"Edelweiss" would strike *every* morning at six o'clock for as long as I lived in Shuho-cho, along with the air-raid siren wailing at noon and a piece of classical music tinkling into the drawing dusk at five o'clock. During school vacations, extra alarms would sound at ten a.m. and six p.m., all of this noise generated by some speaker atop a public building.

That first week, the chimes baffled and annoyed me — blaring sirens and too-loud tunes causing me to jump, disrupting my thoughts. But no one else seemed to mind them. In fact, no one else reacted much at all other than to switch gears, setting work aside and commencing lunch or preparing to go home.

When I asked Sasaki-*san*, he explained that these alerts were a relic of the postwar days, when wristwatches were rare and people needed a way to keep time. Each alarm had its own meaning: gentle "Edelweiss" at six, he said, for "waking the townspeople"; the siren at noon telling everyone to take a lunch break; the music at five saying, "You did a good job today." Supplemental alarms during school vacations alerted children at ten a.m., so they could stop studying and go outside to play, and at six p.m., so they could return home and help out around the house.

That is all very quaint, I thought. But this time-keeping felt like a relic of a totalitarian regime I had assumed, hoped, was long past. Besides, everyone had wristwatches now. And I needed some sleep.

I must have said at least some of that out loud, because soon thereafter, back at my apartment, my doorbell rang unexpectedly. Pushing open the door, I found a petite, smiling woman — or was she a girl? — dressed in denim overalls, T-shirt, and little tennis shoes, lustrous black hair pulled up in a ponytail. She could have been as young as fifteen or as old as thirty. Her arms were full of housewarming goodies: a small brown teddy bear to keep me company, a box of chamomile tea to help me relax, a lavender aromatherapy pouch to insert in my pillowcase to enhance relaxation, grapes, and homemade cookies. She introduced herself as Naoko, the daughter of my supervisor's supervisor, Kashima-*kachō*. Her lips trembled as she spoke Japanese with a few English words thrown in where she could. Was she excited, nervous, or on the verge of tears? She said she had heard I was having trouble sleeping, so she had come to help me settle in.

I would soon learn that Naoko was older than I — twenty-eight — and, like many of Japan's more traditional single women, she lived in her childhood home. In her case, home was a century-old farmhouse she shared with her parents, her smiley *haiku*-writing grandmother, and her fluffy white dog, Paaru — "Pearl." They lived about a half mile from my apartment.

In the months that followed, I would find the three years she had on me made her my *sempai*, my elder, a position that would, apparently, in her mind, give her some authority to take care of me, to watch over me. When I caught a cold, she would deliver medicine, and, inexplicably, a noisemaker and balloon into the newspaper drop box attached to my door. When I had a rough day teaching, she would drop off encouraging notes and packs of my favorite cookies, Alforts, chocolate-dipped digestive biscuits imprinted with grand sailing vessels. To raise my spirits around Halloween, she would corral three neighbor children and bring them to my apartment for an awkward attempt at trick-or-treating.

Sometimes Naoko would pick me up in her shiny dark-blue car and we would leave Shuho-cho for shopping or touring. Each time, I would witness a transformation as she abandoned her casual teen-like appearance and transformed into a princess. The first time we went shopping in a nearby city, she picked me up wearing a neatly tailored peach sweater skirt-suit with contrasting trim and tiny matching shoes. Her long, heavy hair glistened down to the middle of her back, and her face carried only a hint of makeup, which made her porcelain skin flawless. I felt bulky and out of place, a galoot galumphing alongside an airbrushed, perfectly proportioned lady.

* * *

My host parents arrived from Hagi my first Saturday in Shuho-cho, bringing a sense of continuity and stability to my new life. I was not just a foreigner adrift in this new place; I was an errant, ugly-duckling daughter, living on her own an hour's drive from home.

When I opened my apartment door, I lost any stoic pretense. "Okāsan!" I cried, and threw my arms around my host mother's small frame, her head barely reaching my shoulders, as she laughed and hugged me back. Right behind her was Otōsan, generous, serious-mouthed, twinkly-eyed Otōsan. His family's only licensed driver, he was ever ready to answer the call for a jaunt or an errand, donning aviator shades and hopping behind the wheel of his late-model SUV, which hulked through narrow streets, its stick shift inlaid with a stylized scorpion. I knew Otōsan was not a hugger, not a toucher, but I could not stop myself. "Otōsan!" I said, and wrapped my arms around his shoulders. He blanched, standing as stiff and immovable as a short telephone pole, enduring this display of affection from his foreign daughter-of-sorts.

They inspected my new home, nodding their approval that the people of Shuho-cho were taking good care of me, and sat at last in chairs around the brand-new wooden kitchen table, where, I am certain, we shared a snack of grapes. During my early days in Shuho-cho, grapes took up more space in the narrow, chest-high refrigerator than all other foods combined, and I found myself juggling boxes of green, red, and giant purple orbs — the latter being Muscat, flavored like the Grape Kool-Aid of my childhood.

As I accepted a new box from one new acquaintance, I would lie in wait for the next unsuspecting visitor or host on whom I could unload it. I would employ this strategy throughout the year, as various fruits and other foods came into season.

Catching up on the events of the previous four and a half years using my elementary Japanese and the little English Okāsan recalled, I consciously resisted asking whether they knew what had become of Ryota, my one-time love. Even more than that, I avoided the topic that had brought me to Shuho-cho, back into the orbit of their life: my escape from a bad decision. Sitting opposite them, I felt as if I had succeeded somehow in my plot to move back in time to a happier, more manageable place, and it thoroughly affirmed my decision to return to Japan, to shake off the heartbreak and very public fall of a failed marriage.

Soon I confessed my helplessness in my new environment with its mysterious appliances and indecipherable Japanese instruction books: the washing machine with two narrow top-loading bins; the rice cooker with a timer; the little oven, which, after melting cling-wrap around a cob of corn, I had come to suspect was not a mere microwave; the two-ring gas stove that sat on a low stainless-steel counter; the wall-mounted air conditioner/heater/vent in the living room; and the TV and the VCR that sounded like a tiny airplane taking off whenever I rewound a tape. They patiently taught me the basics of each appliance and translated the *kanji* — Chinese characters (the most complex of the three writing systems used in the Japanese language) — that were printed on the buttons of my many remote controls.

That day happened to be my twenty-fifth birthday, and my new neighbors at the apartment building had invited us for a late-afternoon birthday party. Mr. Shinoda's introductory letter had informed me that the apartment I would be living in was owned by the Sumitomo Cement Company, but I had not understood that the three-story building I now called home was actually the company dormitory for the local branch of Sumitomo Cement, a multinational corporation. Every single one of my neighbors was affiliated with Sumitomo, either as an employee (the men) or as a wife or child of an employee, and my unit was on a floor where the executives lived with their families. I was the first non-Sumitomo person to live there, and later I would learn the reason why the Shuho-cho Board of Education had requested that apartment for me: it was the only rental in town with Western-style toilets.

At the appointed time, my host parents and I locked up my apartment and went downstairs to the party room, where we sat on the tatami floor before a long low table filled with food, bouquets, and a banana cake topped with cherries and sliced kiwi and peaches. My host mom sat on my left, and to my right was Hideo, a fit-looking young man with a kind, open face.

We embarked on an evening of introductions, toasts, small talk, and speeches followed by good-natured jokes and questions about where we all came from and what we were about, I doing my best to keep up, flipping through my dictionary with help from Okāsan and, soon, Hideo. At the time, I did not know that twenty-five was considered the high end of the marrying range — at least by the old-timers and perhaps by small-towners — and that I would be nudged about settling down and teased about becoming as stale and unwanted as *"kurisumasu keiki"* ("Christmas cake"), which is no longer appealing after the twenty-fifth of December. Of course, as a foreigner I received some special dispensation, but that night and into the future I was regularly interrogated about whether I had a boyfriend and when I was going to marry, as if I could dictate this outcome. I would not admit that I had only recently become disentangled.

That evening I began getting to know the cement company's local executives and their wives, who lived in apartments on the upper two floors around me; the lower-ranking single men, like Hideo, who lived communally, each with a bedroom of his own, on the first floor below me; and the nurturing middle-aged *obasan*, Mrs. Kawajiri, who had her own apartment on the first floor, from where she cared for the young men and managed the building — cooking, cleaning, making ikebana arrangements for the entryway, and entertaining Sumitomo men visiting from other branches.

I also learned that I had something in common with my new neighbors: we were all transplants to Shuho-cho, the Sumitomo employees and their families having been transferred there from all over Japan, and I arriving from Minnesota. As I learned my Japanese characters, I saw that the name Sumitomo, 住友, contained the characters for "live" — as in "dwell" — and "friend." For me, the name acquired a welcoming connotation. I lived among the "Dwelling Friends."

As the evening continued, Hideo patiently, smilingly helped me negotiate the swirl of Japanese words and comments around me, perhaps even smoothing over my first gaffe: when the head of this cement company branch asked what I thought of rural Shuho-cho, I carelessly replied, "*I like it so much better than Tokyo with all that horrible cement.*"

At the end of the party, my host parents and I retreated to the outdoor staircase that led to my apartment, and Hideo, my new ally, dashed after us to place a couple of English-language books in my hands, one of which, ironically, was titled "Beyond Polite Japanese." The other was a collection of cartoons about a *gaijin* (foreigner) experiencing a year in Japan. Birthday gifts. He smiled his kind smile, nodded his goodnights, and slipped back inside.

6

Yamaguchi's Tibet

Prior to school starting that autumn, I spent about a month in the stuffy, smoky Board of Education office. My mint-condition gunmetal gray desk, well stocked with brand-new office supplies, was docked in a square formation with four others, each sporting dents and scratches like boats that had weathered minor storms. Their navy-suited captains were my supervisor, the boyishly handsome Sasaki-*san*; his superior, the bespectacled Satō-*kakarichō*; our section manager (Naoko's father), Kashima-*kachō*; and Yamamoto-*san*.

How Mrs. Yamamoto fit into the office hierarchy was mysterious to me. She appeared roughly equal in age to Sasaki-*san*, and as far as I could tell they interacted as equals, but sometimes, while Sasaki-*san* took a smoke break or went for a walk, Yamamoto-*san* set aside her work, disappeared through a side door and returned a few minutes later with a full tray of green tea and, sometimes, coffee. She made it for everyone in the office: our group of five, the half dozen people at the bank of desks behind me, and Shinoda-*kyōikuchō*

("Dis is a pen!"), who was in charge of all of us and occupied the private office just behind Mrs. Yamamoto. Drink service complete, she dove right back into her work.

While my new colleagues bustled through their days shuffling and filing papers, tapping on calculators, rushing off to attend meetings and, in Mrs. Yamamoto's case, serving tea, I had little to occupy me, other than sitting as directed at my desk, observing the goings-on around me and greeting everyone who happened to stop by. Some arrived especially to see me. The suave but enthusiastic Mr. Kumagai of South Junior High School, with whom I would be co-teaching, came by to begin planning our English lessons for his students, and others stopped out of curiosity to meet the town's new and only foreigner. But mostly I took part in collateral visits, smiling and nodding with various townspeople passing my desk on their way to see Shinoda-*kyōikuchō*.

Apart from these social calls, I felt awkwardly disengaged from the blur of activity around me — especially after two hyperactive years in graduate school, where I had taught undergraduates, worked side jobs, and studied mass communication, all the busyness serving as a coping mechanism to get me through the emotional upheaval of my breakup and divorce. Now I felt lost without the perpetual demands on my time and, more than that, guilty at having so much of it. I began to feign busyness, jotting down ideas for my vaguely defined master's project — analyzing Japan's newspaper coverage of environmental issues — that I had hoped to complete in my year away but quickly began to dread. And, having realized how important language skills would be to my secluded situation, I began studying Japanese in earnest.

Meanwhile, I kept drinking Yamamoto-*san*'s tea. "*Dōzo*," she would say, placing it on my desk, gesturing with her flat palm. "Please." Cup after cup after short porcelain cup. She executed her tea service four times a day, every day, in addition to steadily working her way through daunting piles of paperwork. The first cup arrived around 8:15 a.m., after *rajio taiso* ("radio exercises"), for which our whole office met out in the parking lot and, following a tradition dating back to the late 1920s, stretched and jumped to a scratchy recording of a man's voice exhorting us, "*Ich' — ni — san — shi!*" over plinkity-plunk piano music. "One — two — three — four!"

Cup number two would arrive at ten, when the wall speaker clicked and launched into a series of local announcements and news broadcasts. On cue, Mrs. Yamamoto and any other women nearby would drop their work and disappear through a side door into a dark hallway that housed a two-ring gas stove and a deep sink, its pipe connected to a wall-mounted, backpack-sized gas water heater. They prepared coffee and tea for their colleagues and themselves, making drinks to each man's specifications, pouring them into each man's favorite cup and bringing them to each man's desk, sometimes with a little bean cake or rice cracker that someone had brought in after a vacation or business trip. Noon and three o'clock brought the same routine.

I watched with some wonderment, faking my busyness all the harder while narrowing my eyes and casting sidelong glances at the men, who I saw sitting at their desks having a smoke, chatting, or staring into space, unconcerned that their female colleagues were working through every break. Yamamoto-*san* never asked me to help, and Sasaki-*san* never suggested it, but with each passing tea time I felt increasingly awkward as the other women hit the kitchenette and served the men ... and me.

But I did not want to serve tea, and I did not want the women to serve me tea, and, perhaps most of all, I did not want the women to serve the men tea. Although I knew tea-serving was part of Japanese culture, particularly in a traditional area like Shuho-cho, it went against everything I believed, namely that women and men are equal and should be treated as such. In my eyes, these women were subjugating themselves by playing a serving role — an unreciprocated one at that — while their office work waited and probably grew in their absence. I wanted no part of this practice. It reminded me of being on the mission trip in college, where tasks were often broken down into women's work and men's, women cooking and doing dishes, men carrying luggage.

So I tried opting out of tea time, saying I could get my own tea. But Yamamoto-*san* would not hear of it. I tried to continue sitting, acting the part of a conscientious tea objector, but that changed nothing. I began wondering whether Yamamoto-*san* and the other women would begin to resent me — or if they already had.

I needed a consult. I called my host mother, Okāsan, a career woman at the telephone company, and explained the situation. She considered my problem carefully, weighed my options and imagined similar scenarios in her office. Finally, she presented her advice: "*You should offer to help, although I doubt they will let you.*"

Yamamoto-*san* had made me feel completely welcome in the office from the moment we met. No matter what I tried to ask or say in her language, no matter what I did, she would respond with a broad smile, shaking her head from side to side, and exclaiming, "*Waaah, Sah-lah-sensei, subarashii!*" — fantastic! She made me feel like a special child — or a superstar.

Now as she rose to make tea, I approached her and asked, "*Tetsudaimashō ka?*" — "May I help?"

She responded with uncharacteristic reserve, a nod and a quiet smile, and — *what?* — she accepted. I wondered whether she had been waiting me out.

When the next tea time came, I joined her in the hallway-kitchenette and under her tutelage began to learn the fine art of tea and coffee service: whose cup was whose, which of our colleagues favored his coffee black, who liked his coffee with sugar and Creap (a mysterious powdery whitener), and who always drank green tea. Her routine was quick and efficient.

As I emerged from the hallway carrying a tray lined with little cups, my chest tightened and my stomach felt heavy. *Hello, everyone,* I thought, *watch me ditch my principles, right here in your office.* Even without my personal sensibilities, this went against every JET orientation I had attended. Each one had emphasized that in addition to improving English education in Japan, we JETs had been hired to help internationalize the country, to enable our host institutions to see their culture from an outside perspective. Now I was contributing my energy to a custom that seemed decidedly un-international, backward even.

But I knew how it felt to be part of the host culture, to welcome people from other countries. When I was a child, my family's church in Fargo had helped families immigrate from Southeast Asia. When the Refugee Committee called for help, the congregation responded with bicycles, furniture, apartments, donations of clothing and furniture, and job leads.

Not unlike my hosts in Shuho-cho.

When the refugee families arrived, they came to church looking a bit disoriented, speaking a foreign language, and smelling of unfamiliar spices. The Refugee Committee helped the newcomers settle into new homes, jobs, and schools.

Again, not unlike me arriving in Shuho-cho.

I could not imagine our newcomers in Fargo, having gotten a bit comfortable in their new environs and their new language, throwing their weight around, telling my church's coffee hour committee how to set up its beverages and cookies in Fellowship Hall between services, or making suggestions about how to run the church potlucks — affairs that are almost as ritualized in northern Great Plains society as tea serving is in Japan.

These people in Shuho-cho were my hosts, and I was more of a refugee than any of them knew, having ditched my marriage and graduate program to run away as far as I could imagine. Yamamoto-*san* and the other women were my colleagues here. I wanted to show them respect by making an effort to fit into their world, no matter how strange it sometimes seemed. Indeed, my second day helping Yamamoto-*san* with the drink service, I would hear her comment happily to another woman, "*Sah-lah has begun serving tea.*" She had no idea how uneasy I was about this conversion.

Sasaki-*san*, my attentive supervisor, intuited my feelings. As I held one of my first trays of coffee, he approached me and asked, "*Do you find it unusual that only —* "

He paused.

"*Women?*" I interjected.

Oh, yes, yes, that was what he was getting at. I told him I found it very "*omoshiroi*" and "*mezurashii*" — interesting and unusual. He explained that this custom was left over from the old days. "*Although the men do not ask for tea service, the women just do it*" — a flicker of what appeared to be genuine bafflement crossed his face — "*especially in the rural areas.*"

I told him that I had joined the women in serving, because as a woman, "*shinakereba narimasen*" — "it would not do not to."

He told me, twice, that I did not need to help, but I said it was for the best. I was in Japan now. Then I asked him to please excuse me — the coffee was getting cold.

A week or so later Yamamoto-*san* gave me a ride home from work, and I brought up the tea service situation. Perpetually upbeat, she echoed Sasaki-*san*'s explanation, it being an old custom. But her view was different, and she expressed it more frankly than I had expected. "*In Japan,*" she said, "*men rank above the women — it can't be helped.*" In future conversations I would hear women rationalize tea-serving as something they do to compensate for the men providing their physical labor whenever an outdoor tent needs to be set up, or office furniture needs moving. That day, I told Yamamoto-*san* that I wanted the men to take turns with us. She kindly refused to consider the possibility.

What I would never tell her or anyone else was that I quickly mounted my own mini-rebellion. When Yamamoto-*san*'s eyes were looking elsewhere, I doctored the instant coffees with too little coffee powder and too much Creap, hoping to steal some of the pleasure from the men, fantasizing that they would beg me to stop serving, or, even better, start making their own damn coffee. Every time I served my drinks, I would watch the faces of my victims for some reaction — any reaction.

No one ever so much as flinched.

* * *

Even without its tea-serving tradition, Shuho-cho was easy to classify as *inaka*, the Japanese word — sometimes used disparagingly — for countryside. It had no train station whatsoever, and although my apartment was a three-minute walk from a bus stop, it saw only six departing buses a day — two in the early morning, two in the afternoon, and two in the early evening. If I rode one of those green, window-rattling, wood-floored buses to Shuho-cho's central business district, I could catch a farther-ranging bus (sometimes after more than an hour's wait) that actually left town and would carry me to the prefectural capital, Yamaguchi City. But getting home again would inevitably be a challenge, as the last bus from central Shuho-cho departed for my neighborhood at 6:09 p.m.

Shuho-cho also exemplified *inaka* for its lack of recreational facilities. I could find no movie theater, no shopping mall and no swimming pool. Although I had already discounted its "town" status, I still held onto my city-oriented assumption that there must be amenities I had not yet had the good fortune to discover, maybe just over the next mountain, perhaps just past where my bike rides ended, *something* that my handlers had neglected to mention or were outright keeping from me so I would stay focused on settling into my work and life in Shuho-cho. I figured I would find it eventually.

But my quest would have to wait. Less than a week after arriving, Sasaki-*san* and Satō-*kakarichō* loaded me and my suitcase into the Board of Education's white Subaru station wagon and drove me to Yamaguchi City, where every JET in our prefecture met for still more orientation. As the only JET to be escorted by her handlers — the rest had arrived via train and bus — I felt like a reluctant kid getting dropped off at camp.

There were four dozen of us, hailing from the United States, Canada, England, Ireland, Scotland, Australia and New Zealand, and in our ranks I recognized bluebloods, Ivy Leaguers, public university grads, professionals, do-gooders, Japanophiles, escapists, and lost souls. Some appeared to be short-term experience-seekers, while others seemed ready to put down roots. As required by the JET Program at that time, every one of us was under age thirty-five, had university degrees, and could renew our contracts, at our sponsors' pleasure, for up to three years.

I would find that most of these JETs had put their lives on hold, some leaving unfulfilling jobs and relationships, others seeking a constructive way to spend a post-university gap year, submitting applications for graduate school or work. And what a grand way to exist on hold, all nicely set up, having made our escapes to well-paying jobs, furnished apartments, and somewhat readymade lives. Everyone recognized that hiring on with the JET program was a savvy financial decision, a way to pay off student loans and credit card debt, shore up savings for next steps, and fund our travel and shopping habits, courtesy of the Japanese government. One ponytailed second-year JET told us newbies about his first payday: he carried his cash-stuffed envelope home, where he and his wife opened it together, tossing the contents in the air, colorful yen falling to the floor like confetti as they laughed and rolled in it, financial worries dissipating. At least for the time being.

Our first official meetings, in which our dour gray-haired prefectural adviser presented various insights and admonitions — "Never walk and eat at the same time" — and returning JETs shared their personal gaffes and missteps, led to unofficial gatherings that served as launching pads for parties, romance and pan-Asian travel, young people comparing what countries they had already seen and which they wanted to visit during upcoming school breaks.

But arriving as I had, mere weeks after the end of my ill-fated marriage and after a month of transitions — leaving St. Paul for Fargo-Moorhead, flying to Chicago for JET orientation, flying to Tokyo for more orientation and then traveling to Shuho-cho — I simply wanted to settle in and try to smooth my ruffled feathers. I had little interest in merging onto the party circuit, running from town to town, festival to festival. And besides, without regular transportation, I had a clear choice to make: either spend a lot of time and energy riding buses and wrangling rides to get somewhere, or resign myself to staying put and diving into Shuho-cho's local scene. Whatever that entailed.

In the coming months I would linger mostly outside the vibrant expat community of JETs and others who lived along the train lines and would periodically hear about their lively weekends, gatherings at festivals, nightclubs and one another's homes, often filled with the drama that results from youthful partying. I would vacillate between smug contentment with my isolation and feeling left out, half-heartedly beginning to search for a car. But my supervisors would always find a reason why I should not lease one, why they would not approve of it — even at my own expense and despite the fact that my contract allowed for driving and I had brought an international driver's license. Wishing to preserve harmony in my adopted community, I would acquiesce.

Perhaps their sequestering of me, so recently wounded by love and fatigued by graduate school, saved me from the part of myself that was ready to cut loose, the part of myself that at this point, newly freed, might not have exhibited the best judgment. When I was truly honest with myself, I knew I had had enough adventure, dishevelment and emotional chaos over the previous few years to last me a while. For me, the JET Program was about finding a refuge, some quietude within which to regroup and discern what was important. I was mostly ready to stay still.

Returning to Shuho-cho after orientation, I embraced my little town, determined to make it my home, blending in as well as would a fully dressed geisha — exquisitely robed in kimono, hair pulled up in a perfect coif, face and neck glowing white — if she tried to nestle into my prairie hometown in Minnesota. I accompanied neighbors to late-summer festivals on the nearby school grounds, I toured shrines and temples with new colleagues, I attempted conversations with townspeople, and learned how enormously much I had to learn about everyday Japanese conversation.

Sometimes I rode my bicycle into the countryside to a small, wooden shrine, weathered to the color of driftwood, and ambled around its grounds, always alert for the venomous pit vipers that were said to live in the area. Unencumbered by anything but my own thoughts, I found a peace there that felt like a visit to church.

Other times I rode much farther searching for that thing, whatever it might be — train station? mall? theater? swimming pool? — that

I had not yet found, sometimes realizing only after I had ventured far from my apartment that yet another typhoon was whirling into the area, winds over the grassy green rice paddies propelling me faster and faster until I stopped, turned around and found I could lean my full weight into the heavy gusts with little danger of falling.

* * *

Sasaki-*san* and I continued my orientation outside the office, running around Shuho-cho to visit the bank, where we set up my checking account, to the neighborhood post offices, where I met the people who would handle my all-important contact with friends and family (I would have no email access for months), and to various shops, including Nattie, where I found everything from vegetables to housewares to those "sundries" I had seen pictured in the photographs included in my introductory letter.

I was one of few Westerners who had ventured to the actual town of Shuho-cho, despite its close proximity to Akiyoshidō, said to be the largest limestone cave system in the Far East. Inside it, visitors could walk a meandering path past formations bearing placards listing their names in Japanese and English — "Superlative Mushroom," "Jellyfish Climbing a Waterfall" — but whenever I went, it seemed I was the only one benefiting from the translations. As far as I know I was the first Caucasian to live in Shuho-cho for any length of time, and surrounded by a homogeneous community of Japanese people, my appearance — brown-haired, blue-eyed and five feet seven inches tall — made it impossible to go about a normal day. My size was both conversation starter and punch line for many encounters in Shuho-cho, particularly first meetings, when new acquaintances would stretch a hand up high in the air to mark my height before lowering it down onto their own heads, comparing my altitude to theirs, laughing, always laughing. "*Yes*," I would admit, "*172 centimeters*" — nearly five feet eight inches. "*Ehhhhhhh?*" they would exclaim. Then I would try to deflect attention by tossing out the heights of my mother and father, both taller than me at five feet ten and six feet three, thank you very much. Finally, I would lob the *pièce de résistance*: "But my brother is *203* centimeters" — about six feet eight inches tall. This nearly blew their minds and, I hoped, showed me to be rather petite, by comparison.

Soon I was running errands and doing business without Sasaki-*san*, engaging people with my rudimentary Japanese and pulling out my pocket dictionary when necessary. There was no such thing as a quick errand in Shuho-cho — and not just because of my sketchy language skills. Every outing functioned as a social call. The whole community seemed to know of my arrival, and early shopping trips involved more time visiting with shopkeepers and other customers than actually putting goods in my basket. After an early foray to Nattie, I walked away with freebies: the clothes hangers I had tried to purchase, a paper fan, towels and a package of steak.

Many of my evenings were conversation-filled too as I ran the *enkai* (party) circuit, some held to welcome me to town, others honoring people and groups I had just met. Wherever I went, I was always asked to introduce myself, to talk about my family, where I was from and my hobbies, and to say a word or two about my aspirations while in Shuho-cho, all in Japanese. Sometimes I was recruited to pour a round of beers, each person lifting his or her juice-sized glass in one hand, resting its base on the other, or to present flowers to a guest of honor. I met a lot of people quickly, and soon neighbors were inviting me to their homes for dinner and reporters were interviewing me for newspapers and newsletters, and on local radio.

The star power I experienced at the beginning of my time in Shuho-cho eclipsed even that of eight years earlier when I arrived in Hagi as its first international exchange student. My strategy then, as a high school student, was to try and blend in with my host sister Miho's high school classmates — despite my hair, my eyes and the height that made me nearly a head taller than most of the girls my age and many of the boys as well (but not Ryota). Working my peripheral vision to the hilt, I had followed the lead of those around me, studying how to eat properly, walk properly, listen properly, and dress properly, trying to avoid attracting attention based on attributes I could control. I came to favor skirts over shorts, covered my broad smile with the palm of my hand, raised my voice to a higher register, and tied a ribbon on my ponytail at the "golden point" on the crown of my head. I evolved something of a Japanese persona, one of which I only became aware on my few encounters that summer with other foreigners. In fact, I tried so hard to fit in that when I was out in public and happened to catch my own reflection in a mirror or pane of glass I was startled to see my small face, ivory skin and sky-colored eyes, on a head of wavy brown hair. I looked strange even to myself.

In Shuho-cho, hired as I was to teach English and bring an international perspective, I would find it even more difficult to fade into the crowd. Instead I slowly became accustomed to people gasping when I rounded corners and accepted that my height and eyes would be frequent sources of shock and amusement — and sometimes confusion. On one of my first solo visits to Nattie, two waist-high children spied me, stopped short and with puzzled faces pointed in my direction shouting, "*Chugokujin! Chugokujin!*" (Chinese person) before greeting me, "*Ni hao!*" in Chinese. I turned to look behind me, but no one else was there.

* * *

One day, after a week or so of feeling at loose ends in the office, Kashima-*kachō* approached my desk and asked me to follow him. We walked out the door into the lobby and began climbing a set of stairs I had yet to explore. The gray floors, gray desks, and smoky air-conditioned atmosphere of the main floor slipped away as we emerged into a different world, one of muted beiges, whites, and browns — woven tatami mats, sliding wood-and-paper doors, open windows and low tables adorned with flower arrangements. I had not realized that above me there had existed another plane, a relic of Japan's past.

We paused briefly before a closed wood and paper door, and Kashima-*kachō* slid it open, revealing a small room, sun-dappled and warm, where several people were setting up long wooden instruments and music stands. Seeing me, their activity came to a stop, and their *sensei*, who had been talking to one of the members, sensed the change in atmosphere, turned, saw me and beamed.

Kashima-*kachō* had brought me to meet an unlikely assortment of townspeople that included his postal-worker wife, the wife of a Buddhist priest, a girlish town employee married to a farmer, a high school student and a male junior high school music teacher. They constituted the town *koto* club, and they gathered once a week to study and play the Japanese zither, the official musical instrument of Japan, a six-foot-long wooden box with thirteen strings running the length of its back.

The group's *sensei* possessed a level of twinkle few could match. She looked like one beloved. Her lined face and long pinned-up hair were set against finely detailed clothing and delicate jewelry, all offset by the energy of a young woman, even a girl, albeit one with wise, friendly eyes. She locked those eyes on mine. "Hallo," she would say. "Howareyou? Hahaha!" I imagined her deeply in love with a debonair gray-haired husband who, now retired, would surely be tapping at his watch wondering why time stood still as he awaited her return to their love nest.

She quickly had me down on the tatami, on my knees, *seiza* position, lower legs prickling and then falling asleep, before a koto, which rested on the floor. On the tips of my right thumb and first two fingers she put leather rings with *tsume* (literally "claws" or "fingernails"). She directed my eyes toward a sheet of koto music — boxes of Japanese characters, beautiful but illegible, read top to bottom, right to left, pages turned with the left hand — set on a short music stand. And she made me play.

When asked to describe the koto's sound, I say it is the stringed instrument heard over sound systems in Japanese restaurants. But diners often eat to the sounds of the three-stringed *shamisen*, a fretless banjo-like instrument plucked with one corner of an elongated plectrum, its shape resembling a windshield ice scraper. A relative newcomer to Japan, having arrived from China via present-day Okinawa in the sixteenth century, the *shamisen* has a jaunty sound, a tennis ball hit hard against a concrete wall, a sound of summer. The koto, part of Japan's music scene since the eighth century, has a less percussive, more serious sound, the sound of autumn, winter, and spring.

That first koto afternoon, the teacher pointed to characters in the music book and then back to the koto's strings, giving me my first experience with tablature, in which the character for one (一) corresponds to the first string and so on, up to thirteen (巾). I understood the concept pretty quickly, but given that I barely read Japanese characters it was nearly impossible for my mind to translate the information on that page into music. This *sensei* seemed incapable, or perhaps unwilling, to believe it.

Somehow by the end of that first meeting, that unexpected lesson, after I had successfully plucked a few notes at the right time, she had me signed up for the koto club, carrying my own pink plastic and red brocade box of *tsume* and orange brocade folder of unreadable music. And she had exacted my commitment to perform with the group at the quickly approaching international contemporary music festival.

It sounded like a real-life version of that anxiety dream where you find yourself standing on stage, expected to do something for which you are utterly unqualified. I protested, "*Hontō-ni, Sensei, dekimasen!*" — "Really, *Sensei*, I cannot!" I had spent fourteen years studying the piano with demanding teachers and would never have performed in public without knowing I had a good shot at executing the music with competence. My new *sensei's* response? "*If you get lost, just po-zu!*" — "pose." She twinkled and giggled in the back of her throat.

It seemed I had no choice. Besides, I felt as if I was saying OK to a pipe dream. An international music festival in Shuho-cho? Perhaps the Japanese word I knew for *international* had different meanings — maybe it could encompass people in nearby communities. I could not imagine performers traveling from faraway lands to Shuho-cho.

Whatever will be, will be, I thought. All I knew was I had a person-sized instrument for a roommate, new music in my head, performances for which to prepare, an expanding community of acquaintances, and yet another reason to study the Japanese language.

7

My Old Hagi Home

I UNLATCHED the black metal gate, and it creaked open to reveal jade-green bushes of hydrangea and gardenia, manicured to look natural and trained to stay clear of people on the walkways — if, like my host grandmother, Obāchan, you were less than five feet tall. Gently pushing through branches, I found her well-groomed pines, the familiar moss-covered stones, the gray stone lantern and then, closer to the front door, pots of blooms, everything growing luxuriant but tidy. Street sounds faded away, replaced by the familiar smells of fragrant flowers, burgeoning foliage, fertile earth, moist air. I breathed deeply. I had finally reached my refuge. "*Tadaima!*" I called out. "I'm home!"

Obāchan stomped out of the house and swatted me across the back.

It was not quite the welcome I had expected. "*Where have you been?*" she exclaimed. "*You were supposed to be here a long time ago!*" In my eagerness to get "home" to Hagi, to see this grandma, who at eighty-three was strong of spirit but stiff of knees, rarely leaving home and garden, I had gotten disoriented at the bus station and walked a fair distance in the wrong direction. As a result, I had arrived later than promised. I bowed, apologizing, and explained my mistake. Then I leaned down to give her a hug. She returned it with warm indignation.

So resumed our curious familyhood, this Japanese household acting as if it were normal to have a tall young foreigner wandering in and out of the house, asking advice, eating and drinking at their table, watching their TV, bathing in their tub, falling asleep in their absent daughter's upstairs bedroom.

My host mother, Okāsan, had made it known — via my host sister Miho, who phoned me from Tokyo to tell me in English — that she would be treating me as a daughter, not a guest. She would not take time off from work when I visited, and she would not refuse my help with dishes. "This way," Miho said, "you will feel comfortable visiting more often."

She was right.

It seemed impossible that eight years had passed since I first dropped into their lives, a high school student assigned to their home, gradually making myself comfortable in Miho's room, sleeping on a futon, a cloud of blankets next to her bed. How quickly I had grown accustomed to the bustling Shinto shrine next door, the lemon-scented interior of the black family van, and a new diet: white rice three times a day (even when tiny frozen pizzas were served on the side), the various varieties of seaweed, the runny eggs, raw cabbage, and tomatoes — always peeled — at breakfast, the *tempura* prawns, and the sweet, peach-colored *biwa* that my host father would pluck from branches outside my younger sister's window, climbing out onto the tile roof of the home's second story. Over those two months, I had come to identify with them and my Japanese life so strongly that when strangers approached us to ask where I was from, I would answer, "Hagi," the name of that small Japanese city, befuddling everyone. By the time I left, though, it had all felt like home, as if I was truly their third daughter.

And how could four years have passed since that winter visit, when I had arrived from India with a workable Japanese vocabulary and we had reconnected as a family over three weeks during which I also got reacquainted with high school girlfriends, introduced my mother to this other world, and fell in love with Ryota? It seemed impossible that I had gone back to America, graduated college, married, wandered through two years of graduate school, and gotten divorced.

But all of that was the truth, and I felt the need to explain the hardest part: how my marriage had not worked out, how difficult it had been, how sorry I was that they had gone to the trouble of sending that glorious Japanese bride doll, which stood a couple of feet tall in her glass box, dressed in a red kimono and ornate white headpiece, gracing our hotel reception hall. As I flailed about in their language, they looked at me with kind, concerned faces, nodding as if they understood me as I flipped through my dictionary looking for words I had never needed to use in Japanese, words like *incompatible* and *sorrowful.* They seemed to sympathize with this crazy American daughter and her travails, as if they did not judge my participation in my home country's divorce culture, so foreign to the Japanese with their society's profound allegiance to marriage, if not fidelity. Gradually my shame dissipated, and I felt some sort of absolution, whether from them or myself I am not sure.

We ate supper that evening, I once again enjoying the flavor of Japanese comfort food — *o-fukuro no aji* (literally "mother's taste"). Then we watched TV and took turns relaxing in the *ofuro*, the bath, where so many years earlier Miho had tutored me in sitting on a plastic stool and using a hand towel-sized washcloth and cup to lather and rinse my body, the stress of the day disappearing with bubbles down a drain in the cool tile floor before we eased ourselves into the shoulder-high waters of the steaming-hot tub and she tried to convince me that it would not be a true Japanese bath unless we sang songs.

Now soaking alone in the celadon-tiled room, its frosted windows tilted open to the night air, I listened to every echoing drip and splash and insect chirp, feeling the water's heat seeping into my pores, my muscles, my very bones, and I began, at last, to unwind from the inside out. By the time nine o'clock arrived, and the city's chimes began to play the slow, majestic theme from Dvorak's *New World Symphony*, my homecoming felt complete.

As the weekend went on, the four of us sat down together for coffee breaks; the three of us women tsk-tsked about my host father Otōsan's habit of sneaking off to play *pachinko* at one of the nearby pinball parlors, so noisy and garish; Obāchan and I visited the shrine next door; Okāsan and I joined hundreds of other townspeople dancing at a *matsuri* (summer festival); and I took off on solitary wanderings through my family's centuries-old neighborhood to visit the seashore, my happy place.

Much as I wanted to believe I had arrived, having taken up residence in my dream world, the place where years earlier I had felt so comforted and so satisfied, something was missing. Ryota. Despite my efforts not to think about the time we had spent together in Hagi, first as high schoolers, then as college students, at the beach, at the store, at the school, at the park, I caught myself watching for him in all of those places, and in cars passing by, even though I knew his appearance was unlikely. Most young people who went away to university did not soon return to a small city like Hagi.

I was too shy to ask his whereabouts, much less to call his family's home. But I had been confronted by the truth. My heart had not let him go.

8

More Than a One-horse Town

DESPITE my early impressions of Shuho-cho as an isolated bastion of pragmatic farmers, I found it did have another side. A few years before I arrived, the town had established a Culture Exchange House, an elegant old farmhouse converted into a short-term haven for international artists and musicians, most of whom came from Europe. Located a fifteen- or twenty-minute bike ride from my apartment, the House periodically kept a visitor or two for some days or a few weeks. These short-timers would work intensely on their projects and then, at the end of their residencies, present gallery shows in the town building, across the hall from the koto room. Otherwise they kept mostly to themselves, having been attracted to Shuho-cho's remote location and its lack of distractions. There was talk of expanding this effort, of building an international arts village someday, out on Akiyoshidai, the plateau. *Are they serious?* I wondered.

The answer was yes. And that is how within a month of my arrival I found myself dressed in a lavender summer kimono and kneeling before a backdrop of gold-leaf screens on a stage draped in vermilion cloth. There, along with the rest of the koto club, I performed on my strange new instrument before a crowd of locals and, yes, international contemporary musicians, including one, a German artist, who literally gargled a song that evening.

Juggling the strange notes on the page and the thirteen strings on the instrument, I did, not surprisingly, lose my place for a while and had to *po-zu*, relying on others to carry my part as I pretended to play along. At the reception afterward, several French and Japanese musicians drew near to ask how I had come to study this fascinating instrument, and I was forced to confess its novelty even to me. I had first encountered it only eleven days earlier.

Musical accomplishments and failings aside, my achievement that night was in making a statement to the people of Shuho-cho: I was investing in my new community. My musical debut, I would later learn, thrilled the town's mayor.

More koto performances followed at festivals and out-of-town music gatherings, where our entire club would kneel on stage to play, I all the while worrying that my legs, which inevitably fell asleep, would betray me, leaving me to crawl off the stage dragging my koto behind me. Before each performance, I would be instructed to stand still like a doll, arms stretched out straight from my shoulders, so I could be dressed by another woman who would unfold a borrowed under-kimono and over-kimono, draping and tying them around my body, adding padding to fill in the curve of my waist, before wrapping a broad *obi* around my middle, not a zipper, button, snap, or pin between me and a wardrobe disaster. A daughterless acquaintance would soon take me under her wing and begin outfitting me with my very own pale-yellow kimono — hers from years past — and a collection of related gear, all of it slowly accumulating in my closet, which began to look like a Japanese trousseau.

My notion of living a solitary year unencumbered, floating in Japan, was unraveling.

9

English, the Dead Language

Fall term started September 1, but there would be no teaching until the middle of the month. My students were outside on their dusty school grounds, dressed in athletic uniforms and busily preparing for the autumn sports festival. I watched, astounded by the amount of time they were spending on seemingly pointless activities — students stacking themselves into five-layer pyramids; girls practicing pom-pom dances; boys working on their "monkey runs" — two boys, each holding one end of a long bamboo pole and running it across the field while a third boy, legs and arms wrapped around the pole, held on for dear life. *This* was the rigorous Japanese education system in action?

Had I been less gob-smacked by all the newness, I would have recognized the hubbub for what it was: a camaraderie-building event that would set the stage for the rest of the school year. But the lack of apparent structure and my ill-defined role in it left me feeling adrift. Having always been busy, studying and working, teaching and writing, I hardly knew who I was when I did not have a title, a role, an assignment, a deadline, or a problem to solve. The only times I had been able to simply be were when I had been pulled out of my element: in Japan, previously, and in India, where culture shock rocked me to the core.

But this time back in Japan, I had a defined role — I was supposed to teach English — and I felt I would be in limbo, dogged by my former life, until I stood before a classroom of students and metamorphosed into a teacher. This sports festival felt like a barrier between me and the life that I was waiting to begin.

I ambled about, and the students, wide-eyed, smiled to see me, but when I tried to engage them, even in Japanese, our interactions quickly devolved into them giggling and whispering, and me awkwardly smiling and nodding. Any conversation we achieved focused on my excessive height, my pale skin, and my blue eyes. I felt enormous, I felt ghostly, I blended in as effectively as a strobe light.

My Shuho-cho honeymoon, in which the newness of the culture and attention of the people had filled my days and my heart, had ended, and I had begun to feel irritable, my anger flashing and sadness welling over incidentals: *Why did everything have to be so different? Why did "yes" so often mean "no"? Why did everyone laugh at my height? Why were apples packed one by one in padded plastic sleeves?*

These feelings were not pretty, and neither were the moments I could not contain them, such as the outing to a museum where a newspaper reporter found me and initiated an impromptu interview. Unable to express myself fully in Japanese and certain he was misunderstanding me, misquoting me, I burst into tears, surprising my handlers, Sasaki-*san* and Satō-*kakarichō*, who swooped in to rescue me, their faces worried, ordering the reporter to kill his story.

I recognized the symptoms of culture shock, that process of acclimating to a new situation, where one set of norms must be traded out for another. I had experienced it as an exchange student, and there was no reason to believe it would not strike again now. It was a normal part of living abroad, and only by recognizing the tension between the expectations of my home culture and those of my host culture, by riding through this dark phase, could I eventually acquire the coping strategies that would enable me to truly adapt to Shuho-cho.

The process of working through culture shock has been illustrated many ways. One uses the letter U, the height of the letter representing the degree of one's well-being and its width signifying time. A person enters the new culture on a high note, enjoying the novelty and excitement. Soon, though, euphoria dissipates and the visitor descends into a place of frustration, hostility even, at the strangeness of the new environment. Finally, as she finds ways to deal with the stress and conflicting messages of her host culture, she rises again, eventually adjusting to the new situation, regaining her sense of well-being.

That U-shaped description always struck me as a bit simplistic, though, and in my JET materials I found a depiction of culture shock that rang far truer to me: a waxing and waning, never-ending wave, the nature of which changes over time. At the beginning of a cultural immersion experience, there are high crests and deep troughs — euphoria alternating with frustration — that arrive and pass frequently. But as time goes on, the wave stretches out. The crests are lower, the troughs are shallower, and waves of strong feelings arrive less frequently. The high highs give way to a more general sense of well-being, and although frustration still occurs, it is less debilitating. Kind of like home.

But knowing all this did not matter. I felt wobbly. I yearned for the structure and boundaries of a real schedule and a real role — the two things that I thought defined a real life; two things I anticipated would bring about my redemption.

* * *

When the first day of lessons finally arrived, I followed my co-teacher, Mr. Kita, to our first class at North Junior High. A small, bookish-looking man, not much older than I, he wore black-framed glasses and a cool attitude. When we entered the classroom, a student's voice sang out "*Kiritsu!*" and a roomful of chairs scraped the floor as the entire class leaped to its feet, standing as straight as green bamboo, faces serious. "*Rei!*" cried the student, and they bowed to us and we to them before they sat down again. We remained standing by the teacher's desk, at the front of the room.

I looked out at a couple dozen students who looked right back at me, their masks softening, some smiling shyly, others transparent with curiosity. The girls wore uniforms consisting of white sailor blouses and blue skirts, plain hair — no perms, no discernible styling — and fresh faces, not a hint of makeup. The boys sported crisp white shirts and black trousers, hair shorn in the *bōzu* (monk) style, prickly short. All of them had clean, white regulation school slippers. I was transported in time back to Hagi, where I had been charmed by the students' professional-style uniforms, which made them seem so timeless, so serious, so dear, as if they could just as likely have lived during my mother's or grandmother's childhood as now.

The homogeneity was striking, but I knew it existed only on the surface. My students practiced a restrained form of self-expression, a rich visual language of handkerchiefs, pencil cases, and key-holders that told stories of extracurricular interests, sports, and beloved *anime* characters. They were so unlike the awkward creatures my friends and I had been in junior high school, all big hair and heavy-handed makeup, ruffled blouses, Forenza brand jeans and white-soled Sperry topsiders, classrooms full of distracting fashion blunders.

Mr. Kita quickly launched into his lesson, directing them to take out their brightly colored textbooks and working with them through a story, explaining its grammatical points in Japanese. I had long envisioned my students soaking up the rhythm of English conversation, growing comfortable with greetings and gradually expanding their conversational repertoire throughout the coming year until they developed the confidence to experiment with their own constructions, their own topics. Now I waited for us to get to the conversational part of the lesson.

Mr. Kita continued to teach, and I continued to wait. And wait.

I began to feel less and less hopeful about my role, and then embarrassed to be standing at the front of the room, so obviously purposeless. I edged farther and farther away from the center, over to the side of the classroom. I took out my pocket dictionary and began passing the time by searching for the words I heard Mr. Kita was using in his lesson: *dōshi* meant verb, *meishi* meant noun, *keiyōshi* meant adjective. I wondered if anyone would notice if I were to slip out of the room and retreat back to my apartment, just across the street.

Now and then, though, Mr. Kita would throw me a bone, asking me to turn to a page in the textbook and read a paragraph in that stilted textbook English, directing the students to listen to my pronunciation. I had been warned at orientation about this role, being cast as a human tape recorder, a classic foreign language teacher archetype. But this, I would find, would be our pattern, Mr. Kita and I. *Good thing I packed up my life and traveled across an ocean for this*, I thought. *Good thing I prepared all those games and songs.* How quickly I was forgetting that this was to be my year of detachment, my year of nothingness, that I had intentionally put my own life on ice and that none of this was supposed to matter. But disappointment hit me like a wave.

The fact was my title in JET Program parlance was Assistant Language Teacher (ALT), the key word being "Assistant." One of JET's primary goals was for us ALTs to work with Japanese Teachers of English (JTEs), like Mr. Kita, to change the way English was taught in Japan's schools, to make the lessons more about conversation and real communication. But as ALTs, we often found ourselves swimming upstream against Japan's traditional way of teaching English, which long had been about rote memorization, infusing students with good grammar and a decent vocabulary that would enable them to read and write for the purpose of passing tests, tests that would help them get into the high schools and universities to which they aspired. English had long been treated as a conversationally dead language, not unlike Latin, so even after studying English throughout junior high and high school, and maybe university too, the best that many graduates could come up with was a set phrase, like "Dis is a pen!" Sometimes even that was too much to expect.

The bottom line was that despite the exhortations I had heard at JET orientations in Chicago, Tokyo, and Yamaguchi City, to work to change the English classroom mentality, my enthusiasm would go only so far. I was an assistant with no actual authority.

I had not fully considered the possibility that my co-teachers would not be excited to see me; that having been educated under the old paradigm, they might not welcome change. I probably assumed they had been the ones to request an ALT for their town. Before I met Mr. Kita, I had envisioned each of my co-teachers eagerly awaiting my arrival, imagining new approaches to their lessons and ways to incorporate a native speaker into their classrooms.

But my first classes with Mr. Kita should not have surprised me. He had not come to see me until school started, and then he had spent his prep time chatting and laughing in the school's smoking lounge, off the teachers' room, emerging from the haze a minute before class was to begin to collect his textbook and me, his real live textbook reader. As time passed, I suspected Mr. Kita dreaded having to brush up on his English speaking skills, which he probably had not used since college, and, more than that, to reveal to his colleagues and students how rusty his English was. The farther he stayed from me the better.

The next day, though, I took a bus to South Junior High School, in the town's central district, where I found Mr. Kumagai, who was as eager to start working with me as Mr. Kita had been to avoid me. As I understood when he visited me at the Board of Education office, Mr. Kumagai not only sympathized with the JET program's goal of changing the Japanese attitude toward English teaching; he was on fire about it. I wondered whether he had been the one to lobby for this little town to join the JET program, to import its own ALT.

A self-assured family man in his thirties, Mr. Kumagai had the appearance of a brainy soccer player and emanated an attractive energy, as serious about his work as he was happy to cut loose with good humor. He was one of the senior teachers at his school — respected, authoritative, and engaged — and had been part of the posse that met me at the airport, climbing into my car and riding with me to Shuho-cho. His eyeglasses, I noticed, had transition lenses.

Mr. Kumagai could hardly wait to immerse his students in the soup of spoken English, and was excited to involve me in lesson planning, giving my ideas, songs and games an enthusiastic try. He embraced my suggestion of presenting the students with names I considered "American" — that is, names of kids I had grown up with. I copied hundreds of them from an old baby name book onto name tags, and when classes began, his students chose their new monikers: Susan, Greg, Brian, Naomi.... The goal was for them to assume English-speaking identities that would release them from their inhibitions. I had seen how effective this could be while working at the Japanese immersion camp in Minnesota, where I had been known as Michi.

That first day teaching with Mr. Kumagai, I met every single student at South Junior High School — about 125 in all. That is how enthusiastic he was. We taught five classes, each of which included a listening comprehension activity: as I slowly described my family in English, the students drew pictures of me and what they imagined my mother, father, brother, and cat looked like. Designed by Mr. Kumagai, the project deftly introduced the students to me and me to the students, while producing a beautiful gift: I went home that evening with armfuls of papers covered in caricatures of my family and me, all of us saucer-eyed, willowy, and friendly looking, like characters from some cheery Japanese *manga*.

10

Shooting Star

Evenings in my Shuho-cho apartment — lit operating room-bright by Japan's ubiquitous fluorescent lights — settled into a routine I could replicate almost anywhere: pasta boiling in one pot, tomato sauce, vegetables and herbs simmering in another, television babbling in a corner of the living room for company.

But evenings that included a party or a meeting, I would arrive home late, chauffeured by a Board of Education staff member, who would deposit me in the dimly lit parking lot of the Dwelling Friends dormitory. Outside at that late hour, I would marvel at how night settled in Shuho-cho like a velvet curtain.

Attempting to exhibit polite Japanese behavior, I would use two hands to gently close my car door and stand on the asphalt bowing and waving, smiling brightly, even if the previous two hours had been exhausting — filled with those first questions asked of every foreigner — "*Do you like rice?*" "*Can you use chopsticks?*" — or deeply embarrassing, such as the time I was introduced to a phalanx of

Yamaguchi University international students from across Asia and the United States, all of whom took their classes in Japanese and who spent an hour pelting me in their proficient common language with complex questions that I, a newly minted English teacher with only conversational Japanese ability, had no hope of understanding, much less answering.

That latter time, after being dropped off, smiling, bowing and waving to my colleague-driver, I wondered how much of a fool I had looked, despite his praises, offered I knew, because he regarded me as *his* foreigner, *Shuho-cho*'s foreigner, the home-team foreigner. I swallowed my tears, cradled my withering pride and told myself that I had done the best I could under the circumstances. I resolved to apply myself more rigorously to the Japanese language studies I had not planned to undertake in my year off from life, so that the next time my Japanese would sparkle, despite the fact that I had no intention of carrying Japan into my future, wherever it might lead.

As my colleague turned his car and navigated toward the gate, blinker flashing, I waved some more, bowed again for good measure and then turned toward the building, pretending to head up the stairs toward my apartment, making a show of it so he would not wonder and linger, worrying about whether his charge, his foreigner, would make it safely home.

As soon as he was gone, taillights disappearing, red dots down the road, I crept back down to the parking lot and followed the line of the concrete building, turning its corner into the dark, not so far around that my neighbors could see me skulking in the shadows of the gravel backyard if they peeked out their brightly lit windows, but just to the side, where it was very dark and, had I been in St. Paul, I would have felt vulnerable. Here, though, I felt embraced by blackness, as if I had become part of the night. No one knew I was there, but I could hear the distant sounds of the Dwelling Friends' televisions, and, more loudly, the rhythmic croaks of frogs, crickets, and whatever else loitered in the moist paddies. I took time to listen and turned my gaze up to the sky where I saw the Milky Way, which in Shuho-cho really does look like milk, a pitcher-full splashed across a slate floor. Then, *fffffffft*, the most elegant solitary firework shot across the sky before disappearing like a dream.

And I thought, "Thank you," because every time I felt depleted, hopelessness settling in, it seemed God sent me a shot of encouragement — a shooting star, a smiling dog, a great blue heron lurching across a blue sky, a visit from a new friend — reminders that I was never alone.

11

Love at First

M Y relationship with my new instrument, the koto, was not exactly love at first listen.

The instrument, often likened to a dragon, is tuned by adjusting its thirteen white bridges, lined up like vertebrae on its back. Beginning tuning is a pentatonic scale known as *hirajōshi* — "tranquil tuning" — D, G, A, A-sharp plus nine more notes rising. To my ear it is less tranquil than pensive, maybe even gloomy. A dragon's solfège. And this is the mournful musical setup for traditional folk songs such as "*Sakura*" — "Cherry Blossoms" — as well as some of the beginner's classical repertoire, like "*Rokudan*" — "Six Pieces" — in which each theme seems more dissonant than the last.

At the beginning of my koto studies, the chord progressions made no sense and intervals seemed random. My Western sensibility told me these composers had written lines of bad-sounding music in willful disobedience to natural rules of good taste. I knew that cultures have different definitions of beauty, but the koto's sound often annoyed me to such a point that I wanted to declare the emperor had no clothes. I envisioned composers through the ages messing with future generations of koto students — *"Ha-ha, let's see if they can find a way to appreciate this little ditty!"*

Even so, I plodded along, trying to find beauty in these new sounds, and, I admit, using the koto for an ulterior motive: to make friends.

It amazes me how the instinct to remain aloof, to preserve my heart was so quickly overwhelmed by the desire to belong. I had envisioned myself living a solitary, perhaps even monastic year, using the peace of single life in a town that had barely made it on the map to process the events of the previous few years.

How quickly I got drawn into the fabric of Shuho-cho, worrying about local tea-serving customs, caring about the progress of my students, trying to keep up with other koto students, and looking forward to Naoko's visits.

The koto club gave me a needed purpose every Wednesday, the day I warmed my chair in the Board of Education office. I would entertain myself all morning knowing that in the early afternoon I would leave my desk and tea-serving duties, climb upstairs, and play and chat with my kindly *sensei*, and sometimes several other students as well. Then, the rest of the week I would encounter my fellow club members around town, and our greetings would go beyond the customary bright greeting of "*Konnichiwa!*" We talked about our songs, our struggles to master them, and our trepidation about upcoming performances. In those moments I could almost forget my identity as the town's resident foreigner.

I used my borrowed koto at home as well. At the front of my apartment an empty tatami-matted bedroom faced the parking lot, and I made it my koto studio. As evening approached, I would crack open the window, slip *tsume* on my fingers and kneel before the instrument to pluck out songs I had been assigned at my lesson. All the while, I kept a keen ear out for the sound of my downstairs neighbor Hideo's car — hoping he would hear me playing, hoping he would remember me, maybe pay me a visit and keep me company, maybe help me learn some of the "Polite Japanese" covered in the book he had given me.

I was not looking for love — memories of Ryota dominated my romantic imagination, and I wondered whether he had become a schoolteacher as planned, whether he was living in the fresh sea air of Hagi or in one of Japan's gray megalopolises. Hideo I wanted for friendship, in part because he reminded me of my congenial, thoughtful, and fun-loving male friends back in the States. After he helped me negotiate my Dwelling Friends birthday party, I had seen him around the building a couple of times and accompanied him, some of his work buddies, and the downstairs *obasan* to the "Italian Restorante" in a nearby town, where we ate pizza topped with octopus and prosciutto. Hideo was kind and entertaining, and, like me, he always seemed to be carrying his dictionary. It was endearing. But many nights his parking spot would remain empty long after I had finished playing koto. Maybe he was busy. Maybe he had a girlfriend. What did I care, right?

But why then was I acting like some kimono-wearing maiden depicted in a woodblock print, sending messages in the music of her koto, messages that would drift on the evening breeze, trying to capture the attention and then the heart of a passing warrior? Silly.

One mid-September Sunday I ran into him outside our building, and he asked if I might be free that Thursday. It was Respect for the Aged Day, so we would both have the day off work. He wanted to take me on an excursion. I said yes. When the day came, we drove around our part of Yamaguchi Prefecture, listening to CDs and visiting as I relaxed into the anonymity of sitting behind his tinted windows. Our tour of the area's high points extended into the evening with a side trip to Yamaguchi City, where we visited the temple Rurikoji and its stately five-story pagoda, built at the edge of a pond in the fifteenth century. Illuminated against the black night, its mirror image sparkled in the still water as the gibbous moon, three-quarters full, beamed overhead. I wondered whether Hideo intended this romantic view as an overture but put it out of my mind.

Hideo's passion was mountain biking, and sometimes he would go directly from work to the plateau or another scenic byway to ride off the stresses of the day — so that was why his parking spot was so often empty. And no wonder he seemed so *genki*, so centered, so healthy. No wonder he smelled of sunshine. I wanted to see him again and continued looking for excuses to cross his path and ways to encourage him to think of crossing mine. I kept practicing my koto, window cracked.

At last he visited my apartment, sitting at my kitchen table, where we drank green tea and listened to music, telling each other stories and laughing in a mix of English and Japanese. He visited again and again, our conversations expanding, he describing his work at the Sumitomo mine on a nearby mountain, where monster machines extracted limestone, and talking about his hobby, rides and races completed, I telling him of the broad flatness and deep snows of my prairie homeland. We enjoyed each other at arm's length.

This friendship, though, was too good to stand still. It did not take long before he told me, "I'm crazy about you," and I wondered where he picked up his English phrases and whether they meant the same to him as they did to me. What I did know was, like my relationship with the koto, this was not love at first sight. I confessed to him — and, in Shuho-cho, only to him — that I had been married before and recently divorced. I told him I did not want to date anyone and that he should not get attached to me. I had arrived in a time machine and would be leaving in it after one short year. He did not need to know that my desire to stay aloof was compounded by my vague hopes of finding Ryota.

There was another complicating factor. Hideo came from a religious family but seemed to hold no belief himself. Having emerged from a marriage that suffered for lack of consensus about how faith should be implemented, how life should be lived, Hideo's lack of belief fluttered like a red flag. No matter how attractive he was, I knew staying platonic would be an easier and safer choice for my heart and his. I would wait for a sign that I was wrong.

* * *

Despite my wanderings, failures, and deep confusion, I held out hope that God would step up and reveal a path to me. Although at that time I wasn't the type to spend time reading my Bible or devotionals, for years I had watched for signs and prayed for guidance — "Tell me what to do!" — but had heard only resounding silence. Impatient, I had plowed ahead, suffering through decision after decision: choosing a college, selecting a major, staying with boyfriends, breaking up with boyfriends, abandoning a perfectly good start in the field of biology to pursue the dream of writing, divorcing an ill-fitting husband, jumping ship for a year in Japan. Through all of those decisions I never felt the sense of clarity that would have allowed my soul to exhale and my mind to rest knowing I had done the right thing. After each decision point, when the result seemed less than satisfactory, I had the sense that I must not have listened closely enough or waited long enough to hear God's answer. I vowed that at the next crossroads I would try again, even harder, to give over the decision-making to God. Maybe then he would help me.

Or maybe he already had. There was that visit to the student health service in the midst of my marital discord, when I met a lovely red-haired nurse who, in the course of a skin check, seemed to say everything I needed to hear. As she methodically looked over my body, she spoke with calm authority: "You need to keep your focus, because no one is going to live your life but you. People will always want to take pieces of you, but you must maintain your priorities and be true to who you need to be. Don't worry whether everyone understands what you need to do, as long as you know why you are doing it."

I listened, rapt. Who was this woman? At the end of the appointment, she opened the door to leave the exam room but turned back to face me. "You are making excellent progress," she said, and closed the door. Alone in the silent room, I knew I had been changed. As I wandered back to the journalism department, I sensed I had been in the presence of an angel.

And then came that sunny May day a couple of weeks later, after my husband and I decided to separate, when I slouched down the stairs of our apartment building, pushed open the old wood and glass doors, stepped outside onto the sidewalk, and was startled by what greeted me. The green of the leaves, the grass and the trees, and the purples and pinks of blooming lilacs and apple trees struck me as ethereal, as if they were vibrating with energy. I stopped in my tracks to gaze at the splendor, to breathe it all in, as if I were seeing spring, colors, for the very first time, as if the grief I had been feeling over my dying relationship had until then been sucking the color right out of my sight, leaving me surrounded with black, white, and shades of gray. Now that I had hope for a different future, my sense of color had been restored. Maybe this was God's answer, his benediction on my gut-wrenching decision.

Perhaps God had not been so silent in the face of my questioning after all. It could be he had been sending messengers and painting pictures for me while I listened and waited for a whisper in my ear. Only my eyes and my mind had been closed.

* * *

Hideo refused to give up on the idea of taking our relationship to the next level and set to work changing my mind. Soon he was visiting my apartment more often, toting boxes filled with dry ice and plastic cups containing perfect scoops of ice cream he picked up while running errands to the city; making me cassette tapes of hit music, Japanese and American, Cyndi Lauper and Akiko Yano; bringing gifts picked up on business trips — from Kyoto a red brocade sachet of sweet, powdery-smelling incense with which to scent my chest of drawers; from elsewhere a porcelain teabag holder shaped as a teapot. On it, in English, was painted, "Let me Hold Tea, Sugar."

I could not help but enjoy his care.

12

Fall Festival

I HAVE a small confession. I tried to contact Ryota before I arrived to teach in Japan.

Twice.

I sent him a New Year's card in January and then a birthday card that spring, right around the time I signed my contract for Shuho-cho. He did not answer either missive, but I told myself that he might have moved on so far from Hagi that my cards never found him. Or maybe his family had moved and my notes had fallen into some black hole in the Japanese postal service. Or maybe his mother had intentionally kept my cards from him, not wanting to add drama to his life. I could not get past the thought that he might be somewhere pining for me as much as I was for him.

It would have made sense, after years of no contact — not to mention that I had no idea how he would, could ever fit into my future life — to let him go. But something between us seemed to have been left undone. This feeling probably originated in the moment I hung up the telephone after he called from California, when I recognized that by not offering to fly out and meet him I had missed the opportunity to close the circle of our relationship, whether that meant reconnecting with him and rekindling our romance or hearing the sad truth that it was over and I needed to let him go.

Now that I was free, and in Japan, it seemed foolish not to find out the truth once and for all.

I lasted a couple of months in Shuho-cho before I could bear it no longer. I figured that since he had gone to university near Tokyo, he had probably found employment there post-graduation. So I looked up the phone number for Tokyo information. Then I sat on it and worried about it and wondered how Japan's telephone service worked. If I were to call and ask for his listing, could the operator click me right through? Would I be instantly out-ed to Ryota? And what if a woman answered? And what if *he* answered? Finally, sick with nerves, I dialed the number, praying I was not about to make a serious mistake. The call went through, and I was greeted by an electronic message that I could not understand. There was nothing to do but hang up, disappointed but relieved. Maybe it was saving me from myself.

Soon afterward I called my same-age host sister, Miho. She asked how things were going in Shuho-cho, and I got an update on her glamorous big-city life. But once we had worked our way through the usual chitchat, I pulled out my best "oh-by-the-way" and, feigning nonchalance, asked her whether she knew anything about Ryota. She suggested I call his mother. I suggested she was crazy.

The next time I went for a visit to Hagi, I took a deep breath and, as my heart banged like a *taiko* drum, I affected my easy-breezy quizzical face and asked Okāsan the same question. Surely she would be more reasonable. But she said the very same thing, and tossed in a Japanese proverb: "*If you don't try, it's the same as being told no.*"

Still, I could not bring myself to pick up the phone.

One November weekend, I returned to Hagi to attend the local fall festival with my friend Kiyoko, whom I had met there in high school. We sat down to eat lunch and began reminiscing about her high school classmates, many of whom I remembered vividly, despite having spent only a short summer with them. I waited and waited through news of person after person for some tidbit about Ryota, and the longer I waited, the more hopeful I became. No news was good news, right? Finally, I could bear it no longer and with as much nonchalance as I could muster, I asked, *What about Ryota?*

Ryota? she responded casually. *He lives near Tokyo. He's married.*

No.

He wasn't.

I must have misunderstood.

But even as I replayed her words in my head, even as my heart took off, thumping in my ears and shooting pains through my chest, even as my face grew hot and my feet itched to run far, far away, my polite, smiling mouth began asking the whens, wheres, and whos of the situation, as if it was the most delightful news and had nothing at all to do with me.

Inside, I wailed. I howled. It could not be true. Kiyoko must be mistaken. I must have misheard. She had gotten the story wrong. But I knew deep in my sickening gut that she had told me the most dreaded truth.

Poor Kiyoko had not known what this parcel of information would mean to me, who Ryota had been to me, that in addition to a treasured fling, he had been a guiding star out of my rocky marriage. I tried not to let my feelings show, tried not to let them dampen the festival mood. When we arrived at a booth offering blood pressure checks (why I cannot remember), the nurse frowned at my unexpectedly low reading, 95 over 60. I did not tell her that I was glad to know my heart was still beating at all.

Although Okāsan had advised finding out what had happened to my old love rather than never knowing, now that I knew, I wished I could reenter my old haze, the one in which I itched with curiosity but where the door to possibility was forever left ajar.

Later I considered the news in my journal:

> *So is it really over? Do I still call his mom and find out for sure? Do I send him a Christmas card, congratulating him on his marriage? Do I write him off completely? To be honest, his image has been getting fuzzier for me as I gather more images and experiences in Japan. But it still was comforting to know he's in this world.*

I returned to Shuho-cho and called Tokyo to report the news to Miho, that his wedding had occurred mere days after I had arrived back in Japan. I told her I was stunned. She commiserated with me for a while, and we hung up.

Not many minutes later, my telephone rang. I picked it up and was startled to hear the quiet, tender voice I knew so well: "*Sah-lah?*"

Ryota.

Using simple vocabulary he intuited I would understand, he told me what I already knew: that not only was he married, but his new wife had a baby in her belly, and it was due in just a few months. He told me he would like to see me again someday, and I said I would like that too. I congratulated him. And his wife too. I wished them well. I hung up the phone.

That's when I came completely undone, crying as I had not cried in many months, crying for the life and the dreams I had lost at home in Minnesota and for those I had lost now, here in Japan, crying for the shock of it all, crying so hard that it felt as if I might turn myself inside out, feeling so desolate that I would not care if I did.

Alone in my apartment in Shuho-cho and lonely for someone in the same time zone who might understand my feelings, not to mention my language, I called a new JET friend, an Englishwoman who was posted in a city a couple of hours away. When she answered, I, bawling, explained to her, as well as to myself, that I had not returned to Japan, post-divorce, to find romance, but now that I had learned Ryota was married and soon to be a father, I did not know why the hell I was there.

My poor bewildered friend listened kindly. A day or two later I received a package in the mail from her. It contained a note of encouragement and a little stuffed hedgehog.

What galled me most was to think that as I was getting over jet lag, licking my wounds from the previous couple of years, greeting hundreds of new students and teachers and neighbors and shop-keepers, taking long walks through the rice paddies, and learning how to recycle my garbage, Ryota was trying on tuxedos and his fiancé-now-wife was enjoying the final fittings for her multiple wedding dresses.

Had I known what was happening, I wonder if I might have instead pulled a stunt à la Dustin Hoffman's character in the cli-mactic wedding scene of *The Graduate*. I can almost see myself abandoning my teaching post and tracking down Ryota to the white-clapboard-look wedding chapel where I envisioned his wedding took place. I would have banged on its flimsy doors till someone let me in, the ceremony on hold, guests gawking, and he would have walked toward me, slack-jawed, eyes twinkling with surprise, and we would have fled together onto a passing city bus, destined for happily ever after.

Or something.

13

The Walls Have Ears

THE walls of my apartment house were thin. I knew this because I could hear animated conversations and laughter coming through the one I shared with the neighbors on my right. They were a smiling older couple, he with high arched eyebrows, she with small, crinkly eyes and a dainty mouth. Every weekend they would hop in their pearl-painted car, its seats covered in white lace, and "*tooooooooooooooooobu!*" — "fly!" — along the freeway, as the wife would say, her fine-boned hand gliding like an airplane down a runway, moving faster and faster away from the Dwelling Friends and the concerns of Shuho-cho, and escaping toward adventure.

The wall on my left side was much quieter. It was home to the slightly rakish *shachō*, the man in charge of the local branch of Sumitomo Cement, and his worried-looking wife. He was a closed-eye smiler and she was a bustler who now and then invited me in for exquisitely prepared suppers, proper affairs with the three of us sitting around their table, cautiously congenial. Other times, she rang my doorbell before I had even begun to rummage for supper in my own little fridge and delivered a shiny lacquered-wood tray laden with flawless, magazine photo-worthy meals: shrimp-stuffed squash, delicately flavored miso soup, and *chawanmushi* — a treasure hunt in the form of an egg custard containing morsels of meat and mushrooms, plus a ginkgo nut. When I told my downstairs *salariman*-neighbor Hideo about these special deliveries, he would shake his head and smile, marveling at the attention I received, and its tasty benefits. Now I wonder if those were nights her husband failed to come home for dinner.

Living in that building but working hard not to put down roots, I assumed myself to be a model neighbor, as innocuous and unobtrusive as an air fern. Late that autumn I would learn otherwise.

* * *

By November, I was ready for a break from Shuho-cho. I still loved my little town, but I felt threadbare from the attention, positive though it was. I observed in my journal, "even kindness can be oppressive." Everyone everywhere seemed to know everything I did or did not do, and I felt a lot of pressure to be *on* — to be friendly and happy at all times, to be the model Assistant Language Teacher, American ambassador, and young lady. It is clear to me now that I was overcompensating for my carefully concealed secret identity, that of a divorcee. I feared — probably irrationally — that if my new community knew this unfortunate piece of my past, they would look askance at me and regard me as a bad influence on their children. Worn down from my quest for perfection, I craved anonymity, just for a little while. So when I noticed the Labor Thanksgiving holiday approaching in November, I saw it as a chance to throw off my growing attachments in Shuho-cho. (Once I determined that a change of scenery was the cure-all for life's challenges, it was hard not to keep going.)

I might have gone off and disappeared alone, but I had too vivid an imagination for that, envisioning myself getting kidnapped or worse half a world away from home. And I doubt I mentioned my plan to travel to my host parents, for fear of causing them concern. So I found an accomplice, a seemingly kindred spirit I had met in August at the JET orientation in Tokyo. A fellow Minnesotan, Robb was posted several prefectures away in a similarly isolated town, and we had been comparing notes fairly regularly on the phone, sharing enough of our triumphs and foibles for me to correctly assume that he would be as ready to get away as I was.

There was nothing romantic between us, at least not of which I was aware. I found his Germanic look — a tall, solid build, dark blond hair, and ready smile — easy on the eyes, though, so I went into our short week away open-minded, not completely averse to the idea of romance but not seeking it either — if for no other reason than that the tone of his voice bore an uncanny resemblance to my ex-husband's.

As I saw it, the best part about traveling with Robb was that he was amenable to my goal: to find the most remote point in western Japan, the place where we would be least likely to run into anyone either of us knew. And while we were at it, that place might as well be warm and sunny. Our agreed-upon destination: Yoron-tō, a tiny island near the larger, better-known island of Okinawa.

This is how you get from my apartment in Shuho-cho to Yoron-tō:

- Walk to the bus stop and catch the 7:29 a.m. bus to central Shuho-cho.
- Transfer to the 7:54 a.m. bus to Ogōri Station.
- Board the 8:51 a.m. southbound bullet train to Hakata Station, located near the northern end of Kyushu, the southernmost of Japan's four main islands.

- Find the 9:45 a.m. subway to nearby Fukuoka Airport.
- Take the 11:05 a.m. flight to Kagoshima, near the southern tip of Kyushu.
- Transfer to the 12:20 p.m. flight to Amami Oshima, an island halfway between Kyushu and Okinawa.
- Arriving on Amami Oshima at 1:10 p.m., make your way to a *ryōkan* (traditional inn) and meander about for a while before eating and retiring early.
- The next morning, board the 6 o'clock ferry for Yoron-tō. Spend the next eight hours on a droning, juddering boat wondering what you are running from, where you are running to, who you are running with and why.
- Disembark onto a thankfully motionless concrete pier at Yoron-tō with your traveling companion, a handful of other passengers and a crate of live pigs, their faces pink and hopeful, their fate less so, and know that you have arrived.

You are now three hundred nautical miles from the southernmost point of mainland Japan, many hours and transfers away from anyone you might know, far from colleagues who fear speaking English and students who giggle at your blue eyes, far from JETs who live along the train lines and have fabulous social lives, far from petite new friends and handsome neighbors who claim to be crazy about you and past loves who live in Tokyo with their pregnant wives. Now, standing on a twelve-square-mile droplet of land inhabited by a few thousand strangers and surrounded by the Pacific Ocean to the east and the East China Sea to the west, you are as close to unencumbered as you are ever going to get.

And possibly as close to paradise as well.

Yoron-tō is an uncrowded island of spectacular beauty — white sands, magenta-blooming bougainvillea, and coral reefs just below the surface of balmy fish-filled waters the color of blue curaçao. Even its outline is picturesque, described by one geographer as the shape of an angelfish. Along with sugarcane and beef cattle production in the island's interior, tourism is the major industry here. But when Robb and I arrived, our fellow tourists were nowhere to be found. It turned out Labor Thanksgiving was low season for Yoron-tō, so we had the island's attractions to ourselves. We settled into our youth hostel and spent Thanksgiving touring the island on mopeds, marveling at poinsettias as tall as one-story buildings, blooming on the roadside; visiting an old-style village of thatched huts, where we were introduced to pillows made of wood, seashells used as kettles, and spiky dried blowfish used as mouse deterrents, installed on ropes between the ceiling and a food hanger; taking a private glass-bottomed boat tour along the coast of the island, watching fish teem below us and visiting tiny Star Island with its star-shaped grains of sand. As evening arrived, we watched the sun set beyond the reefs over open dusky water.

It sounds like a honeymoon, but I recall no spark between us, and had there been even an ember, it would have been doused by the intense curiosity of a few of the islanders, like the grizzled old fisherman who fell in behind us on a deserted beach and began inquiring about our romantic status. Laughing, he recommended we procure some locally caught *uni* (sea urchin) so we could enjoy its benefits to virility, which he illustrated graphically, wiggling his index finger in front of his groin. This lurid style of engagement was certainly different from the attention we received in our posts on the mainland, and it wore on Robb's and my still-new friendship. At the end of our trip, we gave one another a farewell hug, parted ways, and never spoke again.

It was OK. I had found what I had been seeking: a total break from my Japanese reality as well as a chance to reflect on everything that my situation in Shuho-cho offered. It was an opportunity to see I was starting adulthood over and now had the opportunity to establish the life of my dreams.

* * *

My trip with Robb bothered Hideo immensely, and he insisted on meeting me at Ube Airport and driving me the hour or so home to Shuho-cho. I was pleased to see him again, to get back in his car with its tinted windows and return to what had become my new familiar, but we were hardly out of the parking lot before he began telling me about some trouble that had erupted while I was away. His supervisor, at the direction of my next-door neighbor, the *shachō*, had taken Hideo aside and told him that he should not be visiting my apartment. There was talk. It did not look good for the Dwelling Friends, nor for the Board of Education.

I was astounded. My innocent tea times with Hideo were raising eyebrows? No, I was angry. Had my neighbors been spying on our comings and goings? Had the *shachō* and his wife been sitting next to our shared wall and eavesdropping on our conversations, our music, and laughter? I was accustomed to being under relatively constant observation in public places (with children calling out their greetings at the endearing end of the spectrum and the *uni*-pushing fisherman at the other), but I had regarded my apartment as a refuge, a safe place, one where I could clang shut my heavy metal door and inhabit my own private world. I thought I was a good neighbor.

Back in Minnesota, in the relatively small city where I had grown up, I had never sensed my neighbors keeping tabs on me like this. We were friendly, cat-sitting and watering each other's gardens when families went on vacation, but not spying. I had never heard of neighbors making comments or judgments about the boys and girls who came over to shoot baskets on our driveway when I was in high school or to sit with me on the front stoop and watch the traffic go by during college vacations. This level of surveillance was different. Bizarre even.

Had I been more knowledgeable about Japan's past, it might not have surprised me as much. Japan has a long history of neighbors keeping watch on neighbors. Beginning in the early seventeenth century, the beginning of the Tokugawa period, Japan's primary means of social and administrative control was the *goningumi*, literally the "five-person group," units of five to ten families that created a formidable network of social responsibility. Being part of a *goningumi* had its benefits to be sure: it promoted collaboration and created a ready labor pool for rice farming. But this was not a club or even a co-op; it was compulsory, and group members were responsible for one another's behavior and obedience to local and national law, from ensuring that all members paid their taxes to enforcing the shogunate's ban on Christianity.

Compulsory *goningumi* requirements were abolished in the late nineteenth century with the Meiji Restoration, but if I have learned anything about Japan, it is that traditions die hard. The Dwelling Friends dormitory where I lived was approximately *goningumi* size, and I wonder now whether such watchfulness might remain among people who belong to the same company and also live together. There were probably rules — written or otherwise — of which I was unaware that governed life on Dwelling Friends property. Perhaps it was verboten for a first-floor *salariman* — i.e., Hideo — to visit the executive floor, where I lived, without permission from a superior. Maybe misbehavior, perceived or actual, on company property could result in a reprimand or sanctions against everyone at that branch.

I will never know for sure. Had I asked, I doubt I would have received a straight answer. As a non-employee, not to mention a *gaijin* (foreigner), I would never be a full-fledged *goningumi* member. Shuho-cho might have been my floating temporary world, but it was one hundred percent real to everyone around me.

What bothered me even more than being censured by my landlord was that my Board of Education handlers were allegedly in cahoots with him. I dreaded returning to the office and worried that perhaps I was in trouble, my job in jeopardy, for breaking some rule I did not know existed.

This was especially perplexing because I had thought my hosts were happy that I was settling in, making friends and becoming part of the community, unlike many JETs who taught as required but spent their free time meeting up with other foreigners, not dipping as deeply into our host culture — or experiencing as much of the related culture shock — as I was. It had even crossed my mind that the Board of Education might have prevailed on Hideo to spend time with me, that he might have been a plant, used to watch over me, to keep me satiated with ice cream and music, to deliver me to stores where I could buy cheese, to keep me busy in Shuho-cho and encourage me to settle down in that isolated town, perhaps sweetening the pot enough so I would consider a second year. (My employers had made it known early on that they were hoping I would stay on.) To find out now that Hideo was regarded as a troublemaker, a spoiler, made me furious with the Dwelling Friends, not to mention the Board of Education.

The situation made me feel like a *hako-iri musume*, literally "a daughter-in-a-box," a label that can be taken a number of ways. It can refer to a beloved daughter, lovingly sheltered by her family from the difficulties and wiles of the wide world, but it also can describe a girl who is so confined that she is unable to do anything but obey her family and kowtow to social expectations. I had some experience of life as a *hako-iri musume*. When I began dating the man who became my ex-husband, my parents tried to shelter me from what they saw as a questionable match. But from my perspective, as a college graduate who had lived responsibly on my own for the previous four years, my parents' curfews and restrictions all but herded me off the cliff into that marriage.

One of my hopes for my year in Japan was to cut the parental apron strings with absolute finality. I had not envisioned becoming entangled in new ones belonging to my landlord and employers.

It seemed that the Dwelling Friends and my Board of Education bosses were trying to stand in for my parents, trying to protect me — but from what? Making a friend? I had just lost Ryota, or at least my dream of Ryota, and aside from my work colleagues, who were busy with their own lives, I had exactly two friends in Shuho-cho whom I could spend time with: Naoko and Hideo. Would it really hurt to allow me them? All I needed was a job to do and a place to live. And a couple of friends. Beyond that, I needed everyone for whose opinion I had not requested to stay out of my private life.

Embarrassed, confused, ill at ease, and knowing there was no appropriate way to approach my landlord, the *shachō*, about the matter, I backed away from Hideo. How could he not have seen this coming? This was his homeland, his culture, his language, his company's dormitory. How could he have let our reputations be sullied? At the time I assumed that is what the hubbub was about, people's assumptions that we were in my apartment making out, getting overly involved for someone's taste. What they did not know was how hard I was trying to stay out of the fray of Shuho-cho life. As for Hideo and me, we were only drinking tea and listening to music. We were innocent. I had arrived in Shuho-cho looking for a fresh start, thought I had found it and had planned to maintain it. Now I worried I had been branded the town slut. I wanted to crawl into my bed headfirst and not come out.

Hideo seemed almost as surprised about the situation as I was, and that did nothing to mollify me. It only made me wonder: had my desire to find a friend, or my feeling flattered that this man wanted to spend time with me, blinded me to the fact that he was a bit dim? Or naïve? Or foolish? Were my limited language skills handicapping my ability to judge the type of man he was?

When I took a deep breath and considered Hideo rationally, I saw a really great guy. He was different from most of the other young men, more animated, more engaging — in a friendly, not seductive, way. He smiled easily. He was kind. He made eye contact, unlike many of the other guys, particularly the single ones, who avoided my eyes when we passed each other in the parking lot, as if that would enable them to believe I was not really there, as if it would prevent something uncomfortable — me speaking to them? me *jumping* them? — from happening. On the rare occasions they did acknowledge me, it was more apt to be with a grunt and a nod than a smile. And although Hideo's nature was different, I could see he was well-liked by his peers, the older employees and the dormitory *obasan*, who was clearly fond of him.

So what did it all mean? Was Hideo normal or strange in this culture, his culture? And did it matter? He had been a good friend to me.

I took the situation to my unofficial *onēsan* (older sister) Naoko, expecting sympathy and an explanation that made sense. Instead, she piled on. "*Of course,*" she said in a mix of Japanese and English. "*It is not appropriate for a single woman to invite a man into her home. He should know better than to visit you. It doesn't look good.*"

Oh, she made me crazy, talking so holier-than-thou, as if she had always lived the life of Hello Kitty, so much more innocent than

I. As my self-appointed *onēsan*, she seemed to believe she had the right to give me increasingly frank advice on how to negotiate life in her hometown. But she gave me no credit for good behavior, for ignoring sea urchin-pushers in Amami-oshima, or for keeping my tea times with Hideo platonic in Shuho-cho.

In retrospect, though, I wonder if I missed the point of her admonishment. Maybe she was not as critical of Hideo's visiting me as she was of the *appearance* of his visiting me. Perhaps she was admonishing me to pay more attention to the way our comings and goings looked to the neighbors, to take the pressure off the people around us by not giving them something they might think they needed to worry about. Or was she skirting the possibility that the troublemaker was me? Some knew I had gone on vacation with another man, and they could easily have made assumptions about my relationship with him as well as my relationship with Hideo — and decided to protect the latter.

Or it could be Naoko was simply conveying to me a lesson that is innately understood by people who have grown up in small towns: people observe, and people talk. What else is there to do in a place that shuts down at six o'clock every night? This might have had less to do with Japanese culture than with small-town life.

In my embarrassment and anger (and soundly back in my culture-shock trough), I glared at the wall I shared with the *shachō*, wondering if he and his wife were sitting on the other side keeping tabs on me, monitoring whether Hideo and I had discontinued our visits, as ordered. At the Board of Education office, I sat sullenly at my desk. But things there were so normal that I wondered whether my work colleagues even knew about the Dwelling Friends' concerns — or about my friendship with Hideo. Eventually I would conclude the Board's alleged concern had been manufactured for shock value.

As for Hideo, I avoided him for some weeks while trying to sort everything out, trying not to make waves.

And then I realized something: I missed him. He had become irreplaceable. He *was* different, and I liked him for that. Maybe it was his gregarious metropolitan upbringing, or perhaps it had to do with his family's character. Maybe he was different for no reason other than that he liked me and was willing to bend the rules to spend time with me. There was no way I could tease apart the many elements that made up this man, particularly when I factored in his baffling home culture. My heart said I wanted to spend time with him, and to my heart I began to listen.

Inevitably, predictably, the *shachō*'s edict pushed us together. To spend time as friends, we had little choice but to leave town on what were, essentially, dates. I would dash down to his sporty black car, and we would quietly roll away from our apartment building, out of Shuho-cho and toward a nearby city, or a beach, or a tourist site. We went to subtitled American action movies and visited temples. We grabbed suppers of squid-ink pasta and ran half-necessary errands to distant grocery stores.

And once the kerfuffle seemed to have died down, we resumed meeting in my apartment. It was us against the *shachō*, us against the company. Hideo would call to see if I was there, and I would go to my front door and wait. He would tiptoe past the *shachō*'s apartment and, as I felt the vibrations of his footsteps approach, I would ever so slowly turn the knob and push open my door. He would enter and just as slowly close it. We would turn up the music and whisper until we forgot to.

I might have learned the Japanese proverb "*Kabe ni mimi ari shōji ni me ari*" — "The walls have ears and the paper doors have eyes" — but I fooled myself into believing that it was possible to hide.

14

Arrangements

As I was getting to know Naoko, my Shuho-cho *onēsan*, she introduced me to her herbs, which grew in pots and beds around her family's old farmhouse, speaking their names as tenderly as one might those of dear friends — "*ra-ben-da*" (lavender), "*re-mon beh-bee-na*" (lemon verbena), "*ba-ji-ru*" (basil). Bruising their leaves and flowers between her fingers, she held them to my nose while describing each plant's aromatherapeutic and medicinal qualities, as if she were training an apprentice. Some were good for stomach upsets, others soothed the nerves, while still others invigorated the mind.

A high school graduate, Naoko drifted between retail and office work while maintaining a steady presence at home, where she helped with the cooking, cleaning, and gardening. But herbs were her calling. She tended, harvested and dried the best parts of the plants and transformed them into teas, soaps, candles, and sachets of many varieties — sweet-smelling sacks to bury in drawers, lavender-scented sleep-enhancing envelopes to slip into pillowcases, mint- and rosemary-scented tubes to refresh smelly shoes. She sold these products at area festivals, and to hear Naoko tell it, there were few day-to-day problems these herbs could not fix.

But there was one. As I observed her disdain for my relationship with Hideo and gradually heard her own story unfold, I recognized it as the source of her underlying anxiety: at age twenty-eight, she still was not married.

Now that I am a quarter century older, twenty-eight sounds very young, and even then, when I was a newly freed twenty-five-year-old, it seemed we both had many years to play with before needing to get serious about settling down. But then, in the mid-1990s, in her traditional hometown, in her traditional family, or perhaps only in her traditional mind, it was her duty to marry, because at least in theory her single status could hold up the plans of her two younger brothers, who had long since left home for the wider world of university and girlfriends. As the eldest child, she was expected to marry before her brothers.

Not only was Naoko well past the Christmas cake sell-by date; she had been returned to the shelf.

I knew this before she told me, because it is the sort of thing that people love to murmur about, and I arrived in Shuho-cho not long after her wedding had been called off. What I quickly gathered was that Naoko's case was not a tragedy of two young lovers growing apart after the wedding invitations had been sent out. No, it was an unfortunate situation for a whole crowd of people who had been involved in getting them together in the first place. Their marriage had been arranged.

I had trouble believing that the tradition of arranged marriages was still around, even in Shuho-cho, or that my new friend would have been a participant, that her family would have hired a *nakōdo*, a go-between, to sift through the young men in her area and suggest possible matches. But the longer I lived there, the more couples I encountered who had met this way, including one of my teaching colleagues and his wife, who from all appearances were the most ridiculously happy couple I have ever met.

But the matchmaking process does not start off with any manner of giddiness, nor does it begin with the go-between's gut instinct. It starts with all parties submitting photos and résumés detailing their educations, hobbies, careers, incomes and family lines. Every factor is considered before the *nakōdo* suggests a match, before anyone even thinks of meeting.

If one side thinks a prospective partner looks agreeable and the other party concurs, the *nakōdo* will get them together, along with their parents, at some neutral place like a hotel lobby. If the first meeting goes well and both sides tell the go-between they are interested, the potential couple will meet again on their own for a date, perhaps to visit a zoo or go out to dinner and see how things progress without an entourage. This is how Naoko met the man to whom she had become engaged. When I asked her to tell me about him, she described him vaguely, with less detail than she spoke of chamomile or oregano, as if he had been a friend of a friend, not a former future spouse.

I never was certain exactly when or how things had fallen apart, but Naoko told me she had called it off. The murmurers had suggested it was the other way around. What I do know is at about the same time as the breakup, Naoko had lost control of her car on an icy road and broken her back. She spent months in the hospital, recuperating with other patients, mainly old women who taught her how to fold small squares of *origami* paper into animals, into balls, into elaborate decorations that could be glued together and hung from the pull-strings of ceiling lights. She had entered the hospital a wrecked woman and had emerged a paper artist. But it seemed that her fiancé did not believe nursing his future wife back to health was part of the marriage arrangement.

As Naoko told her story bit by bit, her lower lip quivered and her black eyes shone with an emotion I could not quite pinpoint. Was it grief? Indignation? Or something else? My sense was that it was less about loss of love than about the dreaded loss of collective face for all involved, and perhaps just as much about not achieving the married status that would have enabled her — and her brothers — to get on with their lives. Unmarried, working passionless jobs, living at home in a town where secrets were few, Naoko was in a holding pattern, her herbs the bright spot. Realizing this made me wonder why she stayed, chained to her past rather than running. I admired her fortitude. And I did my best to forgive the disapproval she sometimes showed me, an upstart foreigner, escaping to her town and quickly finding male companionship.

What she did not know was that I too had played the role of good daughter, the oldest child, who had done what I thought was expected of me and gone on to experience my own marital drama. I was not yet ready to tell her that I had canceled not an engagement but a marriage, so she had no idea how hard I had worked to get out of my own wrong-headed situation ... how my great-aunt had tsk-tsked to my relatives that I had brought the first divorce to our clan ... how my situation had shocked family, friends, and acquaintances. I had been the subject of murmurs too.

If she knew what I had left behind in Minnesota — a reasonably attractive husband with a job and an agreeable family — would she chastise me for leaving that life? At least I had been married, moved out of my childhood home and, from her perspective, had paved the way for my younger brother's future. Maybe she would say I should have endured the incompatibility, that I expected too much of marriage.

Or would she see us as sisters surviving marriage-related mishaps?

Some months later, Naoko and I would drive to Iwakuni, a city on the far side of Yamaguchi Prefecture, to tour a reconstructed castle and walk a graceful five-arched wood and stone bridge built almost entirely without nails. By crazy coincidence, while we were there, she spotted her ex-fiancé in the distance, walking with a woman Naoko assumed to be his new fiancée, or perhaps by then his wife.

Tiny Naoko, trim and stylish in her black-and-gold plaid sweater and matching skirt, glossy hair cascading over her shoulders like a waterfall, quickly slipped behind my larger frame, concealing herself from the acquaintance she had nearly wed.

15

In Search of Christmas

In December I began watching the sky for snow that never fell. The introductory letter I had received from Shinoda-*kyōikuchō* in Minnesota had described twenty inches covering Shuho-cho the previous winter, and I had taken that as a promise. Instead I was surrounded by naked deciduous trees, half-hearted evergreens, and after-harvest rice paddies that looked scrubby and bleak.

Up to this point I had only experienced one snow-free Christmas ever, and that had been four years earlier in Hagi, when I had hardly noticed what was missing, being so taken up with Ryota and my host family, and then my mother entering the mix. But now, without my usual winter cues, I could hardly keep my mind in the month. This could be November, March, or anytime in between. It bore no resemblance to the glorious Advent seasons of my earlier life.

Christmastime in the Minnesota of my memory looks as it does on Christmas cards, all stained glass and snow, neighborhoods blanketed with shimmering snowflakes falling like confetti. It is a season of traipsing about Christmas tree farms, cross-country skiing, driving through neighborhood light displays, and baking unholy quantities of sweet treats — Scottish shortbread, pink- and green-centered thumbprint cookies, and layered Nanaimo bars — all to be nibbled while listening to LPs of carols performed by Julie Andrews, Mannheim Steamroller, and John Denver with the Muppets.

When Christmas Eve finally arrived, we piled into the car and joined our neighbors clogging late-night intersections on our way to candlelit church services, where we listened to readings chronicling Jesus' birth and children's choirs singing "Silent Night." The next morning we unwrapped and exclaimed over mounds of gifts, taking breaks only to eat iced sweetbreads, sausages and eggs, before donning long johns, wool socks and bulky sweaters, Nanook-of-the-North-style parkas, boots, hats, scarves, and mittens to wander among glittering snowdrifts, looking forward to the meaty, buttery meal we would enjoy that evening.

Christmastime in Shuho-cho — or most of the rest of the world, for that matter — could never measure up. No wreaths or candles hung from lampposts, and there were no holly jolly Christmas events to attend. At North Junior High, the choir slogged through Handel's "Hallelujah" chorus — my students mumbling the foreign syllables *"goh dohm nee poh tent"* to approximate the majestic phrase "God omnipotent" — in a glimmer of Christmas, although it must have seemed strange to sing songs to a deity with whom most were unfamiliar, like a public junior high school choir in rural North Dakota singing praises to Buddha. After a staffroom conversation about Christmas traditions, the school's science teacher hauled a couple of tiny fir trees down from a nearby mountain, so I could decorate them with help from the students. As Christmas cassette tapes played in the background, we cut out paper snowflakes and stapled together chains of green, red, and white paper to hang on the tiny branches. Origami pros that they were, they humored my simple projects.

Back in my apartment I tried to replicate the holiday I had grown up with by hanging blinking colored lights, paper chains, little wreaths — some of which had been intended for the Shinto New Year — and a cascade of cranes folded and strung by the twenty-five students at Shuho-cho's smallest elementary school. Naoko brought in some scented candles from a German gift shop in Yamaguchi City, and my parents sent a painted-wood Christmas tree from home.

But none of these trappings could mask my sense that I was spending Christmas in exile. When I visited Japan four years earlier, I learned that traditional Christmas carols might tinkle in the air of department stores, but Christmas was for lovers. Anticipating Christmas Eve, boyfriends booked hotel rooms and reserved special dinners and entertainment packages costing hundreds of dollars — at least that was what I was reading in the newspaper and seeing on television. When one of my students slipped me a pirated Christmas cassette tape, I popped it in my boom box to hear Mariah Carey's multi-octave sighs beseeching a lover: "All I Want For Christmas Is You," "Christmas (Baby Please Come Home)" and "Miss You Most (At Christmas Time)." I felt hollow.

Surrounded by Japan's version of my favorite holiday, I began to understand what parts of Christmas were truly irreplaceable for me: family and friends, Advent celebrations, and the Christmas story.

The latter two realizations were a bit of a surprise. I had never been a Jesus person. I was uncomfortable with the way the overenthusiastic forced his name — "Jeeezus" — through their teeth and, more than that, I had always found the man himself somewhat unlikable. At that time in my life, I thought the Bible made him sound unnecessarily critical as he berated his earliest followers for their slowness to understand his message and his actions. Sure, he fed thousands of people on just a few loaves of bread, and yes he healed the sick, blind, deaf and dumb, but the miracle that impressed me most was that his disciples left everything and everyone they loved to trail along with a cantankerous stranger.

My other problem with Jesus was his anger management problem. I could handle his being born of a virgin, but I bristled when people described him as being without sin. The Bible showed him losing control and dumping over the tables of the moneychangers in the temple, a scene I imagine as a cacophony of sound — splintering wood, piles of coins crashing, rolling and clinking as they settled on stone, voices yelling, footsteps chasing, hands shoving. This was the Prince of Peace? This was life without sin? It would take me years to realize I believed anger was a sin. Then, one day, jogging up a steep slope, shoes hitting pavement one after the other in the ultimate expression of monotony, my fear of anger would hit me in a flash, followed by a new understanding, my heart softening toward Jesus. A new curiosity took root and slowly, over years, would transform my relationship with him.

But that was later. I know my murky discomfort with Jesus had plagued me at least since elementary school, when in the late '70s it was cool to stick pins on our Mork and Mindy rainbow suspenders. I remember coming across a neon orange button that read, "I'm a Jesus freak." Unable to bear this declaration, I taped the word "cat" over "Jesus" but even so never dared to pin it on, lest the original verbiage be exposed.

Still, I considered myself a believer of the Christian persuasion, perhaps for no reason other than habit, having grown up steeped in Lutheran culture. But in Shuho-cho, surrounded by the trappings of a secular Japanese-style Christmas, I felt more aware of my Christian faith than I had in a long time. And out of this came a desire to reclaim the holiday, the holy day, and to let my students know there was much more to it than lovers and the lovelorn. It was about fresh beginnings, a baby — so much more approachable than the man he grew into — who had come to save the world.

At South Junior High, Mr. Kumagai had given me a hallway bulletin board at the start of the year and told me to decorate it with anything related to the English language or American culture. As Christmas approached, I split this board in half. On one side, I made a paper house and a Santa Claus from construction paper, Santa hopping in the chimney. Then I created a stable. In it, Mary and Joseph stood protectively around a be-haloed Jesus, accompanied by shepherds, wise men, a sheep, a cow, and three angels singing from the rooftop. Below each of these two illustrations of Christmas, I wrote a description in English, as simple as I could make it, with the key words translated into Japanese.

It probably looked like a five-foot-long tract, something I would never have gotten away with in a public school in the United States. (I still remember being eight years old and directing a short Christmas program in my third-grade classroom, two of my classmates wearing bathrobes, walking up an aisle between our desks to a recording of "The Little Drummer Boy," our teacher standing in the doorway, nervously scanning the hall.) But in Japan, I anticipated — hoped — my board would be considered a piece of cross-cultural education, and that no one would be disturbed.

It was not that I wanted to convert anyone, really, but as the town's lone Christian (that I knew of anyway), I felt I needed to say something. And sure enough, once my board was complete, I felt a sort of peace.

* * *

My friend Karla arrived in Shuho-cho during winter break and provided a diversion. We had worked together at the Japanese immersion camp in Minnesota, and she had come to Japan to visit friends. I was thrilled to have a visitor from home, and part of me wanted nothing more than to hole up with her in my apartment listening to Christmas music and bingeing on the cookies my mother had sent.

But Hideo would have none of that. Knowing how much I missed my Minnesota Christmas, he arranged a day trip, inviting Karla and me to accompany him to the city of Tokuyama, a couple of hours away by car, for a festival of Christmas lights and music. There the three of us wandered about chilly, snowless streets, stopping at booths to purchase steaming soy sauce-seasoned corn on the cob and warming our hands and bellies with soup drunk from oversized bowls. At last we heard the event's centerpiece performance: an enthusiastic choir, scores of voices strong, broke into a heartfelt rendition of Beethoven's "Ode to Joy." I stopped in the midst of the reveling crowd to drink in the harmonies as the Japanese choir captured the grandeur of the music and words. *Ah, I thought, Christmas at last!*

And then as soon as the song had finished and the choir dispersed, it was replaced by a band that played a convincing, if out of place, version of "Twist and Shout" — "*Shake it up baaa-by! ...,*" the spell broken.

Karla joked with Hideo that he was celebrating Christmas "*ryōte ni hana*" — a "flower" (that is, a woman) "in each hand," and he smiled his broad smile, seeming at ease. Karla's Japanese was far better than mine, after all, and they were able to have smooth conversations, their dictionary consults few and far between. She had worked as a JET a few years previously and, more than that, she was half Japanese, having grown up with her Japanese mother in Minnesota, near the Twin Cities. It was fascinating to see her against this new backdrop, looking not fully Japanese but also not fully foreign, wielding her nearly fluent Japanese language like an American, peppering the conversation with humor and innuendo, flirting mercilessly. The surprised looks Hideo glanced my way seemed to ask the question: who is more typically American, the convivial Karla or the more reserved me?

Karla took me aside. "Hideo is fantastic," she whispered. "Why are you not involved with him?" I had no good answer.

I certainly had felt jealous pangs, both about her ability with the language and her easy repartee with Hideo, but because I knew she was only to be with us — me — for a couple of days, I did not feel threatened. She was a true Tokyo-lover, bedazzled by the city's pop culture, the music, the food, the happenings. She would not show up in Shuho-cho again, so there was no danger of her moving in and hijacking my friend — or whatever he was. I embraced her warm companionship, vibrant as a scarlet poinsettia, and I looked at Hideo and wondered.

Before Karla departed for Tokyo on Christmas Day, she and I produced a full-on holiday dinner: chicken (because there was no turkey to be found), stuffing, wild rice, corn, and mashed potatoes, topped off with a Christmas pudding my mother had sent. We shared it with Hideo, who, like us, was far from family, the three of us sitting on the floor of my apartment at my low *kotatsu* table, our legs warmed by the heater attached to its underside, listening to tapes of Christmas carols on my Sony boom box.

That afternoon, Hideo drove us to the bullet-train station to say our goodbyes, and with Karla safely on her way to Tokyo, he and I headed toward Tsuwano, the castle town with the spectacular mountaintop shrine I had visited four years earlier on New Year's Day. As we climbed the hill to the shrine, my mind was filled with memories of the time I had spent there with my mother, my host family, Ryota, and the crowds of all ages ambling about in winter coats of black and tan, young women mincing along the path in vibrant kimono, sticking out like spring flowers.

This was a far quieter day, and we had the walkways mostly to ourselves. A shrine maiden dressed in white kneeled and bowed on red steps. Not far from where my treasured photograph had been taken, the one of Ryota and me surrounded by family, the one I had hidden from my husband in plain view, there stood a young woman encircled by several Shinto priests and *taiko* drummers. Not wanting to intrude, Hideo and I kept walking, but he quickly ascertained what was happening. They were performing a ceremony to banish some bad luck, perhaps a ghost, from the woman's life.

Can they really do that? I wondered. Then, moments later, *Would it work even on someone who is not of the Shinto faith?*

* * *

I had experienced something not so unlike this type of spiritual activity before, although not in my Lutheran upbringing. I would have been embarrassed to visit my church and ask a group of pastors or fellow congregants to pound drums and pray for me, and I imagine they would have felt just as awkward. In fact, the one time I had gone to church specifically in search of spiritual guidance, during my dis-engagement to the man who afterward would become my husband and then ex-husband, my pastor seemed as much at a loss as I.

But during my undergraduate save-the-world phase, a friend had invited me on a month-long mission trip that her nondenominational church was planning to take to the Texas–Mexico border. Never mind that I knew nothing about her church. I figured work was work and because I was going to school in Minnesota and they were taking the trip in January, heading to balmy Texas made a whole lot of sense. I envisioned building houses and feeding the hungry amid palm trees.

Certainly we did accomplish some good works — paving a floor at an orphanage, rebottling donated drugs for mission doctors, and handing out clothing in a poor Mexican neighborhood (our naïveté and lack of planning causing a minor riot) — but from the start, the trip focused on bolstering our group's spiritual strength. On our way to Texas, we stopped for rest at a hotel, and after unloading our overnight bags everyone congregated at the swimming pool. I was there to relax and find some peace in the water, but my travel mates turned the place into a revival, performing immersion baptisms on one another — and, for all I know, on other hotel guests as well — as I floated farther and farther out of reach, wondering what I had gotten myself into.

Once settled into the Sunday School wing of an El Paso church, we established a routine of daily Bible studies and worship that included laying hands on one another, praying for healing and spiritual gifts, speaking in tongues, offering words for one another and sharing visions, trying to solve one another's problems with the help of God. I had never experienced such practices before and, thinking such things happened only in biblical times, I vacillated among feelings of curiosity, fascination, and disgust, stealing away for secret phone calls to my parents in which I whispered half-jokingly, "I think I'm traveling with a cult."

It was not really a cult, but as we say in Minnesota, it sure was different, and these activities were almost unbelievable for a girl who had grown up on the northern Plains in the Evangelical Lutheran Church in America, where the order of service is predictable, much like its reserved parishioners. At least we Lutherans kept our hands to ourselves. Members of this mission group raised their hands — and sometimes their weeping faces — to the Texas sky while praying strange-sounding words in an altered state, something far more foreign than any religious practice I had ever encountered, more so even than that of my Japanese host mother, whom I had watched kneel quietly in her living room, hands clasped before a Buddhist altar.

By the end of the trip, I might have been the only one not speaking in tongues, despite the group having laid hands on me multiple times and praying God would grant me the gift. Certainly I was curious what it would feel like to have strange words pour out of my mouth, and I wondered what spiritual power would accompany them. Would it make my prayers more effective? Would God be more apt to answer them? But I felt an insurmountable resistance. Speaking in tongues seemed to be the first hurdle to clear in some spiritual race that had infiltrated the group. I did not want to compete.

I got the sense that some of my companions considered me a failure, spiritually, but I could live with that. What was more difficult was the pressure I felt to bring my beliefs into line with theirs. The pastor leading us was not unkind to me, but he regularly singled me out for conversation, trying to convince me that each dittle and dot of the Bible was God's inerrant word. Seeing I was not going to say "uncle" — I had always taken the view that the whole work was *inspired* by God and written by human hands — he warned at least one member of the group, a handsome, relatively open-minded young man, against spending too much time with me.

The group and I parted ways fairly quickly once we returned to campus. But that young man and I continued our friendship and had a brief romance a couple of years later, a romance that ended the evening he brought one of our old mission group friends along on our date. Afterward, as he was dropping me off, my friend told me our relationship was over, something about my supposed lack of devotion to the Christian faith.

I was incensed. How could he judge me after I had spent thousands of hours at church and in chapel at my Lutheran junior high, high school, and college, singing in church choirs, participating in confirmation classes, teaching Sunday School, reading Bible lessons in church services, reading the Bible myself, taking religion courses, praying, and resisting various temptations? Did he think my critical thinking would hold him back? Did he believe that with me *he* would come to feel unequally yoked?

There was nothing like hearing the message that I was "not Christian enough" to make me want to pitch it all. And to an extent, for a brief critical period, I did. No more than a week or two after that brush-off, I met a new man and, despite my sense that we were leading very different lives, he quickly became my husband. Perhaps my friend and his pastor were right. Maybe I was trouble.

* * *

Walking beside Hideo through Tsuwano's Shinto shrine, I continued to think of Ryota, now married, who should have been as good as a ghost to me, and my ex-husband, and my oh-so-very Christian friend and a few other relationships I had slashed and burned my way through to get to where I stood that day. Feelings of regret dogged me, and I would have loved it if only those Shinto priests — or someone — would have simply exorcised my memories of all those malingerers and my poor behavior as well. But that would require a brand of belief I did not share.

Descending from the shrine, Hideo and I found ourselves alone that Christmas Day amid the old town's samurai houses and carp-filled canals, and as we strolled to a part of town I had not seen before, we were surprised to happen on a small Catholic church. I had not realized that Japanese Christians had been exiled there during nineteenth-century purges, and that a Catholic presence remained. We entered and found a candlelit, tatami-matted sanctuary, empty of people but lovingly decorated with Christmas trees, crèches, and a felt Christmas banner depicting a star shining over Mary, tending Jesus in the manger — Jesus the baby. I felt relief catching a glimpse of what, for me, signified a true Christmas. Slowly ambling about the sanctuary, I breathed it all in, as if I could capture Christmas in my lungs and carry it with me.

I felt more at home than I had in a long, long time.

* * *

Later that winter break, I jogged through Hagi's narrow streets to the beach, where, dodging the sea's wintery fingers, my mind filled with thoughts of Ryota and the fun we had shared in that same place, that same season. I felt as if on that beach, no matter our circumstances, our hearts could still meet.

A crow crouched on the sand ahead of me intently pick, pick, picking at something that was silhouetted in the late-afternoon light. As I neared, the bird floated upward onto the breeze, berating me from overhead. Noticing two objects poking out of the sea-smoothed sand, I slowed my pace and stopped.

The first was the pure-white egg case of a paper nautilus. I picked it up and ran my fingertips over its brittle, wavy, shell-like arc, perfect and complete. I had found a similar one four years earlier, just before Ryota had appeared in my host family's *genkan*. It seemed a good omen. Maybe I would return home and learn he had called, or — was it even possible? — he had dropped by to see me. Maybe he had left his poor pregnant wife.

No. No matter how much I pined for him, that would be more wrongness than I could bear.

But perhaps my presence at the seashore, our place, would somehow trigger in his mind thoughts of me, no matter how far apart we were in miles and in life. Maybe that was enough. It would have to be.

Then the second white object, the crow's prey, came into focus. It was heaving with a desperation that transcends species, genus, or class. It looked like a squid but later I would learn it was the paper nautilus itself — a type of octopus, the one who had secreted the elegant egg case I held in my hands, the one who likely had used it for refuge. I battled with myself: should I pick up the writhing mass of arms and ink, and toss it into the sea or leave it for the crows to finish off?

No matter how sorry I felt for the creature, I could not make myself touch it. Would it sting me? Grab me? No matter how much I fancied myself a Hagi transplant, I was still just a girl from the prairie, and this creature was as foreign to me as an alien from outer space. I looked around for some beachcomber's abandoned bucket but found none. I pulled a twig from a nearby pine tree and tried to nudge the poor bugger closer to the water's edge. I filled the egg case with seawater and poured it over the little animal. It turned scarlet, color pulsating in its legs. I nudged it with its own egg case, which it tried to grab. My skin crawled. Had I understood then that I was holding this animal's home, its own creation, I would have relinquished it gladly, and let her crawl in and reclaim her shelter.

A series of waves approached and pulled the little beast toward the sea, and at one point it looked as if she might make it out into open water. But then another wave heaved her back onto the beach, where she throbbed heavily, a broken heart.

The sky and seashore were nearly dark by the time I gave up, turned and walked away, certain that any good portent brought by the shell would be canceled out by the impending death of the little octopus.

16

New Year, New Life

MIHO arrived home from Tokyo on New Year's Day in a whirl of red-dyed hair, blue-tinted eyes (fancy contact lenses), shiny blouses, and leather pants. She regaled me with tales of her working life in Tokyo and her multiple boyfriends — a dancer, a businessman, and one of the country's most eligible bachelors. But with her parents, she affected an almost childlike demeanor, whining for what she wanted and dropping heaps of dirty clothes in the laundry room, prompting Okāsan to make a face at me. At night she snuggled like a little girl into her grandmother's bed. Miho had always been known, quietly, as the *taifū* (typhoon) of the family, but during her visit it was my heart that would be blown inside out.

I no longer remember how or why this happened, but while she was home, Miho elicited an invitation for us to have coffee with Ryota's mother. What I do remember is that when we arrived at his childhood home and I emerged from Otōsan's SUV, she met me right there and wrapped me in a tearful bear hug before welcoming us into her home. As our coffee cooled, we sat side by side on her sofa — the same sofa where four years earlier, when I was preparing to say goodbye to Ryota, we had sat listening to him play the piano and I had wept into her cherry blossom handkerchief. This time, the piano was quiet, and so was I. She was showing me Ryota's wedding album.

For me the visit was some kind of hell, sitting beside this warm woman, newly a mother-in-law, soon to be a grandmother, looking at photos of her son and his delicately pretty bride. I do not recall crying, but if that is so, it is only thanks to the Easter egg-colored tuxedo Ryota was wearing in the pictures. (Was it lavender or yellow? Either way it looked ridiculous.) I tried not to wish ill on his wife, who my memory dresses variously in a white Western-style wedding gown, a ruffly formal dress, and a traditional red kimono. This is not just paper doll-style imagining; many Japanese weddings feature multiple gown changes, and I am quite sure I saw photos of her in each of these incarnations.

It was unclear to me whether this miserable experience was something typical of Japanese culture or just over-the-top strange. Was it a normal Japanese rite of passage, a way old girlfriends process the loss of a boyfriend to marriage? Or was it the kindest way Miho could imagine to help me exorcise the ghost of Ryota?

Trapped on that sofa, drinking my coffee, trying to be polite, pretending to be fine despite the racket that seemed to be echoing through the living room, the shattering of whatever was left of my heart, I only half understood the quiet conversation between Ryota's mother and Miho, their concerned eyes peering at me, Miho not translating very much at all.

What I do know is I was not the only uncomfortable one. I heard Ryota's mom tell Miho that she had half wanted to see me and half not. She had liked me a lot.

* * *

When Miho returned to Tokyo, I went with her, standing for hours in the aisle of the crowded post-holiday bullet train. My decision to go was impulsive, and I went partly to escape rural Yamaguchi for a bit and get a taste of the big city. But that was not all. I also was tagging along because Ryota had contacted her, and they had made plans for me to meet him in Tokyo. With his wife.

Do I sound like a chump? Yes. Was I a chump? Maybe. Would a normal person agree to participate in yet another obvious opportunity to experience heartbreak? I believe so. Because people are chumps for love.

There was something else at work here too though. Miho truly was my *onēsan*, my older sister in Japan, and had been since I was sixteen. Like an older sister in any family, she had shepherded me through my first wordless, clueless experiences of life in her culture, when I could not speak Japanese at all. She had looked out for me. She had tolerated me. And although we were very different people with dissimilar personalities, I had accepted her authority — not that it didn't make me crazy. But this was her country. It did not matter that she was only nine months older than I, because culturally she had decades on me. We had an established big sister–little sister pattern, and on Japanese soil I generally took her advice. No matter how dissimilar our appearances and our lives, on a very basic level I trusted her. I loved her.

Besides, I was working on a purge here. First my ex-husband, now Ryota. Did I envision anything but more heartbreak coming from a meeting with these newlyweds? Did I think that Ryota might decide over a cup of coffee to bag it all, leave his pregnant wife and company job, and join me at my temporary outpost in Shuho-cho? Or did I think that seeing him in his new situation would give me an opportunity to have the last word, to show him what he was missing and say goodbye forever? I felt a mix of excitement and dread.

Bunking with Miho in her sophisticated single-girl apartment in the heart of Tokyo was invigorating. Her $1,000-a-month pad with its dark hardwood floors and off-white shaggy rugs under black furniture included a narrow kitchen, a tiny bathroom, and a living room and bedroom that together probably equaled the size of a decent-sized American bedroom — and was stocked with more cosmetics and perfumes than food. Her stereo was always on, as with her soundless television set (she hated looking at a blank black box), and so was her heater, which she left on all day while she was away at work, even though the window right below it was propped open. Her washing machine sat outside on a narrow balcony and as I did laundry, I waved at men sitting in a classroom across the narrow street, and they waved back.

While Miho worked, I wandered about the city on my own, spun like a top by rushing commuters, swept along by crowds, accidentally, into a private ceremony at the Meiji Shrine and encountering more foreigners than I had seen in months. Tokyo was truly a world away from my life in Yamaguchi.

The day I was to meet Ryota, I spent an inordinate amount of time choosing my clothes, fixing my hair, refixing my hair, my brush catching on an earring, which ripped into my earlobe ever so slightly, a drop of blood bringing me back to my senses: what I wore, what I said, what I did would not matter. This man was taken, taken, taken by a woman and a baby. Wrenching myself away from the mirror, I padded toward the door of Miho's apartment and reached for the doorknob before remembering I was supposed to call Ryota before I embarked on the forty-minute train ride that would take me to a station near his home.

When he answered the phone, his voice sounded terrible, congested. He was sick with a cold, maybe his wife was sick too. They needed to postpone for a little bit. He would call again shortly.

Another call. I could see that runny noses were not the point. What was unsaid but clear was that Ryota's pregnant wife was uncomfortable about meeting me, or maybe about letting Ryota meet me. At last, they canceled our meeting altogether, apologies all around, and I hung up the phone. Standing alone in Miho's silent living room, I took a deep breath and then whooped with relief.

That was it. Despite the longstanding nature of my attachment, which had played a role in drawing me back to Japan, I felt a sense of release. I had done everything I could — and more than I should have — to reconnect, and now I could recognize the hopelessness of it and that I had been unleashed from it.

Hours later Miho blew in from work, full of questions about the visit I never had. Learning what had happened, she became furious. "What is he thinking?" she fumed. "What if you had forgotten to phone and arrived at his station with no one to meet you? I am so mad. Give me his number. *Give me his number!*" Although it was 11:30 p.m., and I had found some peace in the situation and the end of whatever spell it was Ryota had held over me, it was a little too much fun to see Miho get this worked up. So I handed her the number and sat back to watch her call and chew out Ryota, telling him he and his wife were acting like children. Ryota asked her if I was angry. She told him no, but *she* was.

Miho hung up and gave me the blow-by-blow conversation. No sooner had I been updated than Ryota's wife called, apologizing to Miho, saying it was not Ryota's fault but hers, because she had not been feeling well. Miho could not have cared less and read her the riot act too.

It was such a humiliating conclusion to the whole affair that it was almost gratifying. This relationship, such as it was, appeared to be ending not with a comma, a semicolon, an ellipsis or even a period, but with a boldface exclamation point.

Even after hanging up from that contentious phone call, Miho continued to fume. It was about midnight when she muttered, "I have to call my Mom." She rang Hagi and woke Okāsan, who listened patiently as Miho relayed the entire incident again, in detail.

I listened, detached, as if the drama unfolding were Miho's, not mine. Could it be that ceremony at the Tsuwano shrine, where the priests and drummer had worked to rid that young woman of her ghost or her bad luck or whatever it was, somehow affected me? The events of the day and the relief I felt at our canceled meeting revealed to me what I had not had the courage to realize: the ghost of my relationship with Ryota had faded to a vapor, and there was nothing left for me to grasp.

Still, it was a good thing that this drama took place in Tokyo, where the narrow streets, tall buildings, and ever-lit lamps made it impossible for me to see Ryota's moon.

17

Cold

By the time I returned from Tokyo, Shuho-cho was mired in the damp chill of a subtropical winter. The rice paddies' post-harvest stubble had crisped to pale beige, and the green of the nearby hills had faded to wan, as if the roots of trees and bamboo had drawn the plants' very vibrancy underground for safekeeping, awaiting hope of photosynthetic redemption. Early mornings brought my neighbors, the Dwelling Friends wives, outside with their tea kettles, pouring hot water down the frosted windshields of their husbands' idling cars.

Although this brand of winter was unimaginably mild by Minnesota standards — our outside temperatures in Shuho-cho rarely dipped below freezing — it seemed especially bleak to me, the dreariness stemming in part from my irretrievable loss of Ryota. Although our aborted meeting in Tokyo had sealed the end of whatever our relationship had been, my heart continued scanning for loopholes and fueled my mind's fantasy of a parallel reality in which we would meet up once a year, regardless of our life situations, for delicious rendezvous. I felt guilty even having these thoughts and tried to purge them by writing a short story that went so badly I cut myself off after only a couple hundred words.

There was nothing to do but focus on what was real, and the dreary present occupied enough of my mind. It was hard to believe that Shuho-cho could be less comfortable than the sub-freezing, often subzero temperatures in which I had grown up. In Minnesota I had always been eager to get outside with friends, to build forts, ski and skate, but there we could escape into warm, well-insulated buildings. In Shuho-cho, the chill felt omnipresent. Windows were single-paned and drafty, and central heating was almost nonexistent. Homes and schools were warmed room by room with electric heaters mounted, inefficiently, near the ceiling or with kerosene-fueled space heaters, the latter requiring hourly air exchanges, warm but noxious air released through opened windows that brought in more of the outside chill. Hallways, toilets and bathrooms were left unheated. When given the choice, I gravitated to the Asian toilets, porcelain-lined holes in the floor that required no contact with cold seats.

Having observed my host family's strategy of closing off extraneous rooms in winter, I downsized my quarters to the L-shaped living room and kitchen, which I warmed over and over with a kerosene heater. I also became a devotee of my *kotatsu*, the low, heated table that is a quintessential part of a Japanese winter. In addition to coming equipped with an electric heater attached to its underside, the *kotatsu* includes two tabletops and two blankets that are used to engineer something like a child's coffee-table fort. Here is how you build it:

- Spread the thinner of the two blankets on the floor.

- Place the table on top of it.
- Lay the second, fluffier blanket over the tabletop.
- Place the second tabletop on top of the second blanket, so that blanket is sandwiched between the two hard surfaces.
- Plug in the heater.
- Now sit on the thin blanket with your legs beneath the table and the fluffier blanket draped over your lap.
- Turn on the heater and stay there until spring comes.

It will keep the bottom half of your body as toasty as you please while transferring that warmth to your upper body as well. Sometimes I cranked up the thermostat so high that my legs turned bright pink, as if half my body was in an especially hot sauna.

Once my *kotatsu* was set up, I did almost everything at that low table — eating, reading, making lesson plans, writing, and watching television. I even began sleeping under it. As bedtime approached, I would turn the thermostat to high, spread my blankets out under its fluffy blanket and, once settled in, lay my head on a crunchy buckwheat-filled pillow. Finally, I would turn off the heat and bask in the *kotatsu*'s fading warmth while slipping into sleep.

School offered no respite from the chill, as the classrooms and offices were warmed by waist-high kerosene heaters. They radiated away as we taught, but then, at the end of class, just when the room was reaching a comfortable temperature, the students would shut them down and throw open the windows to clear the air — and any warmth we had built up. When the next period began, the process would start all over again.

As a teacher, I had comparatively little to complain about. I dressed in layers and moved about the classrooms, finding excuses to hover near the stoves. My students, seated in their desks, were required to wear charming but thin winter sailor-style uniforms, which for the girls meant bare legs and low socks. The less hardy girls huddled at their desks, faces cross, hands worrying the hems of their skirts, holding them down around their ankles, making their bodies as small and self-warming as possible, rubbing their legs and chattering their teeth, all while trying to absorb their lessons.

Between classes, we teachers would meet up in the staffroom, where our desks were arranged in a giant rectangle. This is where my colleagues would draw up lesson plans, grade papers, meet with students and socialize, the principal and assistant principal presiding at one end, adjacent to the principal's private office. At the other end was a small kitchen — and smoking room — equipped with burners and insulated jugs of hot water. When I returned to my desk on chillier days, I often would find a cup of hot green tea the consistency of chicken bouillon waiting for me.

* * *

Although both of my junior high schools were chilly temperature-wise, one was cooler than the other in terms of atmosphere. Having one full school term under my belt by January, it frustrated me that I still felt so much like an outsider at North Junior High, where most of the students and teachers continued to give me a wide, somewhat shy berth. It might not have bothered me as much if I had not been comparing them with Mr. Kumagai's students and colleagues at South Junior High. And it surely would have bothered me less had I not become so invested in teaching English.

During the fall term, Mr. Kumagai was always excited to discuss our upcoming lessons and brainstorm ways to incorporate skits, songs, activities and games into our classroom. My desk was a busy place, where I would design and make props for our classes and posters for the hallway bulletin board. The other teachers would invariably get curious and ask me what I was doing, and then offer supplies and advice, using these openings to initiate conversations or to invite me to visit their classes during my free periods. At South Junior High I made pottery bowls with the art classes, listened in on the music class and observed how Japanese students learned math.

Meanwhile Mr. Kumagai and I had set up a program incenting the students to speak English with me. Between classes, the kids would slide open the staffroom door and call out their requests to visit me at my desk. I would welcome them in and we would chat, often using new grammatical constructions from class — "Miss Coombah, habu you ebah [have you ever] gone to Disneyland?" — constructions I would hear so many times that they are still indelibly imprinted in my mind. Our conversation complete, they would reach into their breast pockets and hand me one of the cards I had made for them, cards that read, "I spoke English with Ms. Coomber!" below a flock of twenty balloons. I would take out my *hanko* and stamp my name,

サ

ラ

— "*sa-ra*" — in one balloon each, and they would pocket their cards once again. When they had filled in all of their balloons, I would present them with a little prize, American stamps or stickers. Over the months, we got to know each other little by little as they grew accustomed to trying out their fledgling English.

Across town at North Junior High, I sat at my desk for hours waiting to plan lessons with Mr. Kita, who seemed always to have something better to do, such as smoking with his colleagues. I got the sense that I represented little but added work for him and that it would be easiest if I just let him be and coasted through my days there, doing what was requested instead of inflicting my ideas and enthusiasm on him.

I could have gone along with Mr. Kita's program at North Junior High and used my time in the staffroom to read books, study Japanese, write letters and work on the collection of essays about life in Japan that I had decided to write for my master's degree project, but I could not justify slacking off when I was being paid so handsomely. The previous year in Minnesota, I had worked like a madwoman for birdseed, planning lessons, grading scads of papers, attending training sessions, classes and meetings, and providing one-on-one writing coaching to undergraduate students. In Japan I was earning roughly $36,000 a year tax-free for little teaching responsibility and few expenses, and the sudden ease of my financial situation almost made me crazy.

Add to that my being set up in little Shuho-cho, where surely most people did not earn a salary like mine and certainly not for as little effort. Plus I suspected everyone knew my salary, and this made me self-conscious, particularly because my contract limited me to working seven hours a day, five days a week. The other teachers often remained at school into the evening and most Saturdays as well. Wanting to be part of the team, I initially stayed on with them, but my supervisors soon took me aside and told me they could get in trouble with the JET central office for violating my contract, even if I was the one choosing to stay late. I relented and started going home at four o'clock as requested, but doing so made me feel all the more pressure to prove myself valuable while I was there.

Another reason I had trouble coasting at North Junior High was that the students at South Junior High were making such great progress in English. Even Kazuo.

An eighth grader, Kazuo had some sort of cognitive disability. Like other such students, he was mainstreamed in school, whether he could keep up or not. I do not know specifically what his disability was, but it was clear on sight that he was different: sleepy eyes, broad forehead, out-turned ears, rough skin and a shy, angelic smile. I was told his mental ability was that of a younger child, and it appeared that he barely spoke Japanese.

But there he was in English class, beatifically beaming at me from his desk. When the students worked on written exercises in class, and I walked up and down their rows of desks to review what they were writing, I would find Kazuo at his desk industriously scribbling away: straight lines with little curls sprinkled here and there. It could have been Arabic for all I knew, but it was what he could muster. He tried so hard, and he did so cheerfully. Watching his valiant efforts to communicate and fit in with his cohorts, I regarded him as something of a role model. For me. With our different communication challenges, he and I had more in common than most people realized. I loved being around him.

Just before winter vacation, Kumagai-*sensei* and I assigned skits to the eighth graders. Kazuo's group gave him a one-line part. I forget what the skit was about and what Kazuo was supposed to say, but when his moment arrived, he diverged completely from the script. He began to speak, saying, in English, "I like ..."

I was euphoric with anticipation. What was happening? What would he say next? *What* did he like? Had the clouds parted? Had Kazuo suddenly found a way to make sense?

"No, Kazuo!" shouted his classmates. They did not want him to make a mistake. They did not want him to ruin their skit.

"It's OK," I said, calling them off, and asked Kazuo to continue. But the spell had been broken, the moment had passed. Kazuo was smiling but silent. I would never learn what he liked, or whether his brain was just playing out a random grammatical construction learned by rote. Even so, it was one of my favorite teaching moments: the boy who could hardly speak his own language had begun to express himself in mine.

It did not entirely surprise me though, given the atmosphere Kumagai-*sensei* and I had cultivated at South. It reminded me of the Japanese Village in Minnesota, part of Concordia Language Villages, where our staff had gotten tremendous results from immersing children in the Japanese language and culture for one week, two weeks, or a month. We would watch young American kids, initially unable even to say "*konnichiwa*" ("hello") evolve into comfortable speakers of day-to-day greetings and asking us to pass the rice at mealtime. Repeat "villagers" became confident Japanese readers and writers.

My junior high schools in Shuho-cho could not provide English immersion environments, but a couple of hours a week in Mr. Kumagai's and my classes provided far more opportunity than Mr. Kita's, where he used Japanese to teach English. I wanted all of my students to have the opportunity to learn. I wanted them to see my native language as more than just a subject they needed to study for their high school and university entrance exams.

By the end of autumn term, I had grown accustomed to Mr. Kita's attitude toward English, his prefacing new grammar points in Japanese with defeatist comments like, "*I know this is difficult, but let's give it a try.*" And it seemed he had slowly begun to understand how much I cared about sharing my language and culture with his — our — students. After numerous conversations, we had arrived at a compromise: when I was at North Junior High we would plan our lessons together and work to get the students excited about speaking English. When I was not there, he would teach grammar in Japanese. It wasn't what I had in mind, but it was progress, and it made me hope for more.

Then in January Mr. Kita and I taught our first class of the winter term.

There was no lesson plan, no discussion, and once we arrived in the classroom, Mr. Kita spent the entire period speaking Japanese.

My only contribution was to hold down a spot on the floor. I could not believe it. What had happened to our compromise? Had all my gentle and not-so-gentle requests and nudges been for naught? Were we really back at square one? I had not realized how fragile our progress had been and how much of an outsider I remained. Or just how much I cared. The anticipation I had felt about embarking on the new term was fading fast. Frustrated, after class I vented to a piece of scratch paper:

> I had no purpose there. ... Now and then I read a sentence. ... It could be any half-wit standing there. I began sleeping standing up, with my eyes open. I almost have a master's degree. I'm almost 26. I'm an adult. I've taught journalism and Japanese. On my own. I've been in charge of an entire camp. Here I have no responsibility. I feel like a child. A very large child. It's humiliating.

By the time Mr. Kita and I were heading out the sliding doors of the teachers' room to our next class, I was fuming — and not just about our first class of the new year. Before Christmas I had signed a preliminary agreement to spend another year teaching in Shuho-cho — tentatively committing nineteen months into the future. I had thought it best to keep my options open but dreaded the idea of spending a throwaway year, of being underused. Now that appeared likely.

Mr. Kita and I were running late, as we often were, he needing to finish a cigarette or a conversation with another teacher, and we hustled up the deserted staircase. Unable to bear the thought of a second useless class period, I began to put words to my frustration and my disappointment that we were back to our old, unproductive pattern. And that's when it happened. About halfway up the stairs, tears came to my eyes. I could not speak. I stopped walking. So did Mr. Kita. He leaned in toward me and got in my face. His eyes were angry. "You don't cry!" he menaced quietly. "You are a professional!"

Oh, really? I thought. What kind of professional did he think I was? A professional reader? A professional stander-upper?

I did not reply to Mr. Kita. Instead, I turned around, walked back down the stairs and locked myself in the cold closet that housed the women's lone toilet.

18

The Carp Flips

HIDEO seemed to understand my growing melancholy, at least the part related to my frustration with school — I never did tell him of my near-encounter with Ryota. One January day he suggested we find a change of scenery, go on an adventure. Our mission? To find some snow. We hopped in his car and pointed it toward the northeast.

Riding under gray skies that dropped rain and sleet, I held out little hope that we would find any snow of note. I was a girl of the prairie, and on the prairie the appearance of snow depended on latitude. Minnesota generally had more than Iowa, and Manitoba had more than Minnesota. But as any person who has lived in more varied topography knows, all we needed was a little altitude. So Hideo kept driving and driving, and by the time we reached higher ground near Tsuwano, that touchstone place of one blissful New Year's and one quiet Christmas, we found our quarry.

Hideo and I got out of his car, and slipped and scrambled — exhilarated — up a wooded path, snow covering slick brown leaves, and threw wet snowballs at each other, Hideo seeming as tickled as I to find a taste of winter. The air smelled wet and pure; the chill on my cheeks felt right. This was how real life was supposed to be in January. My bulky down jacket, purchased in Minnesota, finally seemed appropriate, cozy as a sleeping bag. That afternoon, Japan felt like home. And, I realized, Hideo did too.

Was it seeing my friend surrounded by the familiarity of snow that did it for me? Or was it his caring enough to deliver me to the winter I had been craving? I had been evaluating him for a long time, actually, contemplating the possibilities. I recognized from the first time I met him that he was attractive: a couple of inches taller than I, slim without being skinny, and strong. He had wide eyes, a broad smile, strong teeth and a repertoire of endearing facial expressions. It did not take long to see that his face belied most of his thoughts; he was amusingly transparent. And he enjoyed making me happy.

So there it was: I had fallen for him. We had fun together, whether hunting the local hills for *aki no nanakusa* — the seven grasses of autumn — or stargazing in the clear night skies over Akiyoshidai, the nearby plateau, limestone protruding like a moonscape around us. And in my season of recovering post-divorce and pushing through culture shock, he knew how to lift my spirits, by taking me in search of the familiar — Christmas lights and snow — and giving me a break from our Shuho-cho reality — once driving us all the way to Miyajima, the storied island off the coast of Hiroshima. In my photographs, I see long shadows that remind me how we stayed late into the evening, wandering among the old shrines and temples in the chill air, feeding weightless pink shrimp chips to the island's tiny deer until the famous sacred gate — vermilion timber rising from the water several stories high — was lit bright and we ferried back across shimmering sunset water to the mainland.

All of these outings had been Hideo's idea, his way of orienting me to his homeland, of getting to know me, and he had prepared for each of them by packing his ever-present rucksack with maps, travel guides, snacks and drinks, all we could ever need. We never got hungry, we almost never got lost — this in the days before GPS and smartphone apps. Hideo was the epitome of carefulness, a giver of care — a caregiver. And although I did not fully realize it at the time, I was a bit of an invalid, recovering from the loss of multiple dreams, the vanished future I had envisioned as another man's wife in Minnesota and the defunct fantasy of returning to Ryota.

Although my primary goal in heading off to Japan had been to escape my real world and set up a temporary, leave-able one, as the months passed, I seemed to lose my focus, becoming connected to Shuho-cho by more and more tethers, increasingly tightly tied. Naoko and I were becoming mutual confidants, teaching English was becoming a passion, and the koto was becoming a serious hobby. I had even allowed the strongest, most dangerous attachment — love, or whatever it was I had felt toward Ryota — to occupy a fair bit of my mind. There is no denying that the time I was spending in Shuho-cho was impacting the lives of its indisputably real life-living residents, but I continued to entertain the illusion of floating through a year there, as if it were a secondary life parallel to the one I had left in Minnesota. I chose to believe my Minnesota life was clicking along despite my physical absence, fed by letters and phone calls to family, friends, and graduate school advisers. And when Hideo came too close, I would trot out my time machine analogy to prove that it would not be worth his while to fall in love with me. I was a short-timer.

Then, my friend Karla had come for Christmas, and it occurred to me that my stubborn inaction could cause Hideo to find someone else. Imagining him dating another woman helped me realize the truth: we were a good match. Hideo was more than a caregiver. He was nearly everything I wanted in a partner but had been too wary to see. I wanted him for myself, even though that meant sending out a tendril that could easily become another tether to a world I wanted to consider fleeting.

We had spent the day prior to our snow-seeking mission together, driving to Yamaguchi city for a movie during which I conquered the armrest between us, using my elbow to invade his personal space just enough so I could feel his ribs expanding with each breath, testing whether he would reach for my hand. He did not. Who could blame him? I had been working so hard for months to avoid emotional entanglement, to keep our relationship platonic, that I had scarcely noticed my own changing attitude. How could I expect him to know now that my heart felt as if it had come unglued in my chest and might be free for the taking?

After my marriage ended, I had longed for a new boyfriend, for dependable companionship, for someone to cozy up to. But being separated at age twenty-three and divorced at twenty-four, I feared I would be rejected as damaged goods. More than that, I was fearful that despite all the lessons I learned, I would make the same mistakes again.

Before leaving for Shuho-cho, I had made one foray back into dating, going to a few movies with a friend from college. After the second or third one, I let down my guard and kissed him, realizing only then that I was not ready, or maybe not interested in him romantically. It was hard to tell. Still weary from the emotional effort I had expended over the previous couple of years, I saw no way to roll back that new relationship and ended up avoiding that good man, that friend, until he understandably gave up on me altogether. What I recognized from our brief encounter was that I had lost my confidence to choose — or deal with — a partner, and that I had trouble reading my own heart. With that in mind, I set exactly one dating guideline for myself: I would not kiss anyone unless I thought I might die if I did not.

Death is a pretty high bar, and what this hyperbole meant for me was that I would not get involved with a man physically unless I felt a many-layered connection with him, unless I could envision our relationship going somewhere amazingly good and possibly permanent. I had made some small forays into the dating scene since arriving in Japan, going on isolated dates with other expats, and could have fallen into a short-term romance or two, but had never felt that death-defying level of desire, so this criterion served me quite well and prevented my heart from getting clouded.

Plus I was finding that I had one other guideline, one that was deeper than kiss-or-die. I wanted my next partner to respect my faith. He did not need to be on exactly the same page, but I wanted to be with someone who strived to do what was right and, ideally, someone who believed in God, Christian or otherwise. If kiss-or-die did not eliminate most men from consideration, the second guideline certainly did.

Hideo was respectful and curious about my faith and what it meant to me, and he seemed to be working hard to live an ethical life, so I gave him credit for meeting the second requirement. As our friendship evolved, the question had become, *did I feel strongly enough about him to risk it all* — our friendship, the possibility of breaking each other's heart, complications with work supervisors, living awkwardly as neighbors — to take the next step? And would it be unbearable if I did not?

Riding home after our time in the snow, listening to music in Hideo's car, which had come to feel like a cocoon to me, an escape pod from what had turned out to be the not-always-friendly eyes and ears of Shuho-cho, I decided it was time to move forward with my life. But first I had to complete some old business.

As we approached a small bridge spanning a stream of rushing snowmelt, I asked Hideo to pull over. Looking puzzled, he slowed down and parked his car at the side of the road. I took my keys off the keychain Ryota had given me long ago, that ring attached to the *Ouchi* doll, the perfectly shiny, spherical woman painted in bittersweet, black and shimmering gold, now so chipped and worn that it was unrecognizable as anything more than a knob of wood, hard, damaged and worthless, much as I regarded my heart on my darker days. Holding it in my palm, I stepped out of the car into the light of a nearly full moon and walked to the bridge, stroking the doll's familiar surface one last time before hurling it into the fast-moving water and watching it disappear. I imagined it being carried far, far away, along with any residual feelings I had for Ryota.

When I returned to his car, Hideo did not press for information. I did not explain.

Back in Shuho-cho, I smuggled Hideo into my apartment, where he stood over my two-burner propane stove and stirred up a batch of hot cocoa, made according to his grandfather's special recipe. He poured the steaming brew into a pair of jumbo mugs, one green and one peach, some of my favorite acquisitions, procured after months of drinking from Japan's more typically doll party-sized teacups that never satiated my thirst.

Hideo and I sat on the living room floor together, legs stretched out under my *kotatsu*, enjoying the warmth, drinking our cocoa and happily watching a double feature of rented movies. At the end, I thanked him for the day's outing: "Today was fun," I told him. "I love snow."

He looked me in the eyes. "I love you," he said and leaned in, his good-natured face open and unguarded. His lips were calm and warm, and his arms, wrapped around me, felt strong and real. I had found my port. This was where I was meant to be.

That night I crashed my time machine and plunged with Hideo into unknown and potentially heart-endangering waters. But this was intentional, not a kiss of convenience. This development was one of inconvenience, complicating my decision of whether to finish out my JET contract and leave Shuho-cho in July or thoroughly commit to a second year. Now I had a budding relationship to consider — one of which Hideo's bosses disapproved.

Hideo knew I worried about adding wrinkles to other people's lives, fretted about leaving a mark where I should not, in my temporary life. He had told me that no matter who we are or whom we meet — someone from across the world or right next door — we are always making an impact on one another. Live with it.

I might have reflected more on the breaking of my kiss moratorium, of adding complications to my year of detachment, but a catastrophic event occurred a couple of hours after our first true embrace. The Great Hanshin earthquake struck some two hundred miles to the northeast, hobbling the city of Kobe. The focus of the entire nation turned that way, and over the next several days I spent hours glued to my television watching the casualty numbers stack up, watching images of buildings that had collapsed onto streets, lengths of freeways that had tipped onto neighborhoods, cars falling like beetles off a rolled log, survivors stunned and mourning.

My fear of giving my heart to another seemed trite against that backdrop, and the earthquake reminded me of the uncertainty of life, the ambiguity of any future, no matter where it was lived. Legend has it that the islands of Japan rest on a giant carp, a fickle fish that sometimes decides to flip, showing utter disregard for the busy nation built on its back. Just as there is no way to plan for a fish's fancy, there is no way to control when or where love will strike.

Hearing that my neighbors had felt the temblor and knowing I might have too had I not fallen into a deep sleep after staying up late snuggling with my new beau, I began to regard the land mass on which I was building my tentative new life as more brittle and unpredictable than before. Life itself suddenly seemed more fragile, and I was glad to have someone to love, a man who had already proven that he would take care of me.

19

Straightforward as Sunshine

M Y love life was all a-twitter and my teaching experiences at the junior high schools were mixed, but I found a place that was as straightforward as sunshine: primary school.

From the early days of autumn, I had loved watching the exuberant *shōgakusei* — primary school students — skipping and tripping their way to school, boys in black shorts and white collared shirts, girls in shorts or skirts and blouses, every child wearing a cap and hard leather backpack like a camel's hump — red for the girls, black for the boys — comically oversized on the youngest children. Their high, clear voices calling back and forth sounded like cartoon characters — brilliant cartoon characters, utterly confident in the language whose code I was working so hard to break.

My supervisor, Sasaki-*san*, had set me up on visits to a few of Shuho-cho's six primary schools early on, just for fun, and I found my days there to be pure delight. We sang songs, I taught them my favorite playground chase game — pom-pom-pullaway — and they introduced me to their projects, from drawing maps to raising chickens. The children were energetic, enthusiastic, uninhibited, and receptive — and so were their teachers.

This was probably, in part, because the stakes were so low. At the time, English was not an official primary school subject, so there were no curricula to follow, no requirements to meet, no tests to take. If the children happened to learn anything at all linguistically or culturally from my visits, it was simply *shiso* on the rice cake. I appreciated their directness, their honesty, so unlike many of the adults, whose countenances I simply could not read. Like the time I tried to cash travelers' checks — in yen — at the local bank. The tellers looked at me and laughed, saying they could not help me. When I reported this to my supervisor, Sasaki-*san*, he called their supervisor, and we went back and got the job done. He explained to me that in Japan, people laugh when they do not know what to do. In contrast, my primary school students laughed when they thought something was funny and refrained when it was not. They looked confused when they were confused and danced around me when they were excited.

Seeing how much I enjoyed the younger children, Sasaki-*san* set me up winter term to visit a primary school almost every Wednesday morning, a time when I would otherwise be sitting at my desk in the Board of Education office, writing letters home, studying Japanese, worrying about the grad school project I was not getting done, and serving tea. But first, Sasaki-*san* had asked me repeatedly whether this plan was really OK: Wouldn't I get too tired of teaching without my Wednesday desk day? I had assured him that no, the primary schools energized me.

And how could they not? The classrooms and their occupants radiated joy and playfulness. And I could get a taste of what it must feel like to be a rock star.

Shuho-cho's six primary schools — *shōgakko* — varied in size and character from tiny Yashiro Shō, with twenty-five students studying in a century-old wooden schoolhouse on the edge of settled Shuho-cho, to Akiyoshi Shō's few hundred students, whose brightly lit classrooms were stacked atop each other in a new multistory building in the busiest part of that quiet town.

Regardless of location and demographic, when I arrived at the schools, the students would call out to me, welcoming me at the front door and through their classrooms' open windows. They would approach en masse trying to touch my arms and my hair, and to look for the blue of my eyes. They would happily shout, "Shake! Shake!" and I would smile, feeling a bit doglike, and take their generally limp, often sweaty little hands in mine, glad that they were confident enough to use whatever English they had without prodding.

Despite the near hysteria, the mood never remained at fever pitch for long. Once the principal or teachers had introduced me, the children would settle into the lesson at hand, whether I taught them "Old McDonald Had a Farm," comparing animal noises in our respective languages (my favorite being the Japanese rooster's "*kokekoko*"), or they taught me to fold colorful squares of paper into samurai hats, frogs that hopped, and tiny balloons that could be inflated with one breath.

At the end of each class, the excitement would return and I would be mobbed by children thrusting notebooks, pencil cases, papers, and even their bare arms at me, requesting "Sign! Sign!" They wanted my autograph.

When it was time for me to leave the school, to return to the Board of Education office, to my afternoon koto lesson, quiet studies, and tea-serving duties, the school principal would lead me out of the school and open his car door for me — in the early days, I rode in the back like a crazy visiting aunt. As he drove down the school's driveway, children would give chase, waving and calling until we turned onto the street or disappeared out of sight.

Who would turn down such a morning?

These days were about more than living some unearned life as a star though. They were also an opportunity to revisit childhood — not mine exactly — but a childhood of sorts, and sometimes when I joined the students in their classrooms, all of us eating lunch at little wooden desks, the atmosphere of the room would quiet to shy smiles and the sounds of clicking chopsticks, children chewing and the soft thunk of heavy glass milk bottles being set down on wooden desktops. Sitting silently, I could fool myself for brief moments into believing I was one of them.

Truth be told this very enjoyable experience of rejoining the land of innocence also gave me some heartburn. When a posse of senior citizens spent the morning at one school teaching traditional games, or when a *sensei* demonstrated how to use a *shodō* brush to write simple calligraphy, I was not facilitating the students' learning or helping maintain order with the other teachers. Instead, I was placed in a group of children and taught how to juggle homemade beanbags; I was lined up on the floor with the rest of the class, brush in my right hand, following their *sensei*'s air-writing motions and then kneeling over a long sheet of white paper, dipping my brush into freshly ground ink and drawing my own somewhat childlike characters top to bottom,

あ
き
よ
し
だ
い

— "*A-ki-yo-shi-da-i,*" the name of the nearby plateau.

Sometimes I truly became a student of the students. A trio of third-grade boys taught me how to add and subtract using a *soroban*, the Japanese abacus, my little instructors beating me to the answers every time. In the fall, one school had taught me how to harvest sweet potatoes; in the spring, another would show me how to plant rice seedlings in a soft paddy, all of us standing in the muck, red worms swirling around our ankles, mine, thankfully, covered by borrowed boots.

I wondered at times whether it was wise for a teacher to appear so ignorant, so unskilled, to be such a neophyte at activities that came naturally to the students — or at least every other adult they knew. I wondered whether it should bother me that these schools lumped me in with primary school students in the role of learner. I wondered whether this would impact my credibility to teach English or my authority to explain my own culture, to do my job.

But I could not deny that I loved having the opportunity to experience so many aspects of Japan that I would encounter nowhere else, aspects and details that gave me insight into the childhoods of my host sisters, of Naoko, and of Hideo. And truth be told, I had a lot in common with the primary school students. My Japanese language level was still lower than most of theirs, and my cultural understanding was also at a relatively primitive level, perhaps not unlike theirs. Early in my tenure particularly, there was a whole lot of nuance that went over my head. The difference between the students and me was that I knew how much I was missing. The similarity was that, like them, I really was not expected to get it all. In fact, our days probably went more smoothly for everyone when I did not.

I did not need great language skills to understand the impressive level of camaraderie and cooperation I witnessed at the primary schools, where older students looked out for the guileless little ones, and for each other. Or to observe the warmth exuded by the teachers, who offered a kind of wraparound support that seemed to free the children to explore and live out their natural zest for learning, one not yet burdened by fear of failure — or of experiencing that well-known proverb addressing nonconformity: the nail that sticks up is hammered down.

* * *

One Wednesday morning that winter we awoke to the glorious sight of Shuho-cho sculpted white, snow still falling in great fluffy blossoms called *botan yuki* — "peony snow." For once it did not melt after breakfast. I walked to nearby Kama Shō and saw the children on the playground, most wearing their uniforms of shorts and short-sleeved shirts, some with a jacket or sweater, some with pants, most seemingly oblivious to the cold. They were building the Japanese version of snowmen, *yuki* (snow) *daruma*, modeled after the little dolls that represent Bodhidharma, the founder of Zen Buddhism, which are sold with both eyes blank white, one eye to be blackened when a goal is set and the other to be inked in when the goal is achieved.

I had been to Kama Shō a couple of times already, and had sat in the office drinking tea with the school's principal, who seemed to want to tell me about his boyhood memories of World War II. For him, it had meant living on a soup of rice and potatoes, wearing pants held together by patches and attending a primary school where students had no erasers and wrote their lessons on tissue paper. It was a time when the sky blazed red in the distance, the color of bombing. Initially I wondered whether he harbored some animosity toward me or my country, whether these conversations would take an uncomfortable turn, but his earnestness put me at ease, and he would always conclude philosophically, "*It was war.*

That is how it was. It could not be helped." Whether he was explaining it to me or to himself, I am not sure.

Perhaps because of those talks he felt he had sufficiently vetted me and was comfortable giving me the reins at his school, so for this visit, he had asked that I plan and teach my own lessons. Seeing that the day was going to be a snowy one, I focused on the weather, bringing props — a paper sun, a paper snowflake, my umbrella, and a gorilla (a Christmas gift from a junior high school student) that I named Cloudy for the occasion, having run out of time to make paper clouds. In the sixth-grade classroom, the teacher sat back as I introduced weather vocabulary and began to query the children, "How's the weather?"

I grabbed my umbrella. "It's rainy!" they shouted.

I held up the paper sun. "It's sunny!"

"It's snowy!"

"It's Cloudy!"

They got it. They loved it. They cheered for Cloudy the Gorilla.

I must have begun waxing on about Minnesota's glorious snow-falls, reminiscing about making snow angels and playing fox and geese — a game set up by shuffling through the snow to create a giant wheel in whose spokes my friends and I played tag as primary schoolers — because their teacher suddenly asked, *"Do you want to show the children?"*

We made a dash for the classroom door, down the stairs and out the front entrance into the snow. My charges, most wearing short pants and gym shoes, shuffled out fox-and-geese wheels, and chased each other around the spokes. Others lay down, bare skin in the snow, moving their arms and legs in giant arcs to make snow angels. Everyone wet. Everyone laughing.

20

Broken Windows

I LEFT a very meager record of Hideo's and my early life as a couple, and this most likely means we spent most of our non-working moments together. There was no time to write; I was too busy living. Because I am shy about these things, I would like to say the journal entries and letters I did not write are evidence that we were on the road a lot, running around Yamaguchi, going to movies, and hiking. But if that were the case, there would be more photographs in my albums, for in those days I was a merciless documentarian, every new person, place, and event subjected to my camera's lens. Absent those images, I arrive at the most likely truth: Hideo and I spent a lot of time making out.

Let me be clear. Since my divorce, I had become a staunch born-again virgin. The way I saw it, there were three reasons I should wait until marriage before sleeping with someone again: my personal belief that waiting was the right thing to do, pregnancy prevention, and avoiding sexually transmitted diseases. This braided approach worked for me, because there were moments when one or two of those strands began to fray, but even so that left at least one tenuous thread that helped me maintain my resolve. Coming from a fairly conservative family background himself, Hideo respected my position. We did not just hold hands and cuddle, but we also were not sleeping together, not in the biblical sense anyway.

Having kissed only one man once since my ex and I separated two years previously, I had fully reclaimed my physical self and had grown accustomed to the privacy that brings, regarding and interacting with the world as if from behind a glass wall. When Hideo broke through my pane, the closeness of his body and the emotional presence that came with it brought a thrilling shock.

Of course I crashed through Hideo's window as well, and added touch and taste to the senses by which I already knew him, having long ago memorized the sight of his open face, his strong arms and hands; his low, full voice, tinged with good humor; his scent of fresh air and sunshine. As we drew closer, as I became acquainted with his smooth, warm skin, I found he was as pleasant to be near as I had imagined, and that winter we created our own shared perch from which to gaze on the rest of the world. Or draw the curtains against it.

Even when we were not together, he assured me that I was always in his thoughts. When he went on a ski trip to South Korea, he bought me a pair of amethyst and diamond earrings. When I shared a fond childhood memory of eating canned fruit cocktail with my father (vying for the maraschino cherries), he tracked down a can, one packed in Minnesota no less. I wrote to a friend in Minnesota that Hideo was restoring my faith in men.

Winter, it so happened, was the perfect time to fall in love in Shuho-cho, most every chilly day spent in anticipation of an evening curled into Hideo's embrace, snuggling under my *kotatsu* till the wee hours of a dark morning. Then he would rise and pad sleepily down the hallway to my front door, where with one more kiss I would release him to the frosty night, the moon his only visible witness as he tiptoed past the *shachō*'s apartment door, down the outdoor staircase and past the *obasan*'s dark kitchen windows before slipping into the dormitory, the muffled sound of its heavy door whumping shut behind him.

21

A Cat, a Car, Another Contract

You have probably heard the punchline to this joke: "How do you make God laugh?"

"Tell him your plans."

If there is any truth to it, I imagine God laughing before I even left for Shuho-cho, when I assured myself I would spend a solitary year there maintaining an aura of detachment. Or maybe God began laughing when I started jotting down my lists of pros and cons, considering a second year in Shuho-cho but trying not to get swept away by my new relationship. I bet he loved the part where I abdicated my decision by testing the Board of Education's commitment to me by making two requests.

Not long after Hideo's and my first kiss, as the deadline for signing my renewal contract loomed, I told my supervisor, Sasaki-*san*, that I would like to stay for another year as Shuho-cho's JET, but I had two stipulations. One involved a cat, the other a car.

The cat was the fluffy gray stray that had comforted me through my short marriage and longer separation. Although friends were caring for him back in Minnesota, sending me photographic updates, I still missed Thornton's reassuring presence. I could imagine his furry paws padding across the wood and tatami floors of my Dwelling Friends apartment, his green eyes slowly closing as he dozed on the sunny balcony. He would make my apartment feel complete.

The car was a different sort of wish, a standing sore point between my supervisors and me. I had been rattling them about it off and on for months, presenting them with schedules that demonstrated my limited transportation options and promising to swear off alcohol, if it made them feel better (Japan's legal blood-alcohol limit for drivers was zero). But they continued to resist, apparently out of fear that I would get into an accident, causing some tragedy and bringing shame raining down on the school district and the town. It seemed some JET living somewhere in Japan at some time in history had set this negative precedent.

Two important things to note: First, I was not asking the Board to *pay* for my car. Second, my contract stated that I was allowed to drive. Still, in the interest of good relations I did not want to go against my employers' wishes.

But the fact was, without a car I was limited to busing, and that meant I was trapped not just in the town of Shuho-cho but in my neighborhood within that town. And I did not feel comfortable forever soliciting rides from Hideo, Naoko, or my work colleagues. I did not want to be so dependent, or to have all my comings and goings be the stuff of common knowledge. A car would make it easier to visit my host family in Hagi; to take Japanese language lessons in Yamaguchi City; to visit friends who lived more than a bike ride away; to cart my koto to practices and performances; and to run errands to city supermarkets that sold decent cheese, pizza crusts, and canned tomatoes. By this time I knew my way around, and I had a life filled with patterns.

So Sasaki-*san* went to the Board of Education to ask whether I could bring my cat to Shuho-cho with me after my summer vacation in the States, and whether the Board would be willing to stop putting up roadblocks to my getting a car. I waited, wondering if it would withdraw my option to renew.

Giddy with new love, I hoped my requests would be granted, because not so deep down I knew my decision to stay for a second year had less to do with a cat and a car than with seeing how my relationship with Hideo would unfold, determining whether this life in Japan would bring me to the wholeness of which I dreamed.

I was not at all sure it would. The fact that Hideo did not have a faith was a growing concern for me. I would have accepted pretty much any variety of faith, because I believed God was bigger than any one religion and each was designed to lead us back to him. But despite Hideo's coming from a religious family, he followed nothing. I was not a devoted church-goer at the time, but what if that changed? Would he come to resent my faith? Or would he follow me into it? I knew from hard experience that no good comes from entering a relationship hoping a partner will change, but I could not tell this time whether my heart was hopeful or accepting.

Although I had not shared these misgivings, Hideo did understand how important it was for me to make this decision without pressure from him. And my life was not the only one with moving parts. It was possible, he told me, that Sumitomo could transfer him to another office that very spring, but it most likely would take him only as far as a nearby city, a half-hour drive away. I figured a little distance might not be entirely bad. Having a little more alone time would help me keep a clearer head in this romance while getting some work done on the collection of essays I was writing about my experiences in Shuho-cho's schools and with my new friends and neighbors. These essays were more than a hobby; they were the project that would complete the master's degree in mass communication/print journalism I had abandoned in Minnesota the previous year.

I got the answer to my requests fairly quickly. The Board of Education agreed to both. Feeling victorious, I decided it was a sign and handed in my contract.

Locked into another year and a half in Shuho-cho, I actually began to relax. My relationship with Hideo would have time to evolve, and I would get to spend more time with my host family, and friends like Naoko. I would certainly be able to do research for and write more essays, and meanwhile would have more time to spend with my students. Mr. Kumagai and I would build on our already strong teaching partnership at South Junior High, and Mr. Kita and I — having recovered from our earlier falling out — would surely make progress as well.

Shuho-cho had recommitted to me, and I was ready to do the same. Everything was falling into place.

22

Obligation Chocolate

ON March 14, Hideo arrived at my door with a blue box containing a white chocolate heart and two little pots of cacti. *Happy White Day.*

White Day is to Valentine's Day what prom is to a Sadie Hawkins dance. Sort of. In Japan, Valentine's Day is the province of women, who on February 14 present milk chocolate goodies to the men in their lives, lovers as well as coworkers, the latter of whom receive *giri-choko* — "obligation chocolate."

A month later, men reciprocate by presenting white chocolate to the women in their lives, hence Hideo and his gift on March 14. The cacti had nothing to do with the holiday, but I had once mentioned liking them, so he used White Day as an excuse to add to my apartment's ever-expanding indoor garden of purple iris, orange kalanchoe, and herbs from Naoko.

But Hideo's gifts — one sweet, one sharp — formed the perfect metaphor for his visit, because he had also brought some news: he was being transferred — but not to the place he had imagined. He was being transferred to Tokyo. Faraway, cement-encrusted Tokyo. It was a promotion, really, his getting plucked from the field, from the far *inaka*, and sent to work at the cement company's home office. But in terms of our new relationship, not to mention my recent signing on to spend a second year in Shuho-cho, the news was devastating.

I had known that *tenkin* (job transfer) season was on its way, that spring in Japan would bring more than pretty pink cherry blossoms and dewy yellow-green leaves. I knew it would bring upheaval, as schoolteachers, town workers and *salarimen* — Japan's salaried white-collar workers — received new assignments sending them far and wide.

I had watched my host family endure serial transfers with my host father, Otōsan's, telephone company job. As long as I had known them — and for long before that as well — he and my host mother, Okāsan, had kept separate homes, never in the same town. While Okāsan had always lived in Hagi with the children and her mother-in-law, Otōsan had been transferred all over Yamaguchi Prefecture, set up in company apartments like the one where I lived with Sumitomo workers in Shuho-cho. But he always returned to Hagi on the weekends to spend full days with his family working and relaxing around the house, visiting with friends, taking little trips and playing pachinko.

Everyone accepted Otōsan's chronic workweek absence as a matter of course, just as Okāsan accepted a tough decision she had had to make: as an employee of the same company, she stepped off the track to promotion many years earlier, so she and the family could maintain a home base, so the children could stay in one school system, in Hagi. There had been another particularly difficult decision point for them as well. Otōsan could have transferred to Hagi and gotten a promotion to stay there with his family, but when the offer was made, it had come with a serious string attached: Okāsan would have had to quit her job. She told Otōsan that she wanted to keep working, so he turned down the opportunity, and apart they stayed.

It seemed almost cruel how that company kept my host parents apart, like permanent star-crossed lovers, but it did not defeat them. Okāsan and Otōsan chose their own path within the constraints and functioned as a well-matched couple, one that chose to spend its available time together instead of splitting up for guys' or ladies' weekends, as I saw so many Japanese couples do.

What I had learned from observing my host parents was that *tenkin* assignments came when they came, and once the changes were announced, workers — and often their families — were given a couple of weeks' notice to vacate old jobs, homes, and friends, and move on to the new ones. It resembled the Tokugawa-era system of *sankin kotai*, in which *daimyō* lived one year in their home domains and the next in Edo, the capital, enduring — along with their retainers — nearly constant travel and dislocation that prevented them from becoming too powerful anywhere and therefore kept them from becoming a threat to the shogun.

Even though I knew all this, as spring approached in Shuho-cho, I truly believed I was going to be immune to *tenkin* fever, at least at work. It seemed reasonable to assume that the schools and the Board of Education would want to enjoy the benefit of my co-teachers' and my hard-won rapport, our ever-improving lesson plans and teaching strategies, for another year. Little did I know, as *tenkin* season descended, it would bring a great thaw, one that would break loose most of the pieces that defined the life I had been building in Shuho-cho.

Mr. Kumagai would be transferred to Yamaguchi City, to the junior high school at the prefectural university, clearly a plum position. He would later tell me his move came *because* of me: some bureaucrats had observed us teaching together at South Junior High and had recommended him. And Mr. Kita would be sent to teach in a junior high school in another town, his transfer triggered by his recent engagement to a colleague at our school. Like my host parents, he and his wife-to-be would not be able to work at the same organization. In addition to my primary co-teachers' moves, my principals were retiring and several other colleagues would be caught in this fruit-basket upset. It felt as if everything was changing.

When April and the beginning of the Japanese school year arrived, I would be starting over with brand-new co-teachers, establishing new relationships, and working out new lesson plans. The thought exhausted me.

More than that, it angered me. I had signed on for another year and a half of the situation I had encountered the previous August, the one I had been tending like a garden, nourishing and pruning, coaxing my sturdy (and not-so-sturdy) starts along, trying to create an environment where English conversation could flourish, where teaching went beyond preparing for tests. I had not envisioned plowing the whole thing under and sowing new seeds — not to mention doing it without Hideo nearby. Doing it alone.

* * *

Sitting in my living room that White Day, having lost all interest in chocolate and cacti, eight months into what had recently become a twenty-four-month-long contract, I felt adrift. No longer would Hideo and I go driving or walking after work; no longer would I catch a glimpse of him bicycling a byway as I rode the old green, wooden-floored bus home from South Junior High; no longer would we spend lazy evenings listening to music in my apartment, fooling ourselves into thinking we were staying under the radar of my neighbor, Hideo's boss. (Some months later, one of our allies would tell me that he was sent to Tokyo partly in retaliation for us continuing our frowned-upon relationship. I still struggle to understand how punishment and promotion could be so intertwined.)

At least, I thought, I had negotiated reliable transportation for myself. Once I got my car I would be able to drive myself to the train station and hand over the hefty fare for a bullet train ticket that would take me northeasterly toward Tokyo to visit my beau. With all the *tenkin* hubbub erupting, I had yet to make time to find a car, but a fellow teacher offered to loan me his snub-nosed white pickup truck until I did. When our principal heard this, he flew into a tizzy of concern and called the Board of Education, which subsequently forbade the loan.

I was furious. Not only was I losing my beau and key colleagues with whom I had envisioned spending my second year in Shuho-cho, but now the Board was reneging on the negotiated agreement on which my staying depended. I would not continue to be their *hako-iri-musume*, their "daughter" — or employee — "in-a-box," restricted and over-managed by these navy-suited handlers. I was a real live woman, an adult. And a car was the only path I could see to gaining a fuller life, especially given my new circumstances, without Hideo.

I was tempted to quit Shuho-cho in protest, but that would mean taking the fruitless path of my maternal grandmother who, when ordered by her stepmother to stay home from school to care for her step-siblings, quit high school altogether — my family's example of someone biting off her nose to spite her face. No, my resignation would amount to a pointless stand against a system that no one else seemed inclined to fight. I would lose my salary and my ticket to stay in Japan, and with that my opportunity to explore a relationship with Hideo, to spend time with friends and host family, to continue studying the koto, and to wrap up the project that would complete my master's degree.

My leaving would let down my supervisor, Sasaki-*san*, who had gone out of his way to negotiate so I could acquire a car and bring my cat back to Shuho-cho after the summer vacation. And my host family, who had made it clear to my employers and neighbors that they considered me a third daughter.

Quitting now would also let down Hideo, whose life was being upended — for good and bad — probably in part because of our relationship. Leaving his post in Shuho-cho meant not only leaving familiar work and colleagues (and me), it meant leaving a beautiful natural environment where he could go mountain biking on an almost daily basis. Where would he ride in Tokyo? *When* would he ride in Tokyo? Transferring to the home office of a multinational corporation would surely not be a cakewalk. Whatever I did, after all that had happened, I did not want to disappoint Hideo.

Knowing that he would be leaving soon did nothing but fuel my fire for that man. We spent every evening and as many days together as possible, and I no longer cared who knew. The worst had happened — well, other than one of us getting fired — so why not? Besides, in Hideo's mind, I was almost his fiancée. He had told me something I have not yet mentioned: he planned to marry me a year from August. And he accepted that I did not yet share his vision.

This is all to say, although I was a foreigner and a relative short-timer — one that had arrived expressly for a year of detachment — I now had obligations in Yamaguchi that carried far more weight than a box of chocolate. No, leaving Shuho-cho now would send the wrong message, not the least of which was that I could be beaten. Similar to my host parents, who had spent decades dealing with company rules but had found a way to live life on their own terms,

I had a point to make: the Board of Education might be in charge of my employment, and the Dwelling Friends might manage my housing, but neither of them was in charge of *my life.*

My life.

So much for detachment. So much for floating free. I hardly realized it at the time, but having Hideo taken away from me galvanized a sense that Shuho-cho had become my real world. I was engaging in skirmishes and setting boundaries in an effort to preserve a life I had not intended to establish.

23

Worlds Collide

AT the end of March, spring break would mark the end of the school year in Japan and throw every pending change into motion — Hideo's move to Tokyo, my colleagues' transfers to other schools, and my ninth grade students' graduations. It also would bring visitors and sightseeing: my mother was due to arrive, along with her girlhood pal Kay.

For the previous few months I had been building a fairy tale of a travel plan that would follow the cherry blossom front, south to north, while taking us to the major sights of western Japan. Like the sensible-shoed middle-aged models I had seen featured on Japan Rail travel posters, I imagined Mom and Kay posing exuberantly against backdrops of temples, gardens, and castles.

Those posters advertised the "Nice Middy Pass" — ナイスミディパス — a discount ticket for women over thirty who were traveling in groups, ostensibly for weekends away from spouses and kids. I imagine their trips generally included a few cultural sites and shopping sprees, leisurely meals of sushi and local specialties, and, at the end of each day, a bone-soothing soak in an *onsen* where dozens of naked women settled into rock-lined pools of hot, mineral-rich water. Rejuvenated, they returned home rested and ready to make a special supper for their husbands and children.

But that scenario bore no resemblance to the trip I had designed for Mom and Kay. My Nice Middies and I were embarking on a tour de force, with nearly every single minute of the next couple of weeks scheduled. I knew the number and departure time of every bus and train for each city, each castle, each temple, garden, and vista. I had estimated how long we wanted to spend wandering about these places, how much time was required for taking on nourishment and how many hours we needed to allocate for sleep. With this as a guide, I planned to herd my "naisu midi" companions through nine different cities, two of Japan's three "most scenic" places (so designated by the Japan National Tourism Organization) and eight UNESCO World Heritage sites. Our unforgiving expedition routed us from Fukuoka, south of Yamaguchi, through Shuho-cho and Hagi, and then northward to Miyajima, Himeji, Amanohashidate, Kyoto, Nara and Yoshino before ending in Osaka, from where the Middies would depart for home.

I was eager to see places I had read about in books and seen on TV and in movies, and my visitors would get a crash course in Japanese culture. Perfect.

* * *

Our travels got off to an inauspicious start, though, even before my guests landed in Japan.

One clear blue afternoon, Hideo picked me up from South Junior High, and we drove out of town, up the winding roads that led to Akiyoshidai, the plateau. It would be one of Hideo's last opportunities to enjoy the limestone-dotted landscape before moving to streetlamp-studded Tokyo, and Akiyoshidai was particularly beguiling that day, its hills greening, its air touched by that hint of fecundity that heralds the coming of true spring.

As always, Hideo had thoroughly prepared for our outing, having stopped at a convenience store to purchase a selection of snacks, probably our standard favorites: rice balls wrapped in seaweed, some stuffed with pickles, others with tuna; white-bread sandwiches, some spread with egg salad, others lined with thinly sliced, red-rind-ed bologna and cucumber; cans of tea and coffee. When we reached an out-of-the-way part of the plateau, he parked his car in a small, otherwise empty lot, and we walked a short distance — maybe a hundred yards — along a path. Settling down on a large rock, still warm as the evening chill approached, we unwrapped our *combini* meal and savored it amid the quiet beauty of the surrounding landscape.

Maybe an hour passed before we returned to the car, and when we got there, we found it was not as we had left it. The passenger-side window was shattered, and glass chips covered my seat. Inside, my bags and all their contents were gone. My teaching materials, calendars, purse with credit cards, Tanzanian briefcase (a gift from my grandfather, who had worked in Africa), some fish-shaped pottery plates I had fashioned and glazed alongside my junior high school students, $800 worth of yen and $1,100 worth of travel vouchers I had procured for Mom, Kay and me. All gone.

I blinked again and again, slowly realizing that I had made the classic foreigner mistake. I had grown complacent in Japan, relaxing into its pervasive and generally reliable sense of safety. If only I could turn back time, just an hour, maybe two, I could leave my valuables in my desk at the school. Or I could carry my bags with me to our picnic spot. Or Hideo and I could enjoy the plateau from a vantage point closer to the car. There were so many ways this would not have had to happen.

Hideo jumped in the driver's seat and I leaped in the back, and he careened us down the curvy road until we arrived at an inn where we could call and report the incident to police, where I could call and wake my parents early in their Minnesota morning and ask them to cancel my credit cards.

As we raced through the front door of the inn, I ran straight into Shinoda-*kyōikuchō*, the head of the Board of Education, who at that moment was at least two sheets to the wind, relaxed, effusive, smiling broadly. *"Sah-lah-san!"* he gushed. *"Konbanwa!"*

Shoving pleasantries aside, I began telling him what had happened. He continued to grin.

I told him again, and this time my news permeated his buzz. He turned sober and began taking charge, taking care, facilitating my phone calls, engaging the police. The next week, my officemates presented me with a cash gift, money to use for my trip with Mom and Kay. I was touched and humbled. And embarrassed that my colleagues would subsidize my carelessness.

Hearing about the burglary, people told me that there had been some foreigners in the area. (*Foreigners?* I wondered. *Like me?*) They told me my things would surely turn up, maybe scattered on the plateau. This sort of thing had happened before. So for days Hideo and I drove the snaking roads looking for something, anything, nothing. I became a cautionary tale.

* * *

My mother and Kay arrived at Fukuoka International Airport, a few hours from Shuho-cho, in a flurry of hugs and kisses, showering me with greetings from family and friends half a world away. Within moments I shifted from meticulously crafted subject-verb-object sentences and laboriously enunciated English back to my usual tempo, ideas flying in the shorthand of people who understand one another's culture and assumptions, who share a history, both relational and geographic. And I shed the self-consciousness that accompanied my forever being the tallest woman and the only Caucasian in sight. Kay was shorter than I but bustier. Mom was taller and heavier. With them, I could almost disappear in a microclimate of differentness.

Although I had not known what time we would arrive back in Shuho-cho, Hideo found us at the bus station, showing himself to be a doting, considerate boyfriend — and potential son-in-law. After delivering us all to my apartment, he joined us for coffee and pleasantries, and though my mother and Kay seemed to find him quite charming, I could tell they were just waiting for him to leave so they could begin grilling me about my future, one that assumed another marriage: "Where would you live?" "What kind of career would you pursue?" "How often would we see you?"

I was not ready for this. I had no answers and really was still adapting to the idea that I had laid claim to Shuho-cho, signing on for another year, fighting for a car, working to preserve a romantic relationship. Seeing my most familiar person against this backdrop — looking almost foreign to me — and fielding her questions was disconcerting at best.

Over the next couple of days, even while my guests were still slap-happy with jetlag, bewildered by the incomprehensible speech and signage surrounding them, captivated by every shop, whether it sold temple talismans or groceries, I introduced them to my new people. We joined Naoko for coffee, visited the Board of Education office for tea, stopped in at North and South junior high schools, shopped in the local stores, and invited the Dwelling Friends wives and *obasan* for coffee and treats — strawberries and soft, sweet, bean-filled *manju* the women had made fresh that morning, more than we could ever eat.

In addition to playing tour guide and social director, I spent those days interpreting, going back and forth between my mother and

Kay, and my people in Shuho-cho. My handlers and colleagues fed Mom compliment after compliment about my looks (variously and generously compared with Princess Diana and Julia Roberts), my Japanese skills, and my involvement in the koto club. They were exceedingly kind, but it is a cultural tradition to talk up another's child, a tradition that cues a self-deprecating response.

The situation was further complicated by the fact that my people were complimenting me in Japanese, ordering me to translate their kind words into English. I downplayed the accolades, but the Japanese speakers seemed to sense this — or understood enough English to know it. They would make me translate their words again, and it felt even more shameful to compliment myself a second time.

I tried to get my mother to respond with something like, "No, no, no, this, incompetent daughter? I'm sorry for any trouble she is causing you." But instead she politely said, "Thank you!" and beamed, no matter how I pleaded with her. She could not help but agree with them, she explained. After many moons apart, she was too happy to see me and simply refused to play the game. This warmed my heart and made me crazy. Navigating between my two worlds, one a given, the other chosen, it was hard to say which felt more real and which more surreal.

* * *

The night before my mother, Kay and I were scheduled to depart on our grand tour, Hideo drove us to Yamaguchi City and a boisterous sumo-themed restaurant where he had reserved a private stall. There we sat at a low table on the tatami floor and ate *chanko-nabe*, the staple food of Japan's prized wrestlers, who apparently derive their legendary strength (and girth) from this combination of meat, tofu, vegetables, and hearty broth. As it burbled away in heavy clay pots set on gas burners, we worked hard to put a dent in the spread, washing it down with full-bodied Japanese beer, slowly, happily sinking under the weight of it.

Lumbering back outside to the parking lot, we found a blossoming fruit tree, probably a plum, its flowers the color of raspberries blended with whipped cream. The blossom reports on the evening news, complete with special flower maps, had not been serving us well. Word was the blooms were late that spring, and this meant my fairytale itinerary might have us looking at a whole lot of buds. Still, we remained hopeful, and this plum seemed a good sign.

After returning to Shuho-cho and resettling my mother and Kay in my apartment, I left with Hideo for our final drive together before his move to Tokyo, our plan being to see the stars over Akiyoshidai. We had assured each other that this was not farewell as much as see-you-soon, and we planned to talk regularly by phone as my visitors and I threaded our way northeastward. We would meet again in Osaka, about halfway between Tokyo and Shuho-cho, to see off the two of them at the airport and commence the next stage of our relationship, spending time, effort, and money wishing away the distance that would separate us, as if we could fold Japan like a sheet of origami paper, erasing five hundred miles with a few sharp creases.

We had not driven far from our apartment building when the dark sky opened up and heavy blankets of rain dropped onto the road. Hideo veered into the yard of a *nashi* packing plant where workers had spent the previous autumn sorting Shuho-cho's famous greenish-gold pears, packing them for shipping throughout the country. The structure and lot were completely dark, so Hideo pulled under an overhang connecting two sections of the building, switched off his lights and turned off the engine. Sheltered for a moment on the cusp of an uncertain future, we held each other close as the rain crashed down around us.

24

Touring the Nice Middies

IN my care, Mom and Kay seemed almost childlike, unable to speak the ambient language, unsure how to react to bows or gifts, clueless about many of the foods being placed before them. Their questions swirled around me: "Why do we wash our hands before entering the shrine?" "What is the name of those white flowers edged in purple?" "Why are the little *Jizō* statues wearing bibs and hats?" "Why are the children wearing shorts in the cold?" "What does that sign say?" "How old is this castle? ... that shrine? ... that tree?" "Is this raw fish?" I tried to keep up with their questions, but they were testing my cultural knowledge and emerging language skills — and, at times, my patience — to the limit. It made me wonder, *was this what it was like for Hideo, Naoko, and my host family to spend time with me, constantly coaching and fielding questions?* At least Mom, Kay, and I shared a language; my Japanese family, friends, and I straddled both language and culture.

Meanwhile, the tour I had planned for my visitors was challenging every expectation of theirs. In addition to settling into the rhythm of a new culture, they were working to match my pace and keep up with our itinerary, a fire-hose-style introduction to what I had determined were the most stunning examples of Japanese architecture, art, landscaping and culture, our bodies in perpetual motion, rushing to catch trains and buses. Too late I realized that when prepping my Middies for their visit, I had failed to mention that travel in Japan involves countless staircases, and they would do best carrying standard-issue Nice Middy tote bags. Instead, they had brought wheeled suitcases that we rolled bump-bump-bump-bump-bump, up and down dozens of concrete staircases, up to get tickets, down to board a train, occasionally arriving, breathless, at the wrong track and then hurrying back up a flight of stairs and down another to reach the correct platform. Some cajoling was required.

Fulfilling basic needs was also difficult at times. Sometimes, mid-dash, one of my Middies wanted to buy a snack or a souvenir and needed me to help her pick the right coins or bills from her wallet. Other times my visitors balked at the Japanese toilets, floor fixtures requiring deep squats of travel-weary legs, and pleaded for a Western-style toilet, an elusive commodity. There was no grabbing a quick bite to eat; restaurant visits involved language, etiquette, food choice, and chopstick coaching.

Increasingly frazzled, I realized that the spring break trip I had planned was for someone who had mastered the details of everyday life and wanted to delve deeper into the history and culture of Japan. The trip was really for me.

The mother–daughter dynamic also played a role in our experience, mother watching once-helpless child — whose diapers she had changed and whose first words she had cheered — take charge of her short-term fate. It was not that she did not trust me to get us where we needed to go, to keep us fed and slept (although she was right to question my understanding of a middle-aged woman's energy level), but she seemed perpetually astounded that I was able to do these things in a language, place, and culture completely foreign to her, where she was utterly unable to help — or to understand. This lack of control appeared to unnerve her and took the form of not wanting to miss a thing, no matter how mundane. As I talked with people, working out our next step or gathering information about the site we were visiting, she would be in my ear asking, "What is he saying? Where do we go next? What is this? When do we need to go?" I experienced nearly every conversation twice, once in Japanese, once in English, shifting back and forth, sometimes looking at Mom and speaking Japanese, then turning back to a helpful Japanese person and breaking into English. At the end of most days, as my worn-out charges were getting ready for bed, I would leave our room to search out a green public telephone. Sliding in my phone card, I dialed Hideo's number — in Shuho-cho for a few days and then in Tokyo — and get a dose of the person who had come to represent my normal life. He told me stories of his transition from *inaka* to megalopolis, and I shared with him how crazy I felt negotiating the roles of daughter and tour guide. He advised me to take on the attitude of Ha-chan, the orange and white cat he had rescued, who was now the Dwelling Friends' communal pet: "*If your mother does something to annoy you, walk three steps and — 'meow' — forget all about it.*"

Kay provided a good foil, being the more free-wheeling of my Middies, a survivor of the rearing of three rowdy, fearless sons. We had visited her family every year on trips to Mom's hometown in Saskatchewan, and I always enjoyed watching her and her husband loosen up my parents, Minnesotans whose date nights involved dinner and the symphony or a movie. In Saskatchewan, we pored over photos of swim meets, ski trips, and beach parties held indoors in the middle of a subzero winter for which Kay and her husband donned matching grass skirts and coconut bras.

She brought her good-natured irreverence to Japan, making light of cross-cultural frustrations. As we grew bemused by restaurants serving us dribbles of water in tumblers scarcely taller than North American shot glasses, it was she who declared, "If these people would drink their eight glasses a day, they'd rehydrate and be as big as us!"

* * *

A few days into our Nice Middy tour, Mom let me know she was frustrated at our hurried pace. But I was so eager to share my new world — and to see the sights of it myself — that I hoped she would give into my plans and speed up. Observing her and struggling with her over our different tempos and styles, I wondered whether I was seeing twenty-seven years into my future.

When I was a little girl, my father dubbed me Little Eleanor, after my mother, because I so accurately mimicked her intonation, her sayings and her gestures. At the time, this had been the best compliment he could have given me. In my eyes, my mother was like an angel, a goddess and a movie star, all in one, the most mesmerizing, beautiful, wonderful creature I had ever seen. I loved her voice. I loved her cooking. I loved her smell. I wanted to *be* her.

As I grew older, though, I realized I did not want her life, one focused on child-rearing, entertaining, and skillful homemaking. I had never really been expected to follow her path anyway. I was highly focused on school and career, envisioning future success coming outside the home. Besides, I could never come close to achieving her homemaking skills, partly due to lack of interest, partly due to lack of aptitude. She regularly shook her head at my perpetually messy room, my chaotic work style, and my lack of interest in cooking or gardening, and wondered aloud where I had come from.

Even so, I had the sense that some die had been cast, a die that would lead me to a life resembling hers. In college, when I considered a career in medicine, Mom had asked me how I would ever find time to care for my future family. When I abandoned graduate school before writing my final project, Dad had seemed certain I would never return to finish my degree, just as Mom had left her master's degree incomplete. I had busted the Little Eleanor mold by divorcing, but the consensus still seemed to be that my future path would mirror hers.

One rainy day in Japan, as we dodged raindrops and puddles, Kay and I unintentionally outpaced Mom, and I saw my opportunity to ask my nagging question of a woman who had known me as long as my mother had. "Kay?" I ventured. "Am I just like her? Am I like my mom was when she was my age?"

Kay did not hesitate, not for an instant. "No," she laughed, "you're an all-new breed."

And with that, a wall broke down in my mind. I was not Little Eleanor. I was just me, and that meant my whole future was open. Whether I stayed in Japan or returned home to the States, whether I married again or stayed single, whether I pursued some high-powered career or lived my days as a dreamer. The constraints I had imagined did not apply. My life felt more my own and my future more open than ever before. The choices I would make and the life that would follow would be mine alone.

25

Blind

Poised with my heels against a gray rock the size of a bulky backpack, I looked across the stone-tiled courtyard to a second more mottled rock about twenty yards away. Both were wrapped with thick braids of rice straw, *shimenawa*, which in the Shinto tradition sets an area apart as sacred. I drew in a deep breath, closed my eyes, and took a step into that space.

These two stones, known as *mekura-ishi* ("blind stones"), sit in the midst of a Shinto shrine where red-eyed rabbits stand sentinel and shops hawk red and white talismans. Shrines are dedicated to all sorts of causes — education, fishing, abundant food — but the focus here was love, with talismans and prayers aiding visitors who wished to deepen their relationships, marry, and conceive babies. According to tradition, lovers who can walk with their eyes closed, repeating their beloved's name, from one *mekura-ishi* to the other are guaranteed a happy union — proof not that love is blind but that blindness can be used to prove love.

Step ... step ... step ... "HideoHideoHideo ..."

I felt silly embarking on this quest with my mom and Kay watching, my mom surely looking sideways at Kay and shaking her head. They did not know that Hideo had already declared his intent to marry me a year from August, when my teaching contract would end. They also had no idea that I was not only struggling with my decision but with the fact that he had asked the question so early in our relationship. I lacked clarity about whether Hideo was The One, and absolute clarity is what I required. Less than a year had passed since my divorce, and I was in no hurry. But Hideo was.

Step ... step ... step ... "HideoHideoHideo ..."

I had not set out to test my love for Hideo this day. I had not even known of the blind stones when Mom, Kay, and I had left our Kyoto inn that morning. We had set out to see one of my favorite temples, Kiyomizu-dera — the "Temple of Clear Water," a spectacular complex founded in 788 and named for the water that splashes down the Otowa no taki — "Sound of Feathers Waterfall." It is a place where the faithful stand in lines to borrow long-handled metal ladles with which they capture cups of that blessed falling water to drink and wash their hands in hopes of receiving a cure or of preserving their good health.

On this, my third visit to Kiyomizu-dera, Mom, Kay, and I wandered through its front gates, past the snarling stone lion dogs and wild-eyed deva kings, and meandered among various halls before crossing the main temple's massive timber balcony overlooking the city, the place the Japanese invoke when making a major decision, describing it as taking a leap from that very spot.

Although the temple's quiet beauty, dark wood and gray stone, and its ancient roots still impressed me, I had a sense of having been there and done that ... until we happened on the Shinto love shrine, which was set apart from the Kiyomizu complex but still inside its bounds. How had I missed this on earlier visits?

Step ... step ... step ... "HideoHideoHideo ..." *Are my feet still pointed in the right direction? What if I run into a building, or a person? If I miss the second stone altogether should I accept that as a sign that Hideo is not right for me? Does anyone really believe in the stones and their wisdom? Do I?*

I knew Hideo would not have approved of this stunt. On a recent visit to Hofu Tenmangu — a Yamaguchi shrine dedicated to the god of knowledge and a place my students frequented to write prayers for good test scores on wooden plaques the size of a child's hand — Hideo had asked me, *Why do you pray to gods you do not know?*

His question took me by surprise. Over the past several months we had visited many shrines and temples, not because we were on some kind of pilgrimage but because these religious sites were often community focal points, integrated into historic sites and natural vistas. Lots of couples used them as dating destinations.

I approached these places as I had been taught by my Japanese family: climb the stairs; peer into the dimly lit shrine or temple to see its sumptuous gold-embellished brocades; clap your hands; shake the rope attached to a high-hanging, sandy-sounding metal rattle; drop a few yen in the slatted offering box the size of a steamer trunk; bow your head; and press your hands together in prayer.

Didn't Hideo understand? I never prayed to the god of those particular shrines or to the Buddha, but to my own God, the one that as a child I had envisioned as a cartoonish cloud, the letters G-o-d written across it in simple typeface, God of my Christian faith, the one I had grown up believing is present everywhere. Even in a Japanese shrine.

Hideo did not appreciate my religious promiscuity. *When you pray here,* he insisted, *you are praying to these gods, the ones who live in these places.* Although he was neither Shinto nor Buddhist, he seemed to regard the gods that inhabited this world, his world, as real. He would not let me get away with acting as if they were not. I felt indignant. Then I tried to shrug him off, refusing to accept that actual gods inhabited those weathered buildings I loved to visit. For a while.

The truth is Hideo had gotten my attention, and I started to feel strange about saying my prayers in these places. I had always assumed there was no other god but mine, the God I had heard described as "the one true God." But Hideo forced me to think about Old Testament God, the one who rallied his people to focus on him and to leave other gods alone. "Have no other gods before me," he ordered Moses to etch in stone. I had always assumed those "other gods" to be things, like money, power and other earthly pursuits. Did Hideo understand better than I that God was referring to other real gods, like those who dwelt in shrines and temples?

Step ... step ... step ... "HideoHideoHideo ..." *What if I trip over the second rock? Will someone tell me when to stop? Or must I be the one to sense precisely when I arrive at the rock ... or when I arrive at love?*

My mother and I would not have the discussion about the appropriateness of me folding my hands and bowing my head at Shinto shrines and Buddhist temples. Faith had always been a place of shifting ground for us, despite my parents requiring me as a child to attend church and Sunday school every week, despite the fact that they taught me to pray before meals and bed, despite their sending my brother and me to a Lutheran junior high and high school (with mandatory daily chapel services), and Lutheran colleges.

Stories I brought home from school, where speakers shared testimonies of how their lives were changed by God, saved by God, or how faith in Jesus (sometimes pronounced "Jeezus") had impacted their lives, gave her the jitters. "How do they *know* God was at work?" she would ask. "I would never assume God was paying that much attention to my little life. He has better things to do." I would feel all self-centered and naïve, wondering why the stories and testimonies had sounded so plausible to me just a few hours earlier, wondering why it had seemed so likely that God had the ability to pay attention to everyone and to help everyone, even me.

At the same time, I knew that if I had begun rebelling against the faith, she would have grown very concerned. If nothing else, in our family it seemed to function like those bumpers set up for children in the gutters of bowling alleys. It was a way to keep our thoughts and behaviors between the lines. The most important thing, it seemed, was for me to be a *good* person, a *kind* person — and to choose a mate with the same goals.

Step ... step ... step ... "HideoHideoHideo ..."

Part of running to Japan had been about establishing my independence, about learning to listen to myself. To do that, I had felt the need to extricate myself from my parents' influence. I craved their input and, probably, their approval too much, and as I entered adulthood I had continued to listen for what they wanted for me instead of striving to hear the desires and call of my own heart. In college I was on the major-of-the-week plan, vacillating among premed, sociology, English, music, art history, Asian Studies, elementary education, and on and on. Whenever an idea got a toehold, I would share it with my parents, hoping to find the decision that would elicit the response, *Yes, what a perfect plan!* But we are a family of divergent thinkers, and each time they weighed in — negatively or positively — I would begin doubting my latest idea.

The year after graduation, when I was living at home and dating the man who would become my husband and then ex, I found myself encountering mixed messages again as my parents invited my boyfriend to nice dinners but laid down strict curfews that seemed to indicate distrust of him — or me. My parents' and my relationship grew muddled, neither side adapting to our evolving situation.

Although my parents had generously invited me back home after college graduation for that subsidized year of part-time work and internships, I had settled back in like a visiting college student — maybe even a high school student — not a newly minted adult. We clashed over my messy room, my lack of interest in washing dishes, and then my new curfew. I began bucking hard for the first time ever and pulled away from my family. Still unable to hear my own thoughts, I ran to my boyfriend-then-fiancé, the only one from whom I did not receive conflicting signals, the only clear path forward.

In Japan, my relationship with Hideo was part of a new life, my first attempt at true independence. I felt safer seeking counsel from a set of rocks than from my mom.

Step ... step ... step ... "HideoHideoHideo ..."

Still, I had not been above seeking human counsel. I brought Hideo to Hagi to meet my Japanese grandmother and mother, Obāchan and Okāsan, and everyone smiled and bowed and gamely drank coffee or tea as I watched them closely for clues. What did Japanese people, my Japanese family, think of this man? They seemed to be all friendliness.

Later, when Hideo was gone, I prodded Obāchan for her impressions of him, her impressions of us. I had so many questions, most of which were too complicated for my Japanese — perhaps even for my English: *Was I interpreting his behavior correctly? Was he as special as I thought? Or was he some kind of misfit in his native land? (Why else, I wondered, would he pursue a recovering divorcee, especially when his powerful employer — for which he would probably work till-retirement-did-he-part — had declared itself against us?)*

Obāchan patted her age-sagged chest, and peered at me from beneath her long, sparse eyebrows. *"Look not just with your eyes,"* she said in Japanese, *"but also with your heart."*

Step ... step ... step ... "HideoHideoHideo ..."

The longer I turned Obāchan's admonition over in my mind, the more questions emerged. *Was she suggesting that all looked well, but something was amiss beneath the surface? Or was she saying that my situation might appear foreign, but my heart should realize that everything was as it should be?* I was left to chase my wonderings around for months, and still today I harken back to her words, which are probably more memorable for their many possible interpretations. The bottom line seemed to be that I would have to figure things out for myself.

Step ... step ... step ... "HideoHideoHideo ..." Tap.

I opened my eyes. My toe had connected with the second rock — I had made it, sixty feet, eyes closed, all on my own! Hideo and I were guaranteed happiness, if I believed the rocks. I wondered how to interpret this victory, whether it was my own steady heart that had guided me from rock to rock, or a sign from some god — mine, I hoped.

* * *

Some days later, Hideo, true to his word, came to Kansai International Airport near Osaka and found Mom, Kay, and me ready to head back to our respective homes. After kisses and hugs, my mother's soft, cool cheek, Hideo and I waved goodbye, and as I watched her leave me, I felt a sense of unmooring, that tingling, growing bubble of panic and grief that begins deep in my chest and wells up at so many of our partings, rising slowly into my throat, then the back of my mouth, crossing my tongue in a soundless cry, the ghost of a feeling, some artifact of earliest childhood, primal fear of imminent loss. *Will my mother, my world, return to pick me up from the church nursery? from preschool? Or will she disappear forever?* This fear of abandonment, this feeling of overpowering love, despite my desire to step out from her shadow, despite my distrust of her guidance in the realm of love, made me want to run after her, to board the plane with her and hold her hand all the way back to my — our — real-world home in Minnesota.

But instead of a ticket, I had a contract. And Hideo, my rock in Japan.

26

Together Apart

THE rainy day my mother and Kay left Japan, Hideo and I began our new life. Together but apart.

After seeing my visitors through security, he and I left the airport and headed into the city to drift through clouds of cherry blossoms lining the river banks near Osaka Castle. The pink puffs of color so dominated the overcast urban landscape of grays, blues, and dull greens that the scene looked almost contrived, like the backdrop that had caused Mom, Kay, and me to "ooh" and "aah" only days earlier at Kyoto's historic cherry blossom dances, the Miyako Odori. There, in one of Japan's most famous floating worlds, on the broad old stage of the Gion theater, scores of icily elegant geisha and not-yet-so-jaded *maiko* (apprentice geisha) had danced the final exquisite scene amid a haze of painted pink flowers.

Hideo and I dove into the fray, dodging dozens of Nice Middies, men as well as women, their chairs and easels set up across walking paths as they worked earnestly between short rain showers to capture the short-lived flowers on paper and canvas. It was a relief to be back with Hideo, back to our oddly comfortable conversations, a mishmash of English and Japanese, and to our fast-paced explorations, rushing to catch trains and buses, hustling along just for the joy of being in motion, seeing what we could of this gritty city, all the while trying not to focus on the finality of that day, knowing it would be our last adventure together for some time, neither of us certain how we would evolve as a couple living apart.

In couplehood, everyone has a role to play, personas we discover, inhabit, and abandon as the relationship and its circumstances change. We are a teammate or coach, a friend or lover, leader or follower, encourager or hesitater, adorer or the adored, tempter or the tempted, servant or master, inside cat or outside cat, Dudley Do-Right or Nell Fenwick.

No Snidely Whiplash has ever tied me to a railroad track, but that last pair of characters feels familiar. Hideo was an ambassador-lover, rescuing me from my gaffes and misunderstandings, interpreting his culture for me and caring for me within it, all the while releasing me from the residual sadness that had brought me to Japan. When I finally quit resisting, I was quite happy to be rescued. Unlike Nell, I loved my Dudley right back. I wanted to keep him close.

With Hideo stationed far, far from me, I could not imagine how his role, and mine, would change; whether he would work from afar to save and protect me, whether he would want to; whether we might evolve into a new dynamic, whether he would find someone new. Okāsan and Otōsan, and many other couples, lived this way permanently, so it could work. But Hideo and I were not married. The knot was still loose. I dreaded the idea of losing him, but at the same time I harbored doubts that Japan would be my home forever. Perhaps it would be best for him if a new woman did catch his attention and set in motion events that would spell the end for us, what I feared might happen to us anyway. But I did not want that to happen, and he assured me he felt the same.

Our reunion in Osaka, a mixture of hope and tears, was brief. He had his new position in Tokyo to settle into, and I had a fresh school year awaiting me in Shuho-cho, with new students, new co-teachers, and new neighbors. We said our own farewells the following day, he boarding a northbound train to Tokyo and I boarding one southbound to Yamaguchi, kilometers piling up between us like fallen pink petals.

27

Taking off the Gloves

BACK in Shuho-cho, the schools were all upended. In Japan, April brings the beginning of the new school year, so the previous month's eighth graders had taken over the ninth-grade classrooms, the seventh graders had appropriated the eighth-grade rooms, and new students occupied the chairs of the seventh-grade classrooms. I had met the latter group on visits to the primary schools, where they had been sixth graders, benevolent *sempai*, revered by the younger students. Now in junior high, knocked down to the bottom of a new heap, they looked as dewy and wide-eyed as baby frogs.

In the staff rooms too, everything was off. New teachers, new principals, and new secretaries occupied the desks of former colleagues. And I was no longer the greenhorn. I knew these schools, the senior staff members, the students, and the community. I was suddenly a bit of an insider, an outsider-insider.

I met my new co-teachers and found they were nice men, family men, each a few years older than I. They were not interested in running their classes one hundred percent in English, and our lesson plans were more workmanlike than the ones Mr. Kumagai and I had crafted, but they incorporated enough of my mother tongue and my ideas to make staying feel worthwhile.

Still, losing my first co-teachers and all the hard work we had invested in our relationships and our lesson plans had quelled some of my passion for spreading the gospel of English. And this probably made me easier to work with. Teaching became less my preoccupation than my occupation, a way to stay in Japan, pay the bills, and fill time, more of a placeholder until I could meet up with Hideo.

As for Hideo, he and I spoke every evening by phone, at least for a few minutes and sometimes far longer, but I never knew when his call would come. His *nonbiri* days of wearing khaki work clothes to the dusty limestone mine above Shuho-cho, where he worked until five and then took to his bicycle, were long gone, replaced by navy-suited days indoors. Now his mornings began when he rolled out of his new dormitory bed and commuted to Sumitomo's head office in Tokyo, where he sat at a desk until it was time to join his colleagues and superiors for an evening of drinking at a nearby pub, where he drank and ate until he could excuse himself to commute back to the dormitory and fall into his bed for a short night of sleep, day after long, exhausting day. Hideo put on a good face in his new situation — it was a great opportunity, career-wise — but the strain was apparent. He grew serious and fatigued, his exuberant boyishness a casualty of a growing list of responsibilities.

Every evening in Shuho-cho, I would wait, my television tuned to noisy game shows for company, jealous of the time Hideo spent with new colleagues and that he had such colleagues to go out with (even if the outings were compulsory), worried that one day or some night he would meet an office flower, a young female office assistant, whose bright eyes, bluish-black hair, and proximity would cause him to forget about me, all frizzy and far away in Yamaguchi.

What choice did I have but to trust him and wait each night for him to call? I could not sleep until I knew he was safely home and I had heard something about his day, his new life, until I had reported on the latest nothing that had not happened in mine.

* * *

That I pined for Hideo, that I mourned our lost life together in Shuho-cho, that I resented the transfers of my former co-teachers, that English teaching had become a mere placeholder: all that is just part of the truth.

Another piece of it is that all those changes and the feelings they wrought caused me to engage with Shuho-cho in a new way. My growing competency in Japanese, my waning English-teaching zealotry, and my being at loose ends without Hideo altered how I lived. Like a goldfish moved to a larger bowl, I expanded to occupy more of that little town.

I continued studying and performing with the koto club, but I also allowed myself to be lured into the local badminton club. I began hosting a group of vivacious middle-aged townswomen for English conversation practice at my apartment. I started studying Japanese in earnest. I talked with Mrs. Kawajiri, the Dwelling Friends *obasan*, about gardening, and she granted me some space in the shared plot behind the dormitory where I planted a few rows of corn, carrots, tomatoes, mini-sunflowers, squash, and beans in the dry brown soil. With Hideo away and my reliable transportation options still limited to the bus, rides offered by work colleagues and outings with Naoko, my circle of acquaintances expanded and relationships deepened. Everywhere I went I knew somebody.

At the bus stop, I would see Kashima-*san*, a deaf middle-aged man with friendly eyes, who often bicycled past as I waited for one of those rare old buses. Seeing me, he would swing wide and brake to a stop. We would smile at each other (*hello*), he would point to the sun or the clouds (*Minnesota-esque weather commentary*), I would point, smile and shrug (*yep, weather*), he would gesture in the direction the bus would travel (*heading that way?*), I would smile and gesture back (*yep*). I would point to him (*you?*), and he would point vaguely in some other direction (*heading over that-a-way*). We would smile and nod some more, wave our farewells, and off he would go. Ours might have been the purest, least demanding conversations I have ever had.

At Nattie, the little market near my apartment, I would rarely fail to see Masako-*san*, the cheerful butcher who had joined the English conversation group that I assisted with at the town hall. On seeing me in her shop, she would run out from behind the counter, tiny notebook and pencil in hand, to ask me about the pronunciation of some new word or to try out a new sentence structure, her eyes wide and teeth heavy with the new sounds. When I indicated I understood, she would beam and laugh as if she had tossed a ring and landed it squarely around the neck of the best bottle.

At the Board of Education office, I would see Santo-*san*, the mother of two of my students and a town worker who managed the Culture Exchange House. Although she spoke little English, she was in charge of corresponding with and taking care of the international artists who visited Shuho-cho for some days or weeks at a time. (She would draw me in now and then, sometimes for parties with the foreigners du jour, other times to translate in meetings — once, disastrously, to facilitate a conversation conducted in Japanese and German, the latter of which I had not studied since high school.) With her high forehead, dark eyes, little mouth, and long black hair hanging loose down her back, Santo-*san* made me think of Heian-period royalty, minus the layers of voluminous robes. This forty-something princess wore knee-length navy skirts and vests, the uniform of an office worker, and she walked slightly pigeon-toed as she approached our bank of desks, apologetically laughing and deferring to my supervisors until they offered me up — "*Dōzo, dōzo!*" — so we could retreat to a nearby reception area. There we would sit side by side, I helping translate the missives and behavior of her international charges, she lowering her husky voice to ask me about Hideo, covering her mouth as she let slip a deep-throated laugh, elbowing my ribs and crinkling her eyes at me like a knowing older sister.

At the post office, the workers, including Naoko's mother, would greet me warmly, for they saw me nearly every day, accepting little manifestations of my lingering homesickness — letters, cards, and packages I sent to the States in almost constant succession, as if trying to maintain a paper umbilical cord between Shuho-cho and the States, so I would not wake up one day and find myself disconnected, fully birthed into Japan, unable to return to my motherland.

* * *

Another piece of the truth is that school was becoming a different place for me. At South Junior High in particular, the teachers seemed to regard me more and more as one of their own, opening up their feelings toward work and superiors, toward the challenges of life. I too admitted my feelings of frustration — that my handlers were overprotecting me, that my co-teachers and boyfriend had been transferred away.

With this growing sense of camaraderie, some of the rowdier male teachers began teaching me slang, words and phrases they knew I should never and would never use. They told me how I could respond to comments and advice I did not want to hear: "*Yareyare,*" they groaned, rolling their eyes and shaking their heads. "What-EV-er."

Then came "*Irrrransewa!*", a coarse way to say, "I don't need your advice!" The female teachers cringed and giggled as the men egged me on, teaching me to roll my r's and assert with vigor: "*Irrrrrrrr-rrransewa!!*" The salty phrase tasted good on my tongue.

They encouraged me to adopt a strong Yamaguchi accent, goading me to replace polite Japanese questions such as, "*Nani o itteimasu ka?*" — "What are you saying?" — with the ribald, "*NAAAhni iu chun ka?*" something to the effect of, "What the hell are you babbling on about?" — language that might be acceptable among grizzled old fishermen but shocking from a young woman, a foreign one at that. I echoed their intonation with gusto.

I knew they were messing with me, exploiting their resident foreigner for entertainment. But living where I was and working to fit in — a Sisyphean challenge if ever there was one — it was cathartic to shoot off my mouth, even in jest.

But in retrospect, I think the catharsis came not so much from imagining myself telling people off as from having the opportunity to enter the language of men.

I was deep enough into the language and culture to be frustrated by the fact that in Japanese, men and women use different words, different syntax and different intonation to express similar things. Take the basic word for "I": "*watashi.*" It is used by both men and women, but where women have little option beyond the cutesy variation "*atashi,*" men can draw on "*boku,*" a gentle male pronoun, as well as "*ore,*" a gruffer word charged with masculinity and power.

The language of the women around me and the gentle manner with which they characteristically delivered their words seemed designed to keep them in a permanent place of softness, a place where I did not always feel at home, a place that diminished some of what I wanted to express. I had days when I felt dangerous, like a growling *ore*, but there was no feminine way to convey it.

I began wondering what would happen if I co-opted the male vernacular. One day I took *boku* — the gently masculine "I" that Hideo regularly used — for a test drive. Hideo was in my kitchen, washing dishes or frying potstickers or maybe boiling water for tea the first time I threw *boku* into a sentence, declaring something about myself, and he startled and stopped whatever it was he had been doing. He looked at me and chuckled, but his laugh was accompanied by an expression that begged me to never, ever try such a stunt in public. He had no need to worry. I could see that anything uttered after I lobbed a "*boku*" or "*ore*" would be lost in the dust of shock.

I had had a similar experience some months earlier. One day at North Junior High, I was teaching on my own and the students were restless, even after the bell had rung and we had performed our requisite greetings and bows. Growing impatient, I recalled a word Mr. Kita had used to get his students' attention and figured I would give it a try: "*Oi!*" I growled.

It worked — for a short beat of silence. Then the entire class fell apart laughing. *Oi*, I learned, was yet another word that belonged to the province of men.

28

Bus Trip

WAITING outside the lonely bus shelter in the glow of its buzzy fluorescent lights, the Sumitomo dormitory *obasan* and I stood watch against the heavy Yamaguchi night. We spoke little as our hands waved away thirsty mosquitoes floating on the currents of air that rose from early-summer rice paddies, plots of land furry with fast-growing seedlings, hiccupping crickets and frogs burping in the mud.

Mrs. Kawajiri had offered me a ride to the Mito-cho bus stand — probably a half-hour's drive from our apartment building — when I had told her I was planning to catch the overnight bus to Osaka. Keeping me company as I waited, she thrust a tiny blue envelope decorated with cranes and flowers, celebratory motifs, into my surprised hand. *"Just a little something so you can buy yourself some tea,"* she assured me in Japanese. *"Nothing at all, really. Just get some tea."*

We both knew it contained more than tea money, that in the dance of Japanese gift-giving the more something is downplayed, the more valuable it turns out to be. An often-used set phrase used when presenting a gift is *"Tsumaranai mono desu ga ... dōzo"* — "It's a trifling thing but ... please take it." When I presented my gifts to people, I regularly invoked this phrase, adding at the beginning, *"Hontō-ni"* — "Really," because I felt that anything I could give — dish towels, English books, T-shirts, dreamcatchers, pins, stickers, and other items I had packed in my suitcases before leaving Minnesota — truly was dull in comparison to the exotic and thoughtful knickknacks, treats, and housewares I received in Japan from neighbors, shopkeepers, new friends, and even strangers. I never knew when a gift would present itself, or when I should be ready to offer something in kind. As near as I could tell, the ins and outs of gifting were labyrinthine, an art form for which there were no cheat sheets.

I had acquired an English-language book on Japanese etiquette though, one that included a chapter on gifts, laying out in a grid how much money to present to people of varying degrees of closeness (family, coworker, friend, neighbor) when they experienced various life events (marriage, death of spouse, death of parent, birth of child). It also showed how to present the money, how to place it in a white stationery shop envelope — specially folded, inscribed and tied with red ribbon or black, depending on circumstance, colored wires following the ribbon and twisted and rolled into a stylized crane or an elaborate bow. But nowhere did I find advice for everyday life, like when a neighbor loads up your arms with prepackaged foods and homemade yogurt, and then as you head out her door adds a couple of pounds of pancake mix, a jar of plum wine, an apple, and a set of pottery teacups to your load. Or what to present in such quotidian interactions as when one is dropped off at a bus stop.

I did my best to tease out the rules of the game but found myself saying "*arigatō*" — "thank you" — far more often than "*dōzo*" — "please [take this]." This time, I thanked Mrs. Kawajiri, wondering whether she was an unwitting or knowing accomplice in my weekend rendezvous with Hideo. I had not told her that I would be meeting up with my banished beau, but Osaka was roughly halfway between our two homes, a couple-hour bullet train — or overnight bus — ride for each of us. No doubt she had her suspicions.

Mrs. Kawajiri was fond of Hideo and had been sad to see him leave. She had happily agreed to take over his care of Ha-chan ("Little Eight") the friendly, country-wise orange and white cat he had found some years earlier as a hungry, wandering kitten, one who had already used up eight of her nine lives. Although Mrs. Kawajiri and I never discussed Hideo, he had indicated to me that she was wise to our relationship. Even so, I would not tell her that I was going to see him for fear it could make things uncomfortable, causing her to feel that she was aiding and abetting the relationship that had been at least partly responsible for Hideo's being sent into exile, a relationship that I suspected could still get Hideo (if not me) in trouble.

Holding her little envelope, which I would later find contained a five-thousand-yen bill, more than fifty dollars at the time, I made a mental note to bring her a special treat from Kyoto, which was a short train ride from Osaka and a place where everything seemed especially exquisite: handkerchiefs finely woven, pottery gracefully spun, sweets especially refined.

After some time, the highway bus glistened its way to a stop at our station and gasped open its door. The driver and his peppy assistant bounded down the steps and looked expectantly at Mrs. Kawajiri. "Tanaka-*san?*" they inquired.

For a split second I was dumb. Then I got it: Hideo had reserved my bus ticket in his name. I looked at them and nodded, "*Hai.*" The men turned to me with poorly concealed surprise. I did not look at Mrs. Kawajiri.

How different it felt to answer to a Japanese family name, my boyfriend's family name, instead of my own. This is how it would be, I thought. If we married, if I took his name, everywhere I went I would carry with me not only this name but a whole Japanese family, its long history and any related connotations. Whether I was in Japan, back in the States or anywhere else in the world, people hearing my name would immediately know something about me, that somehow, in some way, I was Japanese. In Japan I would be foreign but not as foreign as before. In the States I would become something more foreign. In both countries people would know I had made inroads into Japan, or that Japan had made inroads into me.

Boarding the bus under the name Tanaka, I felt some level of protection. For this moment, I was not just another foreigner; I was an acknowledged foreigner, one who had found a place in a country that does not take ingress lightly.

Settling into my assigned seat in the cooler, drier atmosphere of the bus, I looked out the window and saw Mrs. Kawajiri still standing at the bus stop, her petite feet pressed together, chin dipped toward her motherly bosom. Smiling demurely at me, she waved like an aged beauty queen as we rolled out of sight.

My secret would be safe with her.

29

Perpetual Motion

HIDEO's transfer to Tokyo had made one thing clear: I could not live without him. And I would not, not now. (Take that, Dwelling Friends.)

We became fairly strategic about our monthly rendezvous, usually arranging them over holidays and long weekends so we would not disrupt our respective workplaces or call attention to our continuing relationship. And given the semi-secretive nature of our association, we kept on the move.

Our early trips included an escape to Shimane Prefecture, northeast of Yamaguchi, where we caught a ferry for the Dozen Islands, two hours offshore in the Sea of Japan. A place of plunging cliffs, high winds, and crashing waves, it had served as a place of exile in ages past, and we happily hiked about the islands' windswept moors, where we encountered only wooly horses and sturdy cows, and safely assumed we would encounter no one who knew either of us.

We also met in Osaka and visited Kyoto, where we wandered about the city's sweet-smelling temples and crept stocking-footed through Nijō-jō, a sumptuous castle of dark wood, bright white plaster and gold ornamentation, interior hallways lined with chirping "nightingale floors," their eerie squeaks intentionally installed to alert seventeenth-century residents to intruders.

Once, Hideo even returned to Shuho-cho, where we sneaked in and out of my apartment and drove about Yamaguchi Prefecture, visiting our earlier haunts.

I don't know where Hideo and I found the energy for all the hellos and goodbyes, for the constant touring while together, for visiting old buildings, museums, seashores and rivers, for discussions — punctuated by long silences and bursts of tears — about the possibility and improbability of a future together. Maybe a bond like ours obeyed some variation of Newton's first law: a relationship in motion tends to remain in motion. Perhaps it benefited from distances endured and efforts expended to be together. Had we been left to ourselves, Hideo allowed to stay in Shuho-cho, lobbying me to marry him, our relationship might have sunk under the weight of his hopes and my fears.

Instead, we fed on the anticipation of getting together, on the thrill of moving separately toward our chosen destination and then arriving, alone at a train station where we would experience that jolt of finding each other's familiar face smiling amid crowds. Then at last reaching the privacy of our *ryōkan* room, I would drop my bag and tackle Hideo, pinning him down on the tatami with kisses. The joy and relief of reuniting with a beloved.

* * *

Touring in the larger cities, like Kyoto and Osaka, where more English teachers and foreign business people were stationed and more visitors ambled about, reconstituted my attention-fatigued soul. It was not so unusual there to see a Caucasian woman, not so strange to see couples of different races walking together, although usually the man was white and the woman Japanese. Wherever we went I remained a white rock on a black-sand beach, still a foreigner, but at least I could be one white rock among many. I relished the sense of disappearing in plain sight.

Sometimes as we milled about parks and temples, or walked down narrow lanes packed with tiny restaurants and shops of artisanal brick-a-brack, we encountered other foreigners our age, and Hideo would nudge me to go talk with them, as if it would do me some good. Perhaps like my curiosity about his character among the Japanese, he wanted to check me out too, to see how I functioned among my own kind. But I, all too familiar with the unspoken foreigner code, would nudge him back, saying "Shhhh," as if being quiet would release the others to ignore me, as I often ignored them.

It seemed that on the road in Japan, we *gaijin* went out of our way to avoid communicating with one another, as if we had all taken a vote and decided that common language and culture did not justify acknowledgement. At the time I assumed this lack of camaraderie had to do with keeping our experiences of Japan authentic, free of foreign influence, of hanging onto a sense of discovering places for ourselves. Nothing makes a floating world existence less enchanting than having to look in a mirror, to watch another person of similar background awkwardly bumble through it.

Now I wonder, though, if perhaps I missed the real reason for our mutual diffidence. Maybe everyone else was feeling as attention-saturated and bedraggled as I was and simply wanted, like me, to blend in for a while.

Either way, I imagined I would likely spend much of the rest of my life in the company of foreigners, with or without Hideo by my side, so I wanted to focus on my beau, not strangers, and enjoy the respite that came from being in a place where I could go out dining and touring without wondering who was watching or who knew.

* * *

At the end of one perpetual-motion weekend, Hideo and I drove many kilometers in a few wrong directions searching for the *ryōkan* where we had reservations. At last we found it tucked away up the side of a mountain at the end of a road. The building appeared old, inside and out — not in the picturesque way of a temple, but in an outdated way like a roadside inn that had seen better days.

A stooped old man with yellow-stained hair greeted us at the entrance and handed Hideo a reservation card to fill out. Soon his wife, an old woman with shoe-polish-black hair materialized and hovered nearby, her pink sweater, which would have seemed grandmotherly on most anyone else, appearing medicinal on her, Pepto-Bismol pink. She led us along a dark hall lined with photographs of better times: parties of sunglasses-wearing movie stars, gatherings of monks, and people walking barefoot over red-hot coals, one male devotee to something carrying a crying baby.

Our room was spacious, but there would be no tatami tackle this time. As we set down our bags, our dour hostess kneeled at the low table in the center of the room, poured us tea and inquired whether we would care to eat dinner first or bathe. Hungry, we requested dinner, and the look on her face told us we had chosen poorly, or at least in poor form. She disappeared into the hallway and after a few minutes rejoined us, along with another woman who carried a tray bearing a flotilla of small dishes — sashimi, soup, tidbits of meat, seagrasses, and vegetables. The women arranged them on the table, and Hideo and I compliantly sat on the tatami, settling in opposite each other.

Our hostess joined us. And she promptly informed Hideo that I was sitting in his seat.

Hideo and I looked at each other and our positions at the table. There were no place cards or any other clue. We looked back at her.

She tried another tack. "*Are foreign women particularly prized?*" she inquired in Japanese, her tone vaguely condescending. I am sure my eyes popped wide. What was she getting at? I went on high alert. Hideo and I were mute with confusion. At last she gave up and explained: "*The man should sit in the high position, the woman in the low.*"

If Hideo knew where she was headed, he never let on. For my part, the only difference I could see was the view from our seats: he sat in front of the door to our room and a plain wall. I had my back to the room's *tokonoma* — the alcove, which contained a green vase and a framed picture. He was getting the more picturesque view, and to my way of thinking that was a benefit to him.

She began explaining that the guest of honor or person holding the most power in a room — in this case, the man — should be seated before the lovelier background, and in this case that was the *tokonoma*. Although he would not see the flowers and scrolls, he would know that they formed a backdrop to his presence and that he was the focal point of the room. I had unwittingly sat down in our table's prime spot.

"*Many young people are unaware of this point of etiquette,*" our hostess murmured, "*so I make sure to educate them.*"

Hideo and I looked at each other. This was not the first time we had encountered a part of his culture that made me uncomfortable, or that he found outdated. And this was not the first time he would run interference. He respectfully told the woman that we would stay right where we were.

I loved him.

30

Fireflies

WITH Hideo out of Shuho-cho, Naoko had become my most
frequent companion. She had never liked my beau — she said
he was rude, citing a time when he had failed to greet her as they
passed one another in the Dwelling Friends parking lot. This did
not match up with the friendly Hideo I knew so well. Surely there
had been a misunderstanding. Or perhaps he had been preoccupied.
I silently chalked up her complaint to simple jealousy — that I had
a boyfriend and she did not — but still I sometimes wondered if
my foreign eyes were blind to a character flaw that she was better
able to see.

I might have been less forgiving of her judgment of my taste in
men and her unwillingness to cajole me through Hideo's banishment
to Tokyo, but in little Shuho-cho I had a limited pool of friends. And
Naoko was generally kind, so I tried to overlook her disdain. We did
best when we pretended Hideo did not exist. I spoke little of him.

Hideo was not the only mismatch in our friendship. Naoko's father was my supervisor's supervisor, the man with whom I had been locking horns over driving. He and I were cordial to each other — most of our communications were conducted through Sasaki-*san* — but the fact remained: Naoko's father was the primary obstacle between me and a car, between me and a fuller manifestation of my Shuho-cho life, between me and what I envisioned as my freedom. He was making me crazy, and I suspect the feeling was mutual.

Whether Naoko knew of these aggravations or not, she sometimes invited me over to her home — that is to her parents' home, to my supervisor's supervisor's home. And no matter how frustrated I felt with her father, I could not resist.

It was lovely to be with a family and to get a peek into regular Shuho-cho life. Her family's spacious home was part century-old farmhouse and part decades-old addition. During my early visits there, I was kept sequestered in the old wing, in the traditional visiting room, graced with painted *fusuma* (paper doors) and carved-wood *ranma* (transoms) above them. The back wall of the room featured a *tokonoma* (alcove), the focal point of the room, where a scroll featuring calligraphy or a seasonal painting hung beside a vase or piece of decorative statuary.

On my first visits, Naoko would settle me on the tatami floor in front of the alcove — intentionally — at a stocky hardwood table, where we would kneel, drinking tea and eating little cookies until I could stand it no longer, finally sinking onto my bottom, legs curled to the side. Naoko's cheery grandmother, Umeko, would amble in from the garden to share an elegant haiku she had written, economically evoking the season, top to bottom on thin rectangles of white paper. Naoko would fetch her latest herb projects. Her mother, a woman with a smiling mouth and wistful eyes, just back from her work at the post office, would join us briefly to chat before hurrying outside to do yard work in the waning light or to the kitchen to prepare supper. I wondered what the rest of their house was like, catching only glimpses as my hosts came and went through sliding paper doors.

At last Naoko invited me to dinner, and I graduated from the formal sitting room to a chair in the family's busy kitchen in the newer wing of the house. There I sat, at first awkwardly fraternizing with her father. Perhaps it was the beer, or maybe it was the camaraderie of three generations of women, but gradually he lost his pursed-lipped decorum and broke into smiles, pulling out his camera to record our small, everyday moments.

I began to see that this man was not the same one with whom I subtly dueled in the Board of Education office, the one who did not want me roaming about the country, who did not want me driving a car. In this old farmhouse, enveloped by the moist black night, surrounded by his wife, his mother, and his daughter, he softened, and I realized I wanted to be his friend.

* * *

One June evening, Naoko invited me over for a make-your-own-sushi supper. Using sheets of *nori* seaweed like little tortillas, we made the Japanese equivalent of fajitas, scooping pickled rice onto the seaweed and topping it with boiled chicken and prawns, long cucumber sticks, and slices of rolled-egg omelets, daubed with *wasabi* and plum paste. We were watching our usual early-evening television programs, "ALF" reruns surreally dubbed in Japanese and quiz shows featuring stars playing charades for money and prizes, when suddenly her mother turned to me and asked in Japanese, "*Have you ever seen a firefly?*"

Having been living in Japan for nearly a year, I had already "seen" the autumn moon, the falling snow, and the cherry blossoms — all events that prompt viewing parties. I had not expected insects to make the list of observable happenings.

Just like that, the whole family — Grandma, Dad, Mom and Naoko — were up and headed toward the door. It was time, they told me, to see the fireflies.

I told her mother that I already was familiar with fireflies. My cousins and I used to chase them at my grandparents' home in Illinois. The whole family stopped and looked at me, surprised. *Fireflies in America!* Not to be daunted, they asked if I had seen fireflies in Japan. I replied that, sure, there had been a few in the lot behind my apartment. I felt smug and thought I had this viewing season covered. They looked amused and drew me outside.

I could appreciate taking time to contemplate the changing seasons, but these gatherings were never what I expected. The first viewing party I had attended in Japan had been inspired by a full autumn moon and was held by a group of Shuho-cho town workers. We climbed onto the roof of the community gymnasium, where I was prepared to gaze quietly and appreciatively at the best full moon of the year. But the event, as it unfolded, seemed more an excuse to visit, sitting on a plastic tarp, as we ate and drank our way through a spread of crackers, cookies, beer, and sweet *dango* — soft, powdery, rice-based balls that traditionally are eaten during the autumn moon-viewing. There were few comments made about the full orb shining spectacularly above us.

Then, as spring approached, I eagerly awaited the cherry blossoms and the viewing parties they were said to trigger. I envisioned scenes reminiscent of old woodblock prints, demure kimono-clad figures sitting in a haze of blooms. What a lovely way to celebrate the arrival of warmer days.

Again, the event spawned parties, this time the blue tarps laid out amid the pale pink-blooming trees, which were mostly ignored as revelers drank a special cherry-blossom rice wine, ate treats, and visited and laughed. Although the activity they were participating in was called *hanami*, "flower viewing," they seemed almost unaware of them.

That June evening when Naoko's family led me outside to see the fireflies was warm and moonless, and we simply walked away from their farmhouse toward a narrow, rocky part of the Koto River. We brought no food or drink with us, no blue tarp, not even a flashlight. Soon we were nearing the dark waterway.

"*Look,*" I said, a little surprised at the glittering lights I saw through the trees.

"*Uh-huh,*" they said, unimpressed. "*Come on.*"

I walked with them to a small bridge that spanned the river and saw that by then we were surrounded by hundreds, maybe thousands of fireflies. They were in the rushes, along the grassy banks, in the grove of trees, above us, all around. They blinked on-off-on-off, as fireflies do. Most of them blinked in unison.

It had been years since I had seen fireflies in the United States, and against my expectation I was amazed. It was as if there were a leader in this cloud of insects saying, "*Sei, no — on! ... Sei, no — off!*" I could not help thinking that Japanese fireflies, like Japanese people, have a group-oriented culture. I felt a kinship with the few bugs that were blinking on the offbeat.

The five of us watched the fireflies. I was transfixed, but Naoko's grandmother seemed a little disappointed.

"*The numbers are down this year,*" she muttered.

We all stood quietly together in the dark and watched. And I began to understand Japan's tradition of nature viewing. It is not merely about observing a natural phenomenon; it is about sharing an experience. It is not simply about seeing fireflies, looking at the moon, watching the snow fall or appreciating flowers. It is about giving people an opportunity to be together, to find community. Here, in Shuho-cho, with the full moon, with the cherry blossoms, and with the fireflies, I had found — and joined — a community.

Naoko elbowed me out of my reverie. "*Look up,*" she said. "*Millions of fireflies.*"

I moved my gaze from the riverside grasses, through trunks and branches, to the treetops, to the star-filled sky.

31

Mental Sightseeing

AFTER the rainy season dissipated and summer heat had reclaimed southwestern Japan, my deskmates at the Board of Education broke away from the office to introduce me to Shiraito, the White Thread Waterfall. Located in an especially quiet corner of Shuho-cho, its rivulets of cold water splashed and spilled over a run of dark rocks, bringing a welcome coolness to the area around it.

Appreciating this natural beauty was really beside the point though. Shiraito was all about *somen*, thin wheat noodles rolled shorter and finer than angel hair pasta. Some industrious soul had channeled a section of the waterfall into a bamboo flume, and around this flume had built an outdoor café. Guests sat on either side of the pipe and, chopsticks poised, waited for clumps of *somen* to slip by, sent down the chute by restaurant staff.

The four of us — my supervisor Sasaki-*san*, the higher-ranking, twinkly-eyed Sato-*kakarichō* and my fellow tea-server Yamamoto-*san* — dove after the noodles, our chopsticks scissoring like the beaks of hungry cranes. Laughing at their elusiveness, we pursued and captured these white threads and dipped them in bowls of thin *tsuyu* sauce sprinkled with chopped green onions, all the while keeping watch for the next batch let loose from above.

Once our bellies were full, Sasaki-*san* grew reflective. I had been in Shuho-cho nearly a year, and he expressed regret for not having spent more time with me, for not taking me touring more often. I did my best to reassure him: I had had a good year. I had seen a lot. (Far more than he knew.) He nodded contemplatively and observed that I had seemed busy enough with ... (here he paused briefly, struggling to find the words) "... *mental sightseeing.*"

I had never heard the term before, but it made me feel as if Sasaki-*san* had shone a flashlight into my soul. Whether he knew how much physical sightseeing I had done or not, he realized a greater truth: my internal processing had indeed kept me occupied, playing slideshows that integrated memories of the torn-apart life I had left with the new life I was building in Shuho-cho:

New husband, ebullient on our wedding day. Television images of Kobe's earthquake-flattened neighborhoods. Peony snow tumbling out of a gray sky. Hideo asleep in a Kyoto inn, its paper doors tattered. Ex-husband piling more than my share of our pots and pans into my arms. Old woman telling me I must sit on the low side of a table. Hideo's supply of quirky-flavored chewing gum. Primary school mob scenes. My parents' worried faces. The autumn moon and maple leaves. Hideo's smashed car window. Ex-husband angry and yelling on the telephone. Green tea and bad coffee served with a knot in my stomach. Naoko's gospel of herbs. Hideo stirring hot cocoa. Rain falling in busy Osaka. The baby nestled in the belly of Ryota's wife. Cherry blossoms. The dirty dishes I had been too depressed to wash. Students trading English phrases for stamps on their cards. Hugging my gray cat goodbye. A teacher ordering his struggling junior high school student to stand on his desktop and recite words in English. The ginger-haired nurse who had turned to me and prophesied, "Everything is going to be OK." Hideo sneaking up to my apartment to snuggle me close.

Memories, old and new, tumbled together, forming a *gucha gucha* impression of young adulthood, loss and gain intertwined. I not only had been experiencing culture shock, I probably had some sort of life shock.

By the time Sasaki-*san* drew attention to my mental sightseeing, Hideo was well entrenched as my primary concern, filling my mind and heart, my journal entries, and sometimes the letters and emails I sent home with impossible questions that no one could answer: *Was Hideo the One? If I waited until I was sure, would he give up on me? Would I ever be sure? If I married him, would I be making a second marriage mistake? Was my future in Japan or America? Could I have a career in Japan? Could Hideo have a career in America? How much would each of us have to give up? How much were we willing to give up? Did I love him? Truly? Enough? Would I love him forever?*

Round and round the carousel of my wonderings rattled, even as we were becoming more and more closely linked, referred to in one breath — "HideoandSarah" — by the other JETs, my family, his biking buddies, perhaps even the Dwelling Friends. But the idea of marriage, which he refused to let go and that I refused to discuss, remained a sticking point. He could not seem to understand that I, newly free of an ex-husband (and my dream of a future with Ryota), needed time to be single, to get myself back together, to know who I truly was. I had met him too early.

I had told Hideo that I traveled to Japan in a time machine. I had told him that I wanted to stay detached. Somehow, though, I had become one half of a pair of young lovers struggling to overcome circumstances and the machinations of a heartless corporation, not to mention our own expectations of the future. *Was I sending mixed signals?* Yes. *Was I confused?* Yes. *Was there a future for us?* I did not know.

Hideo was so present, physically whenever possible and, when he was away, by phone and by gift: blue speckled enamelware dishes and cups for my kitchen cupboard; a potted evergreen tree for my indoor garden; bags of real coffee sent from Tokyo — hazelnut, amaretto and raspberry flavors — the smell of which, in that land of instant coffee powder and Creap, was nearly orgasmic. He was helping me feel at home in his culture. He was facilitating my life in his culture — even when my plans did not include him.

Later that summer, a crowd of Yamaguchi JETs would meet up in Hiroshima. August 6, 1995, would be the fiftieth anniversary of the atomic bombing of the city of Hiroshima, and we wanted to attend the commemoration ceremony that would be held near the dilapidated Genbaku Dome, the only building left standing near ground zero after the Bomb had been unleashed. Someone had the idea that we should combine this gathering with a party the night before for those of us with early August birthdays — mine actually being August 6. A group of JETs was planning to roam the city all night, but some of us were hoping for a place to light for a few hours of rest.

More than a month before these events, I tried to reserve a hotel room. And try again. And again. And nine more times. All of the hotels were full. When I told Hideo, he offered to look through his guidebooks and fax me a list of phone numbers. A couple of hours later he called from Tokyo and greeted me with an exaggerated, almost comical groan. "I get to talk with so many people today!" he said. Instead of sending me the numbers, he had called them himself. Forty-five places — *forty-five!* — before finding a vacancy for me and a couple of friends.

With a man this thoughtful, this supportive, this doting, it seemed crazy to dwell too long on my need for singleness. But dwell I did.

It would take me many years before I could see that my struggle was not over the question of whether Hideo was right for me; it was whether I could trust myself to recognize the answer.

32

Self-service

SASAKI-*SAN*'S eyes twinkled as he took me aside to share some big news: he and his colleagues at the Board of Education office had discussed their coffee- and tea-serving situation ...

Oh?

... and they had decided to become a "self-service" office — everyone would get his or her own coffee or tea.

Sasaki-*san* looked at me expectantly, as if I should be thrilled by this news. But I was mortified. Clearly their discussion had been catalyzed by conversations he and I had shared in which I confessed how I felt about serving tea to the men in the office. These were conversations I had not expected to be made public, conversations in which I had asserted that I came from a place where the glass ceiling had long since been shattered, where a woman could live any life or career she could dream, where men and women received equal status and pay for equal work, and women did not serve tea or coffee, especially not to men. Not ever. Period.

Looking back, I love how sure I was of what I thought I knew. At age twenty-five I had spent almost my entire life in school. I had always found success there, and that success seemed to have little or nothing to do with my gender. As a result, I maintained an unbridled optimism that hard work and careful thinking could get a young American woman anywhere in life she wished to go, in equal measure to a man. Or better.

It is also what enabled me to describe a version of America that could inspire social change, for that is what I believed the elimination of female tea-serving would be: a solid first step to positive social change. And if I could get the Board of Education office turned around, surely the local schools would follow, and then....

But first I needed to digest Sasaki-*san*'s news. I wondered how he had presented my thoughts — which I had articulated with the assistance of an English–Japanese/Japanese–English dictionary and the grammar of a grade-schooler. Imagining my colleagues' discussion, regretting my moxie, I felt my face redden. I wanted to crawl under my desk.

But sitting at my desk waiting for the wall clock to read ten a.m. — tea time — I pretended not to watch my colleagues. *Would men put their work aside and amble into the little hallway-kitchenette to boil water and steep tea? Would Yamamoto-san and the other women stay perched on their chairs, working? Would everyone remain seated in some form of a stalemate?*

When the top of the hour arrived, so did my answer. Yamamo-to-*san* pushed her chair away from her desk and stood up, just as she had every other workday since long before I met her, and slipped out the door into the shadowy hallway. No one stopped her. I waited a moment before following.

"*What are you doing?*" I whispered as she filled the teakettle with water. "*It's self-service now, isn't it?*"

"*Yes,*" she replied with a concerned expression on her face, "*but the men can't seem to get their own drinks.*"

Seriously?

I needed a consult with Sasaki-*san*, but when I returned to the staff room his chair was empty. I went looking for him and found him roaming through the lobby.

"*What's going on?*" I demanded, as gently as possible. "*Yamamoto-san is preparing drinks.*"

Sasaki-*san* shrugged. "*She can't seem to help herself.*"

I fumed — at both Sasaki-*san* and Yamamoto-*san*. Both had seemed open to change. And the office had sanctioned it. Yet when they stood on its cusp, each had run the other direction.

* * *

Despite the very feminine roles I played in Shuho-cho — girlfriend to a *salariman*, daughter of Japanese parents in Hagi, friend of the herb-loving Naoko, student of the koto — I had moments in which I felt like a person without a gender.

Certainly my size and some of my mannerisms — the broader walk and wider stance, my tendency to illustrate thoughts with my hands — lent me a physicality that in Japan was more in keeping with male behavior, minus the general stoicism and underlying machismo.

My internal workings — attitudes, dreams, and expectations — while certainly not masculine, also set me apart from the women around me. At work, I expected to be regarded and evaluated on the same basis as my male coworkers; at home, I imagined my future husband would do his fair share — as in fifty percent — of the housework. I did not exude the Japanese feminine ideal: a sweet, hard-working, nonthreatening, male-supporting presence, at work, at play and, presumably, at home.

At least that was what I assumed the ideal to be, based on what I saw presented on television, where popular evening game shows featured doll-faced actresses and personalities who spoke in child-like voices, affecting "I-don't-get-it" innocence in the face of bad jokes and inappropriate male behavior. These women, and actors in many of the dramas too, served primarily as attractive foils for male antics, their innocent, giggling countenances providing eye candy for the camera. Game-show flowers. Drama flowers.

Many of the women I worked with seemed not so unlike these televised images as they affected a manner that was similarly breathless, wide-eyed, and naïve. I struggled with the über-femininity around me, the high-pitched, uncritical-sounding voices, the *genki-na*-sister manner in which they dropped their work and pitched in to help the men when called upon, overlooking their own projects, especially at the schools, where many of the men puffed away their prep time in the smoking room. I would see on my co-workers' faces the familiar struck-dumb expression and hear their accompanying comment, "*ehhhhhhhhhhhhhh?*" with its rising intonation, a benevolent chorus to the men's blustery, animated storytelling. I would observe their laughing, sideways-glancing eyes and hand-covered mouths. When guests arrived at these offices, the women — office ladies, general workers, and teachers alike — were quick to play the half-bowed, eyes-averted supporting role, exaggeratedly hustle-shuffling off to boil water and serve tea. Busy, busy, helpful bees.

Watching the sweetly efficient but bland everywoman on the Japanese screen and in the office made me want to rebel against this brand of femininity, to slow it all down, to feign not noticing the needs around me and to lollygag through my tasks. And these feelings in turn made me feel so very *chigau*, that word that simultaneously and infuriatingly means both "different" and "wrong." Sometimes I wanted to abandon my efforts to try to fit in, to accept the fact that I was the sticking-up nail and drooling mastiff among well-groomed beagles, and simply welcome everyone to regard me as the interloper I truly was.

Despite my desire to live free of gender-based roles, despite my lack of natural girlishness, I did adopt a Japanese-style femininity of my own — when it suited me. I covered my laughing mouth with my hand and shot my voice up to a different register, particularly when answering the phone. And I assumed an innocuous manner of replying to requests. When I was unsure or uncomfortable with what was being asked of me, I would deliver a double raised-eyebrow, wide-eyed expression and utter a sweetly ascending "*Hai?*" — a word that could conveniently convey everything from "Yes" to "I heard you but did not understand" to "Why are you asking me this?" (Never did I adopt the oh-so-tempting gruffness in which my male colleagues had schooled me — "*NAAAni iu chunka?!*" — although it did cross my mind.)

My smiling façade masked a critical eye and what felt like a rebel's heart.

* * *

With Yamamoto-*san* preparing tea in the kitchenette, I struggled to make sense of the situation. Why had she not accepted the new order — the self-service office? Surely she knew the men could figure out how to boil water, add green tea leaves to a pot and pour water into it, and if they did not, they could ask.

I began to wonder what she was really afraid of. She appeared to be one of the most industrious, reliable workers in that office. She was immensely likable and competent. Surely her friendships, social position, and job were safe. *Weren't they?*

I had not yet been in Shuho-cho long enough to understand the glacial pace at which change occurred, and that every habit and every custom existed for reasons that had evolved over years, often generations. As Yamamoto-*san* had told me long before, women serve tea and men do heavier tasks, such as moving desks and setting up tents. This was simply a gender-based division of labor that played to everyone's strong suits.

It made sense on the surface, but what rankled me was that the women's tasks — like serving tea and cleaning up — seemed so mundane as to be unappreciated, while the men's efforts, which occurred only at special occasions, elicited gasps of gratitude and praise. *Had I ever heard my female colleagues feted for their tea-serving prowess?*

When I was sixteen and heading to Japan for the first time, my grandmother was already embarking on a slow slide into dementia. It began with some anxiety that evolved into her losing her grasp on words, then her ideas, then her surroundings and then, at last, life itself. Her decline was particularly heartbreaking for me, because she had been such a doting grandmother, my warmest supporter, and I had to lose her twice, first her mind and then the rest of her.

This is all to explain why the thought she shared before I left for Japan made such an impact on me: "Make sure she comes home," she told my parents. "They don't treat their women very well over there."

At sixteen this did not mean much to me, because I was spending a summer in Japan, no longer. Besides, she had never been to Japan herself. Did she have any idea what she was saying? Still, her words buried themselves in my mind, and I recalled them when I returned to Japan for my college visit, more aware of women's roles; and I recalled them when I taught at and led the Japanese immersion camp in Minnesota, where some Japanese men on staff resented and tried to undermine my leadership position; and I recalled them as a JET watching my female colleagues serve tea and coffee, and exhibit lower-ranking behaviors. "They don't treat their women very well over there."

*Is this what my grandma was talking about? Is this why she would
not have wanted me to dig in and stay?*

That day, as I watched Yamamoto-*san* serve tea, I wondered how
she could not grasp the self-service concept, and I glowered at the
men, none of whom stopped her from squandering this officially
sanctioned opportunity for progress.

* * *

In the years since I left Shuho-cho I have realized that tempera-
mentally, I am not as unlike Yamamoto-*san* and my other Japanese
female colleagues as I wanted to believe. I have smiled and nodded
my way through job interviews and work meetings — receiving
employment offers and positive feedback despite my barely uttering
a word. My habit of active listening has caused people to tell me
how smart I am without my offering a single opinion or an idea. I
too have donned a mask, being helpful when appropriate, laughing
at the right time, and living up to expectations.

When I became a newspaper reporter after leaving Shuho-cho,
I interviewed people on multiple sides of what often were contro-
versial topics, empathetically drawing them out in order to better
understand the issue and to come as close as possible to achieving
journalistic objectivity. Sometimes, after these stories were published,
I would field phone calls from disappointed sources. "I thought you
were on my side," they would say, and I would explain that I had
been reporting their side, not *taking* their side.

Through the years, people have assumed that I align with
everything from conservative fundamentalists to wide-eyed lib-
erals, from the prudish to the worldly wise. I have not tried to
dissemble, not tried to be lukewarm, but like the Japanese women
I encountered, I have gone with the flow when it has served my
interests and when it would simply take too much energy or
time to represent my true feelings. I understand now that my

discomfort watching my female colleagues in Japan should have alerted me that I was seeing something in them that I was not ready to recognize in myself: that I too was capable of donning the mask and playing the game.

But I had not been hired to play the game. As a JET, I had been tasked with speaking my mind. The Ministry of Education conveyed to us time and again that one of the primary JET goals is internationalization, meaning I was imported, in part, to give those who met me a glimpse into what life was like elsewhere, to point out differences as well as similarities. I was all but obligated to explain how the expectations and treatment of women in Shuho-cho differed from how we women were treated back home, in Minnesota. Only later would I learn that I was dwelling less in reality than in the land of my perceptions.

A few years after this failed self-service day at the Board of Education, I would be called into my supervisor's smoke-filled office at an American company. Speaking through the haze, he would confide in me that in spite of the countless fourteen-hour days I had spent producing mountains of copy, I would not be receiving the raise I deserved. The men on his staff needed the money more than I did. "*They are supporting families,*" he explained. "*They have children after all. Surely you can understand.*"

I did not understand but was too dumbfounded to protest. And how could I? My boss had planted the image in my head that if I fought for a raise I would be pulling bread out of my colleagues' children's mouths.

But I did begin rethinking the state of equality in my home country.

While in Shuho-cho, though, I remained blissfully ignorant of such injustices and would never have believed that two decades after I proclaimed Minnesota's glass ceiling to have been shattered, women would be earning less than eighty cents for every dollar a man makes.

Although I did not fully recognize it at the time, I believe my Japanese colleagues were more aware of the shortcomings in their situation than I gave them credit for. I recall catching glimpses of stone-steady knowingness in their eyes and sensing that the submissive behaviors I witnessed were theatrics, outward shows not penetrating to the core.

As time passed I learned that for some of my female colleagues, the portrayed innocuousness was circumstantial, and when we escaped the office, or even when we were in the office and the men were not around, their roles would fall away and masks would come off. Sighs would escape tired lips, shoulders would shrug and eyes would narrow. In private moments colleagues sometimes murmured their actual feelings about drop-in visitors, or clued me in that the male teacher who always stood too close to me made everyone else feel uncomfortable too.

But then again, these women tolerated their role in society. I never heard them bash their male colleagues, and I never observed them using tea-making time as an opportunity for gossip. It was a duty, and it was theirs to perform. They approached it not with resentment but with nobility. In Christian parlance, we could say, "They have a servant's heart," and part of me would admire them for that. And part of me would feel they were being had.

If I could, I would say both to my grandma and to my younger self, "It's complicated."

* * *

That first self-service day I drank my cup of tea along with everyone else in the office but enjoyed it less than I had ever enjoyed a cup of anything, the taste of bitter disappointment.

Then it was time for the cups to be collected.

Matsumoto-*san*, a thirty-something married, athletic sort of guy who sat at the bank of desks behind me, suddenly rose up and began gathering cups from all of the desks, a study in efficiency. Yamamoto-*san* stood up from her chair, frowning, protesting. Others in the office sat at their desks, watching the unfolding drama wide-eyed.

As Matsumoto-*san* carried the cups into the kitchenette, Yamamoto-*san* shadowed him, and I could hear her imploring him to stop and him politely refusing her offers of help. The water came on, and I knew what he was doing, squirting dish soap on the dingy yellow sponge and sudsing up the little clay cups, following a process I had helped with countless times before.

Before long the water was shut off and Matsumoto-*san* emerged, smiling tightly, with Yamamoto-*san* following. He was shaking his head and waving away her profuse thanks. She gradually quieted and smiled, a bit uncertainly.

33

Shaken

"MEET Chad," said my friend Brant, a brassy Michigander, as he introduced a group of us Yamaguchi JETs to his friend, a tall fellow, even by U.S. standards, with reddish brown hair and a sprinkling of freckles.

I had just arrived in Kobe for a mandatory three-day conference for JETs who had signed on to teach another year. I had not really wanted to go, knowing it would be a busy, boozy affair that would turn our hotel and its surroundings into a spectacle of English-speaking revelry during which our loud, un-nuanced voices and gestures would demonstrate yet again that foreigners could never truly fit into Japanese culture — the exact opposite of what I was trying to prove in Shuho-cho.

But as I closed in on the hotel where the conference was to be held, I encountered scattered individuals and then groups and crowds of foreigners, vigorous and youthful, their many colors of hair, eyes and skin dazzling to my eyes, their accents — North American,

European, Australasian — so pleasing to my ears. After an initial feeling of cultural vertigo, I began embracing JETs I had not seen since the previous summer at Tokyo orientation and palling around with the Yamaguchi-based JETs I normally saw only at prefectural meetings a few hours a month. Here, now, all of us were comrades in arms, all of us a tribe.

I had been standing with Brant and several other Yamaguchi JETs when he had hailed Chad, who he told us was a longtime friend, teaching in another part of Japan. "Chad," he said pointedly, "is the nicest guy in the world."

I smiled at Chad, this allegedly nice man, who was attractive in a boyish, rather innocuous way. Then our mutual friend turned to him and said, "Chad, meet Sarah, the nicest woman in the world."

No, no, no, I shook my head. I was not that nice — certainly not as nice as Brant attested (we all knew he was prone to hyperbole), and not as nice as Brant assumed. He did not know I felt like a total fraud, having abandoned a messed-up marriage and life, flown to Japan and then ever since kept the story of that sorry past under wraps hoping, I guess, to appear nicer and more innocent than I was. Only Hideo, my host family and by then Naoko knew my story, along with a couple of female JETs, whom I had sworn to secrecy.

Brant the Michigander would learn the truth some months later when, sharing a seat with him on a crowded public bus, I would confess my divorce, and he would whip around to face me and bellow "NO!" his voice filling the vehicle and causing dozens of Japanese and the few of us foreigners to nearly leap out of our seats. I was sorry to have catalyzed such a reaction, but it did confirm my fears: if people knew my truth, their impressions of me would be altered forever. By then I was on the home stretch of my JET contract and had less to lose. It was OK to come clean.

But in Kobe I still maintained the sheen of niceness, and when Brant introduced Chad and me, and pointed out what he regarded as our common trait, the idea of "us" became a potentiality in my mind, and I was alarmed at how quickly that occurred.

* * *

Only five months previously Kobe had been the epicenter of the Great Hanshin Earthquake, which hit the night Hideo and I got together. I had imagined we would encounter a sober place there, all of us foreigners stumbling about the rubble, disrupting a city where so many people's lives had so recently, suddenly, and irretrievably been shattered. How long would it take to right such a topsy-turvy world? I had been unable to imagine Kobe being livable or visit-able only these few months later.

I had never experienced a major earthquake, but a couple of months previously I had felt the earth move in Shuho-cho. Out for a jog, I had heard — or perhaps sensed — a roar like a low-flying airplane, the asphalt beginning to undulate, my feet moving without me, as if I was a marionette. My first thought was that the cement company had blasted away another piece of the mountain that was slowly shrinking above my neighborhood. But the roar continued, and I felt myself spinning in a slow-motion pirouette on a Silly Putty road.

And then everything was normal again, so steady so fast that it could have been a neurological blip. I looked around. On the soft hill to my left the trees and bamboo were still. The rice paddies to my right were calm, the ground uncracked. Nearby the mountains stood intact, and no one fled into or out of the farmhouses that squatted here and there on the small plain.

I turned around and cautiously padded home. Against all logic, I wanted to hide inside, behind the metal door to my apartment and among its hollow-sounding walls, sandwiched between the first and third floors of a three-story building. As if that would be safe.

Having grown up on the northern Plains, when it came to hazards I had focused less on the earth than on the heavens. It was there we saw spectacular lightning shows and kept a lookout for the greenish tone that could herald the odd tornado. It was from there that fell unpredictable quantities of snow and rain, and when the latter fell too hard and too fast, or the former melted too quickly, the water would overwhelm our rivers and flood our stubbly fields, no hills to block the flow. We spent the next days barefoot in damp basements sopping up the mess, the whirring of electric fans making it too noisy to talk.

But I had never questioned the earth's stability. The idea of the ground moving of its own volition was unsettling, as if my life raft of land was bobbing on magma. The Japanese archipelago seemed much thinner and more tenuous than it had just moments earlier.

When I reached my apartment, I telephoned Hideo. "*Did you feel anything around six o'clock?*" I asked him.

"*No.*"

"*I think I felt an earthquake.*"

"*Uh-huh...?*"

"*Yeah, and it spun me around.*"

He was quiet for a moment before he asked with a patient voice, "*Could you stand up?*"

I felt like a child. "*Yes.*"

"*No problem,*" he said, clearly amused. "*You know the Earth is alive.*"

Alive? Did he mean in the way James Lovelock described it in the 1960s with his Gaia hypothesis, the Earth being a single organism and we humans to her body what those creepy-crawly, eyelash-dwelling mites are to us — merely one of many factors affecting (or not) her systemic health? That would make the motion I experienced on the road the equivalent of a stretch or a twitch.

Although I imagined my minor event could easily have Richter-ed up a few notches into disaster, Hideo's attitude was reassuring: he viewed a quake as a function of the world in which we lived. Like that legendary, petulant carp on which Japan is said to rest.

Perhaps this attitude explains why in Kobe I found parts of the city still teetering in disrepair, wafting dust particles that caused my lungs to itch, a cacophony of construction sounds assaulting my ears, but in adjacent areas life appeared perfectly normal, people eating at restaurants, people shopping, people carrying on.

* * *

Located on the city's harbor, the Portopia, the elegant hotel hosting the JET conference, was one of these carrying-on places, an oasis. Popping with two thousand foreigners, nearly all English speakers, it was easy to forget we were visiting a quake-ravaged area — or that we were even in Japan.

I no longer felt like that odd creature I was in Shuho-cho, where my hair, befuddled by Japanese shampoos, tended to be frizzy, where my size-nine feet hung off the end of women's large-sized slippers, where my height and mass gave me the appearance of a different species, where my long, drapey clothing was nothing like my colleagues' tailored looks, where my pierced earrings dropped below my lobes, and where my face, so expressive, stood out among the placid countenances that surrounded me in every photo.

Moreover, at the Portopia I felt insulated from the perpetual *gaijin* fascination, absolved of the responsibility I felt as the sole foreigner in Shuho-cho, trying at all times to offer the best representation of my homeland. It was shocking how quickly the Portopia became my new reality, little Shuho-cho fading to a dreamscape. I began to relax. I spoke English rapidly. I shared stories of disastrous class lessons and intransigent colleagues. I ate Italian food. I went dancing. I drank until I could not stop smiling.

And I entered Chad's orbit, wondering whether indeed he was the nicest guy in the world, speculating about his situation and, as we ate group dinners and joined a swimming expedition at the hotel pool, I obliquely gathered intel on him: hometown, college major, future goals. I do not recall learning anything of his faith, whether he had one or whether that even mattered to him. Still, I was drawn to him and told Brant that if I were not dating Hideo, I would be interested in Chad. About whom I knew next to nothing. Meanwhile another part of my brain wondered what was wrong with me for having these thoughts and saying these things. I was dating Hideo, whom I had actually experienced and truly knew to be among the nicest men in the world. I felt terrible turning my gaze on Chad. But not terrible enough to stop.

During those few short days in Kobe, something happened to me: I became aware of a dangerous fault in my relationship with Hideo. Glassmakers speak of inclusions, foreign objects enclosed in a piece of glass. Some inclusions — pieces of metal or air bubbles — are intentionally added to enhance a work of art, while others show up by accident when a fragment of metal or clay contaminates the medium. If the inclusion is too large, if it expands and contracts at a rate different from the glass itself, or if it exerts significant pressure on the glass, it can cause the object to shatter.

Hideo and I had not found anything specific about each other that could destroy our relationship, nor had either of us done anything that could cause our bond irreparable harm. But spending time with other foreigners in Kobe caused me to focus more intently on an inclusion I had long ignored that had been obvious from the very beginning: we did not call the same place home. Not geographically, culturally, linguistically or spiritually.

We did share many commonalities — our way of treating other people, a love of family and an appreciation of nature. But Hideo's and my relationship required a lot of hard work. Ground I could cover with Chad in fifteen minutes — thanks to the cultural shorthand, language and assumptions we shared — might, with Hideo, require hours or even weeks due to the interference of our different languages and cultures. At that time, I was working pretty hard to convince myself that Hideo's and my lack of shared background would prevent us from getting bogged down in the minutiae of life by forcing us to skip the petty arguments, because they would not be worth the linguistic effort. Instead we would focus on what was really important: living and loving.

That argument might have worked better for me had I not been married before and learned that love and passion are not enough, and that the minutiae are what make up the bulk of daily life. In fact, I think I had made a similar argument to myself before I married my ex. In that case, we did share a language, a culture, and a geographical home, but our lifestyles, values, and goals had differed. We knew this before we married, but we had no idea how perpetually bogged down we would get in the particulars of daily life, whether deciding which bills to pay when or how to spend our free time. We never could get to the bigger picture. *Despite* a shared language and culture.

If Hideo and I were to stay together, we would have to deal with the daily decisions — not to mention big-picture issues like which hemisphere to live in — against the backdrop of our not-always-congruent attitudes toward work and family obligations — as we flipped through our English–Japanese/Japanese–English dictionaries.

Although nothing but conversation happened between Chad and me, what meeting him did was raise a nagging question in my mind: *all other things being equal, if I were actually to have the good fortune to choose between the nicest guy in the English-speaking world and the nicest guy in the Japanese-speaking world, whom would I pick?*

When the conference ended Saturday morning and we JETs were milling about the hotel lobby saying our farewells, I could not help but glance around for Chad. But as I peered about, it was not Chad who entered my sights but Hideo, my dear Hideo, fresh from Tokyo and smiling broadly, startling me back to the real life I had found in Japan. I went to him.

We were planning to spend a short weekend in nearby Kyoto, running about the city seeing temples and shrines. In the evening, back in our room at the *ryōkan*, we would talk in circles about our nebulous future until we both fell into tears, not recovering till ten o'clock, when, hungry, we would step out for convenient-store takeout, rice balls and cucumber sandwiches, bowls of hot noodles and bottles of tea.

Before all that, though, as we collected my bags and prepared to leave the Portopia, Chad appeared at my side.

Awkwardly, I introduced two of the nicest men in the world.

34

Stirred

AFTER nearly a week away in the hubbub of Kobe and Kyoto, Shuho-cho once again felt like a tiny dot on a map. The streets all but emptied by suppertime, and the nights were quiet but for the muffled sounds of television sets and the regular brouhaha of insects and other creatures in the rice paddies. My apartment echoed with the sound of my slippers slapping the hardwood floor as I shuffled from room to room, alone. Hideo's absence weighed heavily.

I wanted for female company as well. Naoko and I had recently had a falling out, the cause of which was unclear to me even then. It seemed to begin one evening in my apartment when I confessed some unvarnished feelings of isolation, loneliness, and melancholy. My tears started coming and I was unable to stop them, unable to maintain my *genki gaijin* (happy foreigner) façade. She had departed abruptly in the midst of my grief, which was probably standard-issue culture shock triggered by my return to rural Shuho-cho, and I was left feeling embarrassed and confused. Had I been too honest? Had

I shared too much? Naoko was my friend, my closest in Shuho-cho. I thought I should be able to speak openly with her.

I was still learning to negotiate the delicate nature of *tatemae* and *honne*. Used in Japan to preserve harmony in a group and in society at large, *tatemae* is one's public face, what a person conveys to the outside world. By contrast, true feelings, *honne*, are mainly kept to oneself and perhaps shared with family and the closest of friends. I must have stumbled that evening into the land of *honne*, and Naoko was not ready to join me.

Later I apologized, not understanding exactly what had happened, and she said it was OK. Even so, our relationship remained testy, and I noticed she was less forgiving of my efforts to speak Japanese — our primary vehicle of communication — jumping on errors I made in her native language, no matter how hard I studied or how carefully I spoke. I fell deeper into my trough of culture shock, rejecting my host culture as it seemed to be rejecting me. In my mind anyway. The Japanese are not the only ones to employ *tatemae*.

Although I interacted with many people daily, at the schools, the Board of Education office, the post office, the grocery store and on the street, I had few social outlets, people to go out with for a beer or invite in for supper and a video. And I had begun to realize that sometimes I was learning about social gatherings after the fact, parties held by groups of which I thought I was a member. My favorite co-teacher, Mr. Kumagai, who had been transferred away in April, sent me a note thanking me for some translating help I had given him, and in it he mentioned his disappointment at not seeing me at a recent get-together of South Junior High teachers. He assumed I had been invited. I had not.

I was crushed but not terribly surprised. Although South Junior High was the workplace that had most embraced me, I had come into the care, socially speaking, of a single female teacher. She was warm and amusing with a ready smile and struck me as an innocuous, everybody's-sister type. But although she and I were friendly, giggling together in the staff room, there were times that she neglected to fill me in on various happenings. And when I was included in staff gatherings, I noticed she would try to send me home at the earliest opportunity. In my first months there, I went along with this, figuring I should trust her, another *onēsan* (older sister) watching out for me. Perhaps she knew best. Besides, I did not want to inflict my linguistic and cultural cluelessness on the other teachers for too long when they were looking to kick back and relax.

But as months passed, as I began to get the cultural drift, I started ignoring her efforts and instead announced that I wanted to stick around after the first party of the night and then accompanied the group for its second and third parties — and had a great time. The teachers expressed their surprise, saying they assumed I always wanted to get home early. And then they offered me additional invitations. I came to suspect that she had been trying to keep me from siphoning off some of the attention.

In my lonelier moments, such as when I learned I had missed the party with Mr. Kumagai, whom I would not see any other way, I felt marginalized, compartmentalized, as if once the workday ended, my colleagues would have me return home to my box until the next time I was scheduled for an appearance. Like a cuckoo retreating into its clock.

Or, to be more dramatic about it, like a geisha.

This might be a leap, especially since a geisha's role is to make social events sparkle, and I was being left out of gatherings, but here's the similarity: similar to JETs, geisha are part of Japan but set apart from Japan — geisha as entertainer, JET as teacher and interpreter of Western culture. Each one's life is interwoven with

Japanese society while being kept intentionally and adamantly separate from it.

A little history: the geisha — "arts person" — came into her own in the eighteenth-century floating world, those places set aside for the recreation of all classes, where usual class-based rules did not apply — as long as you had the money and were savvy to this walled-off world's highly scripted etiquette.

A geisha usually got her start as a young girl when she was adopted into an *okiya* and put in the care of an *onēsan*, an older "sister," who would lead her along the path to geisha-hood. Unlike the more flamboyant *yūjo* ("woman of pleasure"), whose *obi* (belt) was tied in front for convenience, the geisha sold not her body but her skills in music, dance and witty conversation, her ability to turn a party into an event.

So as geisha evolved to fill a need in Edo-era Japan, JETs, beginning in the 1980s, were brought in to satisfy a twentieth-century desire for improved communication and global understanding. Like geisha, whose rules and hierarchies are dictated by the "willow and flower world," separate from broader society, JET life is circumscribed by rules, obligations, contracts, and housing set up by host institutions and the Ministry of Education.

In my case, I was paid a generous salary for work unlike that of my colleagues. I lived in a lovely apartment, kept at the ready for teaching and events that benefited from an international presence or English interpreting, kept without access to convenient transportation, kept, sequestered even, as an independent operator in a country organized by teams and clubs. Yes, I felt something like a kept woman.

From this perspective, my expectation to be included in the daily and nightly life of my colleagues challenged our natural and engineered separateness. I was probably the only one in Shuho-cho who imagined myself becoming part of a Japanese diorama.

* * *

At school, classes continued through much of the summer, and as my new co-teachers settled in, I was back to spending a lot of time sitting at my desk. In my bleaker moments I felt as if I was being kept in storage, missing out on my youth, stuck in a holding pattern. *What kind of life is this?* I wondered. *Had I escaped an unsuitable marriage and dismal future only to land in Shuho-cho, lonely and underutilized?*

I recalled the refugee families from Southeast Asia that my childhood church had helped in the 1970s or early 80s. As each family arrived, there came a flurry of activity as church members gathered clothing, repaired bicycles and painted a donated apartment. Then more activity as they helped the family settle into a new home, community, jobs, and schools. We saw them at church most Sundays, and as the months passed, the children began wearing trendy sweatshirts, and the adults grew plump. Although they never blended in, they had become part of our congregation, part of our landscape.

I recall a Sunday when our pastor announced that one of these families was moving to California.

What? How could they? I thought. *All that time and money spent, and now they were leaving?* I naïvely figured that these people (who of course had survived unspeakable tragedy) could not handle the northern winters.

As a foreigner living in Japan, I began to understand the decisions these immigrants made. Like them, I had received a warm welcome and had been set up with a place to live and a job. But despite the beautiful apartment, the gifts of towels, hangers, and the electric fry pan, the "hallos" in the street, the invitations to play the koto at various festivals and to attend some *enkai*, I felt lonely and out of place being the only one of me. This feeling encompassed far more than my appearance and my language issues. It permeated my existence there, all the way down to the careless manner in which I peeled my oranges. The discarded peels of my Japanese acquaintances looked like flowers.

Around me, everyone else seemed to share common understandings about almost everything. Japanese acquaintances expressed their opinions as if they were endorsed by the entire country. They began explanations with the phrase "*Wareware Nihonjin ...*" — "We Japanese ... ." While some seemed to earnestly believe they shared a common consciousness, others appeared to seek refuge there, finding safety in numbers. By explaining a custom as "the Japanese way," they absolved themselves of responsibility or embarrassment. One of my co-teachers explained the rationale to me: "We don't want to be alone. We don't want to *do* alone."

As a JET, I had been brought to Japan, to Shuho-cho, to learn about this Japanese way while sharing my culture and my language. At times, though, I felt like a virus being attacked by a strong and efficient immune system made of millennia-old traditions and ideas. *What did I know? What did my culture have to offer?* Sure, one of my offices had attempted to implement a self-service tea situation, but it would not reach fruition.

At some point that year I learned about the Japanese system of *uchi* and *soto*. *Uchi* refers to people on the inside — those belonging to a certain school, office, or town. In Japan, one introduces oneself first by the group name, and then by a personal name: "I am Shuho-cho Board of Education's Sarah Coomber." This group identification is cemented with mandatory recreational activities like annual volleyball matches and hot springs trips, where one sits naked with same-sex colleagues in a steaming pool of mineral-rich water.

The flip side of *uchi* is *soto*, which refers to outsiders. The character for *soto*, 外, can also be read "*gai*" and is part of the commonly used word for foreigner, *gaijin*, meaning "outside person." In Japan, foreigners are the consummate outsiders, but the *uchi/soto* concept works to our advantage initially. Most short-term visitors are enamored with Japanese hospitality, as they are treated like honored guests: taxi drivers present gifts, passersby drop everything to take us to our destinations, and shopkeepers offer free postcards and souvenirs.

Foreigners who stay a bit longer find the special treatment ends, but they are not allowed to blend in and enjoy group benefits like sure-fire invitations, shared secrets, and nearly unconditional acceptance. For the most part, we do not enter the *uchi*, but we also are no longer completely *soto*. I do not know whether there is a name for that purgatory between the two.

In my case, as the first JET to live and work in Shuho-cho, people did not know quite how to classify me. Was I a long-term guest or a new staff member? Was I a JET or a colleague? Although I was required to be present at my scheduled schools and their functions, my name did not appear on staff rosters. Toward the end of my time there, a co-teacher would get married, and I would hear later that, except for me, the entire school staff had gone to her wedding. When I asked another teacher, with whom I had near-*uchi*-like rapport, why I was not invited, he said, "Maybe Miss Miyamoto forgot about you."

At the time, my mind categorized incidents like this as peculiar to Japan, things that would never happen in my homeland, a land of immigrants, a nation of diversity. But then I remembered that refugee family, and several more after them. I began to imagine what they must have experienced living on the northern Plains, being separated by language and culture, by cuisine and smell, by expectations and hopes — not to mention the culture shock they must have experienced, emerging from war, from famine, from the maws of death and into the stillness of Fargo, North Dakota. We never invited them to our home for dinner, nor did I hear of my church friends' families doing any such thing. I felt too shy to say more than "hello" in the church hallway, fearful that a longer conversation would lead to misunderstandings or some other awkwardness. But it took living in Shuho-cho, living on the flip side of the situation, for me to realize that the refugees' defection to California most likely had far less to do with escaping snowy winters than with finding a community of compatriots in a place where they could belong.

Now, with the benefit of many more years and experiences living in various cities and states, in urban and rural areas, I have found another way to understand my isolation: in Shuho-cho I was a newcomer who alternated among two junior high schools and the Board of Education office, never visiting one place more than two days a week. They were all I had, but from my colleagues' perspective, I was a part-timer, mostly absent. My loneliness probably had less to do with being a foreign teacher than with parachuting into a small town where everyone was busy raising children, raising crops, and trying to balance work and family.

* * *

That June, when I decided I was less a part of my community than I had imagined, I was invited to a funeral. The father of Mr. Fuji, a popular teacher at South Junior High, had died after a lengthy illness, and his memorial service was to be held on Father's Day.

I attended with another teacher, a friend my age, and she helped me negotiate Buddhist funeral etiquette as I purchased a condolence envelope of soft white paper into which I tucked three thousand yen, roughly thirty dollars at the time. After refolding it, I replaced the stiff loop of twisted silver and white paper strings that would hold it closed, and on the outside carefully signed my name, サラ・クンバー. I slipped on my black dress, black stockings, and black shoes, the prescribed attire for mourning.

The ceremony is a foggy memory: a Buddhist priest chanting incantations, grass under my feet; people in black suits, black kimono, black dresses; bowing and lifting incense to my forehead, then dropping it in a burner, bowing again; praying to my God to comfort my colleague and his grieving family; Fuji-*sensei* thanking me in English, his puffy, red-rimmed eyes meeting mine; the hearse, a black car fitted with what appeared to be its own shrine, brilliant metallic gold sculpted into dragons, snakes and flowers, departing; presenting my condolence envelope and receiving a blue box that contained green tea and "helthy drink" mixes, its cover declaring "Recollecion If you would be happy, be good. Many thanks."

Joining my colleagues to share in this grief, a feeling that knows no limit of culture or language, I felt as if I was being gathered back into the fold of community.

35

The Price of Progress

O n a Tuesday in July one of the South Junior High teachers was out of the office, and the principal asked me to take over his classroom for the lunch hour. Even though it was only lunch hour, I sat a bit taller at my desk that morning in anticipation.

In Shuho-cho this was my dream, to be entrusted with classrooms full of students, to be given responsibility, to be treated like my colleagues, to be recognized as the adult and the teacher I knew I was. I had been handed the reins to lead classrooms on my own a few times before — including the time that had led to the notable "*Oi!*" incident of some months earlier — and the opportunity to try out my teaching ideas always left me hoping for more. I had begun envisioning a post-Shuho-cho life plan that included finishing my master's degree, getting a few years of experience in journalism and then teaching writing at the college level, either in Japan or the States, depending on how things evolved with Hideo. The only thing I could see standing between me and a more teacherly life at the moment was the expectations of my handlers in Shuho-cho.

The classroom I would be lunching with that day had caught my attention that summer. It had been one of my favorite *kumi* the previous school year, but since April, when its members had been promoted from eighth grade to ninth, its atmosphere had changed. It gave off an air of cockiness, and I was observing some mild disrespect toward teachers, including myself. I knew that I might not have the smoothest lunch hour.

When the time arrived, I headed toward that classroom, where a few students had already donned white aprons and hair scarves, and were on their way to meet the district's school lunch delivery truck from which they would receive stainless steel vats and haul them back to the classroom. There they would take charge of setting up a serving line for their classmates. These lunches included all kinds of foods, from Japanese home-style soups and rice dishes to items that might be considered delicacies in the United States, such as the shocking *shishamo*, a fish stick lookalike. (I got a few bites into that one before I realized I was eating an entire fish, breaded and fried, full of its own tiny eggs. I was not a member of the clean plate club that day.)

This particular lunch hour, as the class representatives retrieved our food, the remaining students pushed their desks together into groups of four or so. At lunches when a homeroom teacher was present, I would usually join one of these groups, sometimes eagerly welcomed and other times ignored. This was junior high, after all.

Because I was in charge, I sat at the front of the classroom at the teacher's desk, looking out at my charges and keeping a special eye on Kazuo, my student with the cognitive challenges. Since the classroom's atmospheric shift had occurred, I had begun noticing that Kazuo's classmates, who had once been supportive and encouraging, had become less so. I had observed them teasing him and tricking him into doing things that made the rest of the class laugh. I tried to read these behaviors as a maturing class's awkward way of including him, but I was having to work pretty hard at it.

I had come to regard Kazuo as my comrade in arms in Shuho-cho, enamored with the good-natured attitude he maintained even in the face of confusion. Plus we had camaraderie. Every time Kazuo saw me, he broke into a smile, one that slowly, shyly spread across his face. Maybe he understood that I too was out of my element. Perhaps he wondered, as I did, whether we were two birds of a feather.

As the end of the lunch period neared, I watched the other boys piling their dishes and trays on Kazuo's desk.

This was new. Before, the students had always played *jankenpon* (rock-paper-scissors) to determine a loser, and that loser would put away the trays. Today Kazuo told them he wanted to *jankenpon* for this duty, and the other boys agreed. Good. But when I watched them play, I saw they were waiting shrewdly until the instant after Kazuo had signaled his choice of rock, so they could make theirs paper. Kazuo signaled scissors and his classmates flashed rock. He had no hope but to lose every round and either did not see their trickery or lacked the ability to defend himself. His face showed his disappointment, and I felt a slow burn ignite within me.

Before the students cleaned up their dishes, they always chorused, "*Gochisō sama deshita,*" a rote pleasantry that means literally, "It was a feast." That day, I waited for them to say their *gochisō* and then rose up from my chair. Trying to keep my anger in check, I inquired why Kazuo had so many trays to dump.

The answer was silence.

"*Kazuo should not have to dump all of the trays by himself,*" I admonished in Japanese, my voice trembling in anger.

More silence.

Then, one of the boys, who I had always regarded as a level-headed kid, addressed the others. "*Let's help him.*"

"*Good idea,*" I said.

I remembered junior high school all too well and could see this boy had been ensnared in the ugly groupthink and was happy to take the escape I offered. He and a couple of his classmates walked over and began assisting Kazuo.

Seeing that my special charge was now in good hands, I moved in on two of the boys who remained seated, not helping, and whose smart-aleck attitudes had been trying my patience for some time. I glared at them and warned them quietly, in Japanese, "*It would be a good idea for you to be a bit nicer.*"

They looked straight ahead. I eyeballed each of them in turn, now growling, "*Wakarimasu ka?*" — "Do you understand?"

Each nodded.

Retreating to the teachers' room, I shook with blazing anger, upset at the way Kazuo was being treated. I also worried that as a JET, an assistant teacher, I had overstepped my bounds.

Two days later, that class's teacher was still away, and again I was assigned to spend lunchtime with them. I took a deep breath and entered the room, closely watching the boys, wondering whether I would encounter some sort of rematch from the other day. Instead, they were on their most *kanpeki* behavior: no one picked on Kazuo, and everyone dumped his own tray. I was not so naïve as to think I had fixed the situation, but I had drawn a line that said "not on my watch."

When the homeroom teacher returned, I confessed what had happened. He told me he had already heard about it from the girls in the class. And he thanked me.

* * *

When I signed on for a second year in Shuho-cho, I imagined that it would involve an easier, more predictable day-to-day life. My handlers and I had, after all, worked out my role in their — now our — community, and we had pretty well settled on our expectations of one another. None of us was getting everything we wanted, but I think we were mostly content.

Plus I had emerged from numerous cultural and pedagogical missteps mostly unscathed, acquired more Japanese vocabulary and grammar than I had imagined or planned, embraced my seemingly predestined koto hobby, abandoned my doomed fantasy romance with Ryota, grudgingly accepted Hideo's transfer to Tokyo, and figured out where to buy my staples like canned tomatoes.

But there was an unforeseen complication. Instead of my increased knowledge and experience leading to a more predictable, tranquil existence, my hard-won skills were causing a fog to lift. I was gaining confidence and trusting my understanding of what was happening around me. And that was a double-edged sword. Now my days as a bystander and observer, insulated by a bubble of foreignness, of ignorance, of blinding culture shock were past. I began to feel more responsibility to engage and speak my mind as I did when I observed bullying in Kazuo's classroom. This cost me whatever remained of my identity as an innocuous visitor — and probably cost those around me some peace of mind as well.

This is the irony of learning. In striving to achieve a new skill, we assume it will make our lives better. But there is no way to imagine the repercussions of acquiring competency, nor is there a way to turn it off and make it go dormant again, to put things back the way they were. The genie is out of the bottle.

Moving forward, I would find that in some ways life had been easier when I had nothing to fall back on but smile-and-nod diplomacy.

36

Home Again

SUMMER vacation took me back home to Minnesota, where I woke up for several mornings in my old bedroom, my bed covered with a many-colored quilt, pieced and stitched for a Lutheran bazaar by some unknown woman using squares as exact as the nearby fields, acres of blooming sunflowers and ripening barley.

White eyelet-lace curtains blew in a warm breeze as I stepped out of bed onto plush green carpet and swung open my door. Crossing the threshold of my room, I took in the vaulted ceilings of my parents' home, a glorious amount of space poured into rooms of varying shapes, what used to be mundane now exotic. Heading outside, I stood on the soft green lawn and ambled about my mother's garden blooming lavishly with purple coneflowers, red and yellow gaillardia, spiky purple liatris and simple white daisies, butterflies lighting and lifting, lighting and lifting. A short walk away, I stood on a gravel road that ran between farmers' fields and looked out at the horizon, the lip of a translucent blue bowl resting lightly on the land. Everything was exactly as I had left it.

Mom and Dad were there. My brother. My grandfather from Saskatchewan. Later, my grandmother from Illinois. I fed them all *somen*, noodles made from a kit sent with me by the Shuho-cho Board of Education and served in a foot-long chop of fresh bamboo carved into a serving dish, and smaller chops cut into dipping bowls, little bits of Japan that had accompanied me home, as if to say, "*Wasurenai yō ni ...*" — "Don't forget ... " *What? To return? That it was real?* Very quickly, in the light of the northern Plains, it did seem like a dream, like maybe I had just awakened from a deep sleep.

Some days after my homecoming, though, part of my Japan followed me home, confirming that the previous year had been no dream. Once my jet lag had begun to settle, and the green carpet and the green lawn and the unlimited supply of cheddar cheese and cookies had begun to seem normal again, I drove back to the Fargo airport and stood at the mouth of the arrivals chute. And out walked my smiling Hideo.

Damn, he was brave. He had boarded an airplane in Tokyo, transferred somewhere in the States and ended up in Fargo, where he encountered terrestrial flatness the likes of which he had never seen. Flying in, he would have observed what some identify as bleakness and desolation but what I see as a patchwork quilt of yellows and greens, designed to perfectly set off a spectacular, ever-changing skyscape. Swinging down from high over Fargo, he would have seen meandering rivers with wide curves cutting S's through green farmyards of barns, gravel drives, and parked tractors, all looking from the air like someone's well-tended model railroad diorama. The pilot would have casually announced his pending arrival, the airplane floating lower and lower, its descent punctuated by little lifts and falls, updrafts of heat rising from hot black soil, then wheels connecting to flat concrete beneath the overwhelming sky.

He had entered my world, so familiar — his touch, his scent, his clothing, his smile — yet now, for me, everything about him seemed so foreign. Or was it that being with him made everything around me feel foreign? This part is difficult to remember. What I do know is that having him there with me made me feel more complete but also off kilter. I could not tease out whether it was home or his presence that did not quite fit.

Although my hometown has always been home or at least a refuge to a varied population, my experience there had been anything but diverse. I grew up visiting my father's office on a Lutheran college campus and going to schools and a church that were populated by Norwegians and Swedes of the Lutheran persuasion. Those who were not Norwegian or Swede by heritage became de facto Scandinavians by proximity, homes filled with Scandinavian knickknacks, rosemaling painted on breadboards and trays, hardangar embroidery on their tables, painted wooden trolls providing touches of levity to their shelves. As my friends packed off to Norwegian camp each summer, I had been left behind, feeling like an oddball minority, my family's background being English, Scottish, and German.

Back in Minnesota, though, I felt completely standard-issue, at least on the outside, blending in in a manner that had been impossible for the whole previous year (save a couple of JET conferences), blending in as Hideo did every day in Japan. Now I was the one roaming about with someone exotic by my side, translating conversations and acting as a social go-between. I was the one in the know, who belonged, who had invited along an interloper.

And my interloper was smiling.

This was not surprising, because Hideo is a natural smiler, not hyper-smiley, but erring on the side of being friendly and engaged, of making the people around him feel comfortable. This is not to say Hideo lacks a serious side, because he has that too, doing business, making reservations, procuring information, expediting.

The latter Hideo did not come to Minnesota. Instead, I saw Hideo take his congeniality to a new level with a wide-eyed, listening, trying-to-understand, trying-to-keep-up, not-quite-knowing-what-was-going-on expression. I realized I was looking in a mirror, seeing the most common expressions I probably used in Japan. I did my best to keep him informed, probably offering him more patience than I had given my mother when she visited me in my other world.

I kept no journal of our Minnesota travels, the week Hideo spent in the midst of my three-week furlough home, my only record being photographs: Hideo at the Fargo airshow with my parents, my grandfather and my brother in his Grateful Dead-inspired beard and tie-dyed T-shirt; Hideo standing in hay stubble on the pink sunset prairie beside a giant round bale of hay; a self-timer shot of Hideo and me at our lakeside campsite; an ebullient Hideo smiling beside Gooseberry Falls near Lake Superior, handsome and muscular in his gray tank and green shorts; me sitting on a sofa with my beloved gray cat, who, in the tearful end, I opted to leave in Minnesota with his caregivers — my friend and her fiancé, and their new black kitten, with whom he had become fast friends.

My mind holds onto memories that are even more vivid than those stored in photo albums: sitting beside Hideo in the Episcopal church (to which my family had transferred), hoping he would connect with my Christian faith, sensing his discomfort, wondering if this would be, should be, a deal-breaker; stopping the car to ogle a towering moose beside a northern Minnesota road, marveling at its size; breathing in the blackness of the north woods at night; feeling an awareness of Hideo's vulnerability in my home language, in Minnesota's outback, recalling unkind comments that had been lobbed at some Japanese camp staff members a few years previously.

I wanted to quarantine Hideo from any danger, protect him from any discomfort — like the prim owners of the bed and breakfast near Lake Superior who, realizing we were unmarried, repeatedly offered us separate rooms. I could not bear the thought that something untoward would happen on my watch. I felt indebted to Hideo, that I owed this man my very life. He had brought me out of the on-again off-again funk I had entered on my honeymoon and that had deepened as I had lost hope and had evolved into embarrassment, guilt and shame as my husband and I separated and then divorced before I turned twenty-five. When I arrived in Japan, serious and reserved, it was Hideo and his exuberance that had brought me back to playfulness, to liveliness, to life.

Yet he continued pushing the idea of marriage, unable to let it go, and it was making me want to run. If in Shuho-cho my wounds in the heart department had begun to heal, Minnesota was irritating and even opening them again. Our traveling, our camping, the open-sky scenery, the presence of friends and family who had seen me through my crisis ... having left as soon after its resolution as I did, these people's view of me and mine of them had not kept up with real time. My Minnesota life had not clicked along in my absence as I had hoped it would.

The upshot was, as much as I wanted to keep Hideo happy and safe, and despite my deep gratitude and feelings for him, I could not protect him from myself.

My starkest memory: we had brought my family's canoe on our camping trip, and one blue-bright sunny day, we took it out on a lake, slicing across the water, the shoreline ahead dense with dark evergreen trees. When we turned around, the waves and wind rose against us, slapping the bow. My memory has Hideo, an experienced paddler, steering us parallel to the waves, setting us up for a precariously tippy situation. I demanded a perpendicular approach, insisting I was the expert, based on my experience of Minnesota lakes. We went back and forth, arguing how best to paddle and steer, all the while straining to make progress back to shore. When at last we reached the beach, I scrambled out of the canoe and lay down in the sand, exhausted and crying for frustration.

Hideo was baffled. So was I.

What I was unable to tease out then was that my tangled feelings and tears were not about paddling styles or marriage proposals. They were about needing some room to choose the colors and patterns that would best suit my future, so I could get the blocks arranged before stitching the quilt of my life, just so, into place.

37

Right of Way

UNLIKE my Minnesota hometown, laid out with broad streets and sidewalks, Shuho-cho was a place of narrow roads where pedestrians and bicyclists on *mamachari* — bell- and basket-equipped granny-style bikes — jockeyed for position with the ubiquitous white, snub-nosed pickups local farmers drove from rice paddy to rice paddy. Some of these roads were bounded by steep drainage ditches on each side while others snugged right up to the green fecundity of darkly forested hills and mountains. There was little room for error.

But I had brought back from Minnesota a pair of brand-new Rollerblades, and I was ready to join the fray. Once unpacked, I buckled on my new blue skates and, a bit self-consciously, rolled through my neighborhood, probably the first inline skater ever to hit the local roads. Over the weeks and months that followed, I ventured farther and farther afield, toward the nearby mountains, my ride varying from semi-smooth blacktop to a jaw-jiggling aggregate. It felt little like the smooth glide I had experienced soaring around Minneapolis's Lake Calhoun, but the feeling was even more exhilarating — in part because my skates gave me the ability to attract attention on my own terms, flying past earthbound pedestrians, most of whom had never seen inline blades, and startling people with my speed.

One day my travels led me through a rice-farming area on the far side of a nearby mountain. Ahead of me I saw a couple of bent-over old women preparing to emerge from the paddy where they had been working. I neared them just as they were stepping up from the field, onto the road, and by the time they caught sight of me, I was almost beside them, their faces perplexed as they tried to register my extra-tall, fast-moving presence, their mouths cracking open with surprise. Once past, I heard their laughter. I looked back, smiled and executed an off-kilter rolling bow.

* * *

My Rollerblades were not the only wheels I acquired after returning to Japan. Now in my second year of employment and working under my negotiated contract, I quickly headed off to the local car lot, a couple of blocks from my Board of Education desk. I had just begun inspecting the used cars when a kind-eyed woman with an easy smile emerged from the shop and introduced herself. She was the mother of one of my South Junior High students, a congenial joker of a kid with high-water pants.

She invited me inside, and we sat in chairs across from one another at a low table, drinking glasses of pulpy orange juice below a calendar advertising car parts or oil and featuring a photograph of a topless Caucasian woman in a provocative pose, surely intended to appeal to gearhead guys — not this sweet mother and me. Trying to keep my eyes on the real live woman in front of me, I explained what I was looking for — a safe little car that I could drive around Shuho-cho and to Hagi. Soon her grizzled, smiling father, wearing an oil-stained mechanic's jumpsuit, sat down with us. They offered me a lease: 20,000 yen, roughly $200 per month, including repairs and maintenance, for a white mini-car, a Suzuki Alto L'Epo hatchback. There would be no written contract, no deposit. We stood up, smiled, and bowed. Done.

Over the next year I would drop by with cash once a month, each time greeted by a different Western nudie, each time wondering whether anyone there was imagining that under my conservative clothing I might look like those women. (I did not.) I tried to envision a parallel car shop in rural Minnesota doing business below a pinup calendar of Asian beauties.

Part of the deal I had made with my handlers to get the car was that I would bring them along on my maiden voyage. So, a couple of days later, Sasaki-*san* and Sato-*kakarichō* went with me to take possession. Only my car did not look quite the same as the day I had first seen it. Now it had a chevron-shaped magnet, half yellow, half green, attached to its hood and another stuck to its hatchback: *wakaba* marks.

The *wakaba* ("young leaf") mark is a signal to everyone that the driver of the marked car is new to the road, fresh from driving school. I reminded Sasaki-*san* that I had been driving for ten years. "*Well*," he replied, "*you're a new driver to Japan.*" I swallowed my protests and smiled, inwardly fuming but conceding the point. Truth was I would be adapting to driving on the left-hand side of the road, my driver's seat on the right side of the car, stick shift in my left hand. And if I were ever to pass a sign that read "*Bridge out*" in Japanese, I would most likely not be literate enough to read it.

When I later complained about my *wakaba* marks to Hideo, he suggested I buy more of them. Then I could stick them on the right-hand door, the left-hand door, the roof and the undercarriage too. Just in case. *Ha ha.*

I started up the car, one supervisor beside me and one behind, and feigned confidence, hoping I would not make everyone's fears about foreign drivers come true, praying I would not turn their wives into widows. Leaving the car lot, I stopped at a red light and saw it was time to make my first right turn, from the left lane of one road into the left lane of a perpendicular road. When the traffic light turned blue (Japan's version of a green light), I held my breath, said a quick prayer and stifled the voice in my head that yelled *hug the curb!* As my life in Shuho-cho so often required me to do, I abandoned one of my longest-held assumptions, this time beating back everything I had ever learned about driving or riding a bicycle in the States — and made a wide right turn, letting go of a move I had done by rote ever since early childhood.

And I made it. The system worked. After that first successful turn, my brain shifted, and I never looked back. This was Japan. Up was down, and right was left. As for the *wakaba* marks, I soon stopped complaining. The car granted me my freedom, and the *wakaba* ensured I always got the right of way.

38

On My Own

As the autumn equinox neared, brilliant red *higanbana*, a type of amaryllis, began shooting out from the rice paddies' earthen banks, each bloom a mini-bouquet of slender petals and long, curved stamens that arced like fireworks. Wild pink and white cosmos, gaudy along the roadsides, soon followed, along with graceful blond blades of *susuki* grass, swaying patiently, graceful tassels bowing to the gentle fall breezes, one of the seven grasses of autumn that Hideo and I had hunted the previous year. Seeing this season turn made me realize that since starting college eight years previously, it was the first time I had experienced a second autumn living within the same four walls. So this is how it felt to get settled.

But unlike the previous autumn, whose landscape I soaked in slowly on foot and from the seat of my *mamachari* bicycle, this season I watched the colors glow through a windshield, my cassette tapes of Hootie and the Blowfish and Toad the Wet Sprocket providing the soundtrack. As I turned onto the road that wound its way from my neighborhood toward central Shuho-cho, I dialed up the volume in an attempt to cover up the car's built-in chimes that ding-ding-dinged whenever I hit about forty miles an hour, the recommended speed limit on the open road, which always seemed too slow.

But I happily endured my car's stubborn reminders, because now I was free. Free to drive over to Hagi to visit my host family, free to go to Yamaguchi City for private Japanese lessons, free to run errands, free to skip the early bus and wheel instead under my own power into South Junior High's parking lot at the last minute before morning bell. And I was free on early holiday mornings and weekends to hop into my glorified golf cart of a car and putt-putt the hour or so to Ogori, where I would abandon it in a parking lot, make a frantic dash to the train station, buy a ticket, and scurry to the platform for the northbound *shinkansen*, always northbound, toward Kyoto, Osaka, and Nagano, wherever Hideo would arrange to meet me despite his amped-up schedule of long work hours followed by mandatory nightly after-work parties with superiors and co-workers. I was free, at last, to feel like an adult, independent, in charge of my own life.

By the next month, though, I would be even more independent than I had imagined or wished. One October day I went to the Board of Education office and found the seat next to me, Sasaki-*san*'s, empty.

I had no idea exactly how old Sasaki-*san* was, but he looked young to me, even among Japanese people, who to my eyes show their age less than most Caucasians. Part of Sasaki-*san*'s apparent youth had to do with his expressivity. His eyes would widen when he was listening hard, and there was a gentle boyishness about his reactions, the way he would smile and shoot a look my way to see if I was picking up on what was happening around us. Plus, like me, he appeared to have been blessed, or cursed, with the tease-ability gene, his colleagues exploiting it good-naturedly, Sasaki-*san* smiling and bowing his head.

When I was first getting to know him, I figured he was a few years older than I, so not much over thirty. Like many Japanese men, he wore no ring, so I wondered whether he was attached. Soon I learned that not only was he married, but his son was a student at South Junior High, and his daughter was an elementary schooler. Much later I would realize he was eighteen years my senior — forty-three years old at the time of our first meeting.

Earlier that year Sasaki-*san* had missed a day of work to check into the hospital. Many of my colleagues took time off for *ningen dokku* ("human dry dock"). A comprehensive medical examination designed for healthy adults, it functioned as a health maintenance program and took its name from the work a ship undergoes after a voyage. During *ningen dokku*, medical staff put most every bodily system to the test with a battery of exams, fluid draws, and imaging options.

I had not heard that anything untoward had been found, and I wondered how the doctors could have missed this fault. Or perhaps his condition had come on so suddenly that it could not have been prevented. The reason he was absent from work that October day was he had had a stroke. No one could tell me his prognosis.

I was bereft. First that this kind man and his family should be going through such an experience, especially at his relatively young age. And secondly, selfishly, because Sasaki-*san* was my advocate, my buffer. Especially now that Hideo was gone, he served as my cultural interpreter and my confidant in matters related to work. When the JET program's national office began cracking down on us English teachers, curtailing our holiday travel plans, trying to keep us in-country and more closely tethered to our assignments, Sasaki-*san* had convinced his superiors that it would do everyone more good if I were allowed to travel, whether in Japan or internationally, rather than sit at my desk with little to do. The more I learned about Japan and the world, he asserted, the more I would be able to share with my students and the "townspeople," as he referred to his fellow Shuho-cho residents. His superiors ran his thoughts all the way up to the town mayor, who recently had been hospitalized and to whom I had, perhaps fortunately, sent flowers. He concurred with Sasaki-*san*.

Now my number-one local supporter was in dire straits.

Against the advice of my remaining handlers, I figured out where Sasaki-*san* had been taken and drove the mini-car he had helped me acquire to Yamaguchi City, about an hour's drive away, through the nearby mountains. There I found him in a hospital bed, his right hand and leg suddenly foreign to him, the right side of his handsome face sagging helplessly.

He would be there more than a month, and I visited him a couple of times, bringing treats and books, hoping to cheer up my supervisor and coax him back to health, back to Shuho-cho.

Returning to the office, I reported that I had seen him, that he was making progress. I was glad to have the opportunity to share observations, to act like an adult, to prove myself part of the community.

39

Waterloo

ONE very early morning not long after Sasaki-*san*'s stroke, I sped to Ogori and boarded a northbound bullet train that carried me past Hiroshima, Himeji, Kyoto, and Osaka, and up to Nagoya to meet Hideo. We were long past the tension of our Minnesota trip and re-immersed in the culture where we had fallen in love, where his habit was to watch over me and my habit was to let him.

He met me in his car at the Nagoya station, I hopped in, and after what always seemed to be an insufficient number of hugs and kisses we turned up the music and headed off to nearby Nagano Prefecture, our seats thumping and the air around us growling with Apache Indian's infectious "Boom Shack-A-Lak."

It was liberating to be back in Hideo's car, unbound by train and bus schedules, camouflaged by tinted windows, free to sing and car-dance along with his ever-expanding collection of English-language and Japanese CDs, the music of Sheryl Crow and Lisa Loeb and Yumi Matsutoya. As we drove, I studied the faces of other young couples we passed, all apparently Japanese, riding in their similarly sparkling-clean late-model cars — no beaters ever anywhere — and wondered if they felt as self-possessed, as dispassionate as their faces appeared. Hideo and I were so animated by contrast that we must have looked like escapees from some ward. Of course, the wards we had abandoned were his days and evenings of never-ending work in Tokyo and my loneliness for him in Shuho-cho. We had escaped our own versions of madness, to each other.

It was November, and we were off to Kamikochi, a spectacular area of the Japanese Alps, a place so prized for its natural environment that private cars were not allowed. As we neared our destination, Hideo parked the car, we grabbed our backpacks and camping gear, and caught a bus into the Chubu Sangaku National Park for our newest adventure.

The clear, sunny air carried that unmistakable alpine chill, and I was glad to be there with my beau, someone I could snuggle up to. We got our bearings, made our way to the campsite and found a quiet spot to pitch Hideo's tent before heading off to hike. We wandered through stands of birch, their white trunks glowing against coniferous larch, greens fading to gold. We traced pristine rivers gliding over rocks that had been ground through the millennia into smooth, round balls. We paused to dip our hands in lakes so clear and cold that we could see their rocky bottoms dropping deeper and deeper away from the shore. When the waters stilled, we shifted our focus to the glassy surface that mirrored the mountains surrounding us.

Despite being together and surrounded by great natural beauty, it did not take long for me to start feeling on edge. Hideo had been trying to nudge our relationship toward marriage for months, peppering the idea into everyday conversations, speaking as if we had already set our wedding date for the coming August, just ten months away, ignoring my pleas to let the topic rest until more time had passed, until I felt strong enough in our relationship and, more even than that, until I felt strong enough in myself.

When we had started dating the previous January, I was only six months past receiving my divorce decree. Prior to that I had exerted fourteen months of effort and cajoling to get my life disentangled from my then-husband's. Before that, I had spent ten months trying — in my mind, in the counselor's office, in our home and everywhere else — to pull that doomed union out of the death spiral that had begun on our honeymoon. Or, more likely, before. Not even including the vicissitudes of our nine-month courtship and engagement, this added up to a full two years spent trying to fix and then flee a doomed relationship. Although I must not have shown it on the outside, relationship-wise, I was spent.

But Hideo and his advances had been irresistible to me. I knew that if I had remained set against them, him, and stayed in my time machine to wait until my heart was truly ready for love, I might have sequestered myself for another few years, or many more months at least. And when you are twenty-five and everyone around you seems to be having a good time and getting on with life, every opportunity, every potentiality feels so fleeting that to hold back for even a few weeks or months seems like waiting a hundred years. I feared that in that time, I might miss everything, especially the opportunity to engage with this attractive man, who could easily have found other women to date, what with his mountain biking meets and business trips. Even when I had sometimes felt crowded with him living right downstairs, and after his move, by the hours we spent on the phone each night, my broken-down heart could not help but love him.

But the idea of marriage seemed to itch Hideo like a mosquito bite. He could not stop scratching it. *Did he think if he stopped bringing it up, I would forget? Or that the possibility of us marrying would disappear altogether? Why wouldn't he leave it alone for a while? Why couldn't we just be us, HideoandSarah, boyfriend and girlfriend?*

As we made our way through the park, we encountered a marshy area, and the softening trail led us to a narrow log bridge installed to keep hikers from sullying their boots in the muck. I watched as a middle-aged man approached the opposite end of that log, and I knew that as a woman in Japan I should defer to him and wait until he crossed before I set out for the other side. But that day, in addition to being irritated with Hideo's talk of marriage, I felt a global frustration that had been building over the year-plus I had been living in Japan. Annoyed by the expectations that culture had of me as a foreigner, a teacher, a temporary worker, and a woman, I felt frazzled and frayed, tired of trying to measure up, weary of working to blend in, sick to death of being *chigau* (different) and exhausted especially by all of the men who assumed that I should and would serve their tea, let them walk through doors ahead of me, and listen as they showboated their interminable stories.

Watching that middle-aged, vacationing man start across the log toward me, seemingly without a thought as to whether I might wish to cross too, I thought, *"Not this time,"* and threw my shoulders back, marching forward over that same narrow log. I set in motion a game of chicken.

As I made my way toward the other side, I forced that man to notice me, and I essentially dared him not to move for me. I cannot recall with absolute certainty whether I won or lost the match before he and I, Hideo and the rest of that other man's party, all of us, with tremendous awkwardness, eventually reached our intended destinations on opposite sides of that log. What I do remember is that I embarrassed the hell out of my long-suffering beau, who, when we regrouped on the other side, remarked on my poor behavior.

In my harried state, his comment sounded like evidence that despite his many kindnesses and sacrifices on my behalf, he was, at heart, as biased and close-minded as the rest of "them," meaning every other Japanese man who in one way or another had ever trod on my good nature. I feared he was revealing a side I had hoped was not there, for I had been warned by more than one Japanese woman: "*Everything changes once the ring is on your finger.*" With Japanese men, they said, the ardor disappears after the wedding when the new wife wakes up to find herself transformed in her husband's eyes from lover to mother, responsible first for his care and upkeep, and then for that of their soon-to-arrive progeny. I began to imagine Hideo as the caricature husbands I watched in Japanese television dramas. Perhaps he too would roll in later and later from the office and after-work drinking engagements, not with hellos and kisses but with that hollered infantile command: "*Gohan!*" — "Food!" It had seemed so funny on TV.

I thought he and I were special. Surely we could surmount our cross-cultural challenges. Surely we would figure out our different approaches to work, to family, to faith. He would not be with me if he were not open to a new type of future, a life on equal footing. Right?

Now that my mental train had gone down a different track, I began obsessing over every warning I had received, every fear I had conjured. What if it were true, that his attraction would last only as long as we dated, and that our form of "different" — *chigau* — would cross over to the other meaning of that Japanese word and become "wrong"? Earlier in our relationship, Hideo had been understanding of my frustrations, even supportive of my minor rebellions, when I began adding too little instant coffee and too much Creap to my colleagues' drinks. He had seemed to enjoy seeing his own culture through my eyes, studying its quirks and customs alongside me, eager for a new perspective, mine. The log bridge incident felt like a betrayal, as if something had changed, as if maybe we were both realizing he was more a product of his culture, the parts I preferred not to see, than either of us had believed.

We did, after a while, move past the log bridge brouhaha and for the rest of our weekend put on brave faces, "ooh"-ing and "aah"-ing over the delicious views, enjoying the warmth of our campfire and the closeness of our tent, but I felt a sense of foreboding. When I was honest with myself, I knew that even when we had been flirty and honey-sweet with new love, I had been unsure whether I wanted to marry Hideo, whether I was ready to contemplate forever ever again. But I thought I had time to work it out. We were only dating. As he turned up the pressure, though, I felt forced to make a decision, and I still did not know whether my evasion had to do with a feeling of "not yet" or "not ever."

What I had realized was that I could not get past the magnetic pull I felt toward the place I considered my real home, Minnesota. I could not imagine it ever fully waning, and that caused a growing certainty in me that nothing and no one would be able to keep me in Japan forever. So I found myself asking myself a question parallel to the one my ex-husband had put to me when I suggested we go to Japan: *what would Hideo do in America?* I came up with no answers.

I considered letting life make some decisions for me: *what if I were to sleep with Hideo, just roll the dice and let fate take the reins?* If I got pregnant, we would marry and most likely stay in Japan. If not, I would leave Hideo at the end of my contract, head home to the United States and return to my previously scheduled life.

I never made this suggestion to him — in part because I knew it was stupid and went against the way I knew I should be living my life. More than that, he was a man who knew his worth and never would knowingly have agreed to serve as a fallback plan. As much as he wanted me to buy into his marriage dream, he would not have accepted less than an unequivocal yes.

At that time in my life, though, I was only equivocal. In addition to being relationship-fatigued, I was still buffeted by waves of culture shock, having been transplanted from city to village, Minnesota to Yamaguchi, graduate school to teaching children. Some days I hardly knew my own mind, my own heart.

At the end of our short weekend of hiking and sight-seeing, we broke camp, packing up Hideo's tent and supplies. After carefully rolling up my sleeping bag, I visited the campground restroom to prepare for our bus and then car ride, a little more touring and our all-too-familiar train platform farewell. When I returned to our campsite, I found Hideo rerolling my sleeping bag.

And that is when I snapped. My memory of how exactly I snapped has, thankfully, been lost to time. I imagine I stopped short, watched him for a moment, my eyes widening, and, unsuccessfully trying to keep my voice at a whisper, demanding, "*Naze mō ikkai tsutsundeimasu ka?*" — "Why are you tying it again?" I probably grabbed the sleeping bag away from him and unfastened his tidy ties. Did I jump up and down on the bag? I certainly wanted to. Did I throw the bag on the ground and stomp off? Maybe. Did I cry hot tears of fury? Definitely. Did I look utterly crazy? Absolutely.

It seems ridiculous even to me that our relationship, one of great complication and devotion, one that had endured such challenge, one with which I identified so fully that our mismatched names — HideoandSarah — blended naturally in my ear, would encounter its worst storm yet with an event as trifling as this. But there it was: his seeking a more perfectly compact sleeping bag than I could deliver had pushed me over some edge neither of us knew existed.

Just like the canoeing incident in Minnesota had not been about canoeing, and the log bridge fiasco had not been about getting to the other side of the muck, this moment was not about a sleeping bag. In fact, it was almost not about Hideo. What it represented for me was a microcosm of the Japan I could not and most likely would not ever be able to satisfy. It was just another example of how in Japan I was *chigau*.

Japan favors the compact, from people to cars to *bento* boxes. Everyone seems most comfortable when everything fits: a place for everything and everything in its place. One of the ultimate Japanese compliments is to say that something or someone is *"kichin"* ("just so"). And "just so" often means compact.

I was not *kichin*, not physically, and not in the way I lived, my tendency toward entropy, papers spread across my desk, projects in varying stages of doneness lining the walls of my apartment, my eclectic and last-minute style of planning and decision-making, my lack of attention to the details of life. Early in our relationship, Hideo had noticed the way I neglected my umbrella, quickly scrunching the fabric together, snapping it shut and tossing it in my bag. Once, he rescued the poor bedraggled thing, shaking loose its nylon fabric and carefully, precisely rewinding it on its shaft, forming each crease as sharp and true as the leg of a well-pressed trouser before snapping it shut and handing it back to me. "You must be a lady," he admonished me with a smile. I was charmed. That might be a fun persona to try, I thought. I could be a lady.

But after a year and a half of feeling like the big galoot — the most unladylike person — in every room, in the school, in the town, on the train, in the temple and now in a national park, I was tired of trying to be someone I was not, tired of being wrong. And that is exactly how his redoing of my task made me feel: I was simply *chigau* — "wrong" — and this time at something I had experience with — rolling a sleeping bag, something that was culture-neutral, something in the physical world, a task for which I should have been on level footing. I had done my bit and thought I had gotten it right. But yet again I was *chigau.*

Maybe my going off the cliff had something to do with the ante being upped. Hideo's parents, whom I had not met, had invited me to join the family, including Hideo's older sister and her husband and children, for the upcoming winter holiday. I imagine the nearing of this visit was causing Hideo to look at me with different eyes, with his family's eyes, and to begin expecting more of me — more compliance with, or at least tolerance of, the mores of his culture. Perhaps the closer he came to bringing me to his family home, the more he began to envision me there, worrying whether I would fit or reveal myself to be a bull in the china shop. Or maybe it was in my own mind that this question was weighing most heavily.

What Hideo might not have understood was that although I had a growing awareness and understanding of his culture, and I worked to fit in as much as possible, I did not want to be fully absorbed by it. It probably is not too much of an exaggeration to say, however ridiculous this might sound, that on some level I wanted to *change* it — yes, change this culture that had been functioning without my intervention for thousands of years. I wanted women to have the same opportunities and rights as men, and I wanted foreigners to be allowed to blend in more deeply, to not always be regarded as special cases and exceptions.

At the same time I knew I was about as likely to change the Japanese culture as a lacey snowflake landing in a puddle could turn water droplets into snow.

All the pressures I felt closing in on me — the visit to the parents, the talk of marriage, the culture shock of not fitting in — caused me to fill with self-righteous indignation. At least that is my excuse for playing log-bridge chicken with a middle-aged man who was probably trying to escape all of *his* cares and woes amid the beautiful scenery of Nagano. It is also my excuse for becoming incensed at another man, my man, for rerolling my sleeping bag.

But I make these excuses in retrospect. At the time, having lost my temper, I went further, taking a step I had been considering, and dreading, for a while: there, in that peaceful, picturesque campsite, I announced to Hideo that I needed a break from our relationship.

He was stunned. And once the words had left my lips I felt as if I had let the string of a bright helium balloon slip through my fingers. As it rose up, up, up through the treetops, as it floated toward the lake and caught a draught toward the craggy mountains, I hastened to explain that I needed time to figure out my heart without the pressure of playing the to-marry or not-to-marry game. I told him that I loved him, but I was confused, that I loved being in Japan, but the culture was making me nuts, that I could not envision living out my life in that country, or how I would support him in mine, that I could not imagine life without him, but neither could I see a way to be forever with him. I had been diving for a long time in the deep sea of our relationship and needed to come up for air, needed to see where — and who — I was.

For him, my coming up for air seemed to mean that I would soon be climbing aboard a waiting vessel, drying off, and sailing away forever.

Later that day, we drove, faces tear-stained, to Shirahone — "White Bone" — Onsen, a famous hot spring with milky-looking water containing pure-white mineral shards that are supposed to heal most anything that ails. Hideo entered the men's changing room, and I entered the women's, which was empty but for me. Sitting on my little stool before a bank of mirrors and water spigots, I washed with sweet-smelling ylang ylang soap, trying to scrub away the grime of camping and the sadness of our morning. I felt little better, though, as I pushed open the door to the outdoor soaking pool. Naked and alone, I eased into the hot water, letting it envelop me to my chin.

Several rough-hewn logs had been stacked to form a rustic privacy barrier between the men's and women's areas of the bath, but through the narrow gaps I could hear a couple of men in animated discussion. Their voices and splashes began moving closer and closer to the logs until all at once I heard Hideo's voice. Then silence.

Afterward, in the car, Hideo told me the men had been eager to take a peek at "the *gaijin*" — the outside person, the foreigner, me — but he had interrupted their game, telling them that he would charge them for the view.

Odd as it was to hear myself described as a commodity, I warmed to his protectiveness, knowing that he had been defending my honor. In that moment, in the midst of a hard, sad day, it was bliss to know he still regarded me as his.

40

No Limits

For the record, my maniacal-sounding dream of change for Japan was not one of simple selfishness. I did not want Japanese society to transform just so it would be friendlier to me, or to other foreign women. I wanted it to change also for the sake of the girls I taught, the ones who dreamed of becoming the future OLs (office ladies) of Japan.

The previous March, I had watched the South Junior High ninth-graders graduate. Sitting with the other teachers, I spent much of the ceremony with a lump in my throat, mourning the pending loss of those students, many of whom I had come to care deeply about and knowing that once they transferred to their various high schools I probably would never see them again.

I felt a growing tightness in my chest though as it became clear that the show was being run almost entirely by men: the school's head teacher emceed the ceremony, the vice principal offered greetings to those gathered, the Board of Education head and assistant mayor gave speeches, the principal spoke and presented diplomas, and fathers thanked the school on behalf of parents' groups. The only women playing active roles were the school nurse, who silently delivered the tray of diplomas to the principal, and the music teacher, who provided piano accompaniment to the national anthem, school song, and "Auld Lang Syne."

Realizing that the primary adult involvement would be one hundred percent male was disappointing enough, but when the students lined up to receive their diplomas, I watched in disbelief as all of the boys walked across the stage first, the girls trailing afterward.

It was like watching a dramatization of situations Jane Condon described only a few years previously in her 1991 book *A Half Step Behind: Japanese Women Today*, which had been stoking my ire as I witnessed how ubiquitous Japan's limitations and expectations were when it came to women. Although I did not hear anyone overtly telling the girls to aim low in Shuho-cho, situations like the graduation ceremony seemed to send clear messages: boys have greater value to the world of education and work; boys are more important.

At the time, in the mid-1990s, four-year universities drew almost 39 percent of male high school graduates but only 21 percent of females. Junior colleges served nearly a quarter of Japan's female high school graduates but only 2 percent of males. Why? At least part of the explanation was an assumption that women would quit work when they married — at age 26.3 in 1995 — so those who attended junior college would have more working years to offer than graduates who spent more time on four-year degrees.

Unless Japanese society were to change drastically, a substantially greater percentage of these ninth-grade boys would end up pursuing four-year degrees and finding a wider world of opportunity than the girls — although the girls were the ones who excelled in my classes.

One of those girls was Reika, and she gave me reason for hope that graduation day. Despite her obvious handicap — being a girl — she was selected to speak on behalf of the students. Reika was a standout — bright, friendly, athletic and polite — and she imagined a spectacular future for herself: she wanted to be an astronaut. I wanted nothing more than for her to achieve that dream, or whatever her true calling would end up being, so she could return to Shuho-cho and share her story, inspiring more girls to dream big. But I knew societal pressure was against her.

After the ceremony, I needed some answers. I asked my colleagues, *"Why did the boys receive their diplomas before the girls?"*

The answer: *"Well, they were presented in the order of the class lists."*

So I asked the next obvious question, *"Why are the class lists divided, with the boys always at the top?"*

The answer: a look of surprise. I might as well have asked why summer follows spring.

Locally, few women held leadership positions in education. Seats on the Board of Education were filled with blue business-suited men, and among the leaders of the town's two junior high schools and six elementary schools, there was only one woman — vice principal at a twenty-five-student elementary school. As for teachers, only 30 percent of Shuho-cho's junior high school teachers were women, and that included each school's nurse and secretary. Of the non-school offices I visited, I saw women serving mostly as clerks and OLs.

This was not unusual. Nationally, women accounted for nearly 40 percent of Japan's labor force but only 2 percent of all officials and managers, according to the 1990 census. Of professional workers, like physicians, accountants, lawyers, and university professors, fewer than 20 percent were women.

What disappointed me even more than these facts was that the trend did not seem to be changing. In 1995, more than 80 percent of female university seniors seeking jobs at the Tokyo Student Employment Center were looking for clerical work, keeping the office lady dream alive and well. And although 133 jobs awaited every hundred male college graduates, there were — stunningly — only forty-five available for every hundred female graduates, according to a survey of six thousand companies doing the hiring.

No wonder so many of my female students told me they wanted to grow up to be OLs. Given their role models and experiences, other choices would require swimming against a strong current. If becoming an OL was their true calling, Godspeed. But I wanted them to take that route out of desire, not for lack of imagination or opportunity.

* * *

When I was a teen, I had a bulletin board behind my bedroom door, and it became a repository for all sorts of flotsam: movie tickets, achievement certificates, photos of friends, magazine clippings, and a small print of Jesus.

One of the push-pinned items I remember most clearly was an advertisement. Part of a bank's direct-mail campaign, it was a photograph of a landscape somewhere on the northern Great Plains. Taken at eye level, it captured the moment of quiet that arrives just after sunset on a late-summer day, the sky glowing a nearly uniform pink over a flat green field. On the right side of the image sat a simple clapboard house. Superimposed was the sentence, "There are no limits."

The ad was intended to alert customers that the bank had abolished lending restrictions, but for me it depicted a perfect marriage of image and idea, the familiar flat, wide-open topography reflecting the mindset I grew up with.

The region where I was raised is a place where there are, in the physical sense, no visible limits. It took only a short drive or bicycle ride to get to the edge of town and find an immeasurable vastness, no hills and few trees to block the view. Get a little ways out on a county road and there is the horizon, 360 degrees of it. Take a drive in the rural night and you are gliding through a jeweler's black velvet-lined case, a glittering pendant lighting a nearby farmyard, a strand of pearls stretching down a small-town Main Street.

I did not always recognize this starkness as beauty, and there was no denying that Fargo-Moorhead was less glamorous than "The Cities" — Minneapolis–St. Paul — 250 miles to the south, and nowhere near as cool as "D.L." — Detroit Lakes, Minnesota — forty miles to the east, which achieved high notoriety when *Playboy* named it one of the country's top places to get picked up on the Fourth of July. But when the bank mailed my parents this ad, it sparked in me a deep pride and made me feel as if I lived somewhere more special than I had realized. The slogan "There are no limits" became my rallying call — one that I bought into with all my literal, optimistic little heart. Where I came from, there was at least the illusion that everything was within reach, and if not within reach, at least within sight.

Perhaps this is why I grew up assuming that if I used my head I would be able to solve any problem that arrived in my backyard. My family is fond of saying, "No one can sneak up on you here," and I guess I figured if some danger were circling, literal or figurative, surely I would see its shadow approaching, and that would give me time to make a plan. Failing that, a faithful neighbor would surely bail me out. As the years passed I found myself wrong on some counts, optimism crossing into unlucky naïveté, but in general this attitude of limitlessness served me well.

In Japan as a young adult, I felt as if I was struggling against a philosophy that came with a very different tagline. "*Shikata ga nai*" — "It can't be helped" — was an oft-repeated sentiment, and I was especially loathe to hear it from my students, who used it to explain away their too-busy schedules of sports practices and after-school tutoring sessions, or to rationalize why the girls received their diplomas after the boys. To my mind, "*Shikata ga nai*" could be translated as "There are limits. Don't even try to breach them." Anathema.

I wonder if there is a correlation between topography and attitude. In contrast to the part of Minnesota where I grew up, Shuho-cho — and much of Japan — is broken up by low, soft mountains that make it impossible to see into the next neighborhood, much less the next town. There are visual limits everywhere. Do these translate into aspirational boundaries as well?

Or were these limits a product of the eyes and ears that everyone knew were at every window, every wall? Eyes and ears that caused the townspeople to maintain the status quo, that required women to drop their work to serve tea and girls to set their sights on becoming OLs, as boys expected to be presented with their diplomas, to hear their names, their futures, called first.

* * *

I must have been grumbling, because that autumn one of my co-teachers invited me to speak briefly about my observations on gender issues to an auditorium of students at a gathering he was facilitating in a nearby town. I prepared and presented a short speech in English. It seemed to go OK, but I wondered how much anyone understood.

Word somehow got out, though, and I was invited to expand my presentation to a thirty-minute talk for a gathering in Shuho-cho of some fifty adults, from young people to grandparents. In Japanese.

I felt sick to my stomach at the idea of standing before this group, townspeople to whom I was connected by an intricate web of students, their children and grandchildren, and common acquaintances in the koto club, in the town English conversation class with which I assisted, in the shops and the neighborhoods. I wondered if my critique of their culture, in their language, would cause them to look at their situation anew, or at me anew, or both. The net effect could be negative, and I would not know until it was too late, until I had taken off my mask and revealed some of my *honne*, my true thoughts.

When the time came, there was nothing to do but dive in. I began with a disclaimer: I was not arguing that either the American way or the Japanese way was correct or incorrect. I was merely sharing the perceptions of one American woman living for a short time in Shuho-cho. I took the tack of presenting the cultural differences I had encountered as "surprising" to me. There were a lot of surprises.

I described going to the *ryōkan* (which, for propriety's sake, I camouflaged as a traditional restaurant, rather than an inn) and being informed that I was sitting in the high position, where my male friend should have been sitting.

I spoke of my American grandmother's surprise that I was serving tea at the office. She had worked decades earlier at a county court-house in Illinois, where tea and coffee had always been self-service, every employee washing his or her own cup.

I told them about my dismay with Children's Day, May 5, which until 1948 was known as Boys' Day, and from what I could see remained the province of boys, as homes with sons flew giant cel-ebratory carp banners from the rooftops. By contrast, Girls' Day, March 3, was kept quiet, inside the house, where elaborately painted dolls were set up in stepwise fashion on red fabric-covered risers — and put away quickly lest a prolonged display would, as super-stition claimed, have a negative effect on the girls' marriageability. Again, the message was clear: the presence of sons is broadcast to the wide world, but daughters are kept like secrets.

I related what I had read about the Japanese idea of *koshikake*, meaning taking a seat for a short period of time, and how the term was used to describe the way in which women would occupy a position in the labor force only briefly, filling time before leaving to marry and have children. Hence young women's predominance in junior colleges, and service and clerical positions.

In my little town, I saw many women in the workforce — some single but many married with children and grandchildren. I wondered how many had decided not to shoot for their dreams because of the idea of *koshikake* ... but found themselves working during much of their lives anyway. I shared my worries about the middle schoolers and elementary schoolers I was teaching — especially the hard-working, enthusiastic girls with bright ideas who, I feared, had little sense of how broad and diverse their futures could be. I told them I wanted the girls' dreams to be as exciting as the boys'. But how could they be, when most of their teachers were male, when their names were listed below the boys' on class lists, when their diplomas were presented at the end of the ceremony? The implication was that their education was worth less, and that it would lead to short-term work anyway. How could these future women buy into a notion of their own equality?

I walked my audience through its own history, beginning millennia ago when Japanese women were rulers and warriors, before Japanese scholars brought Confucianism home from China, an import that caused women's status to plummet with its declarations that a girl was to obey her father, then her husband and then her son.

I reminded them of the women's movements that began in the Meiji period, when everyone was said to be equal, but women still had lower status. And I broached how after World War II, the Americans and Japanese worked together to create a new constitution, one that forbade discrimination, including against women, and required schools to provide the same education to girls and boys.

I also acknowledged that the United States and Japan shared some problems, which I was just beginning to recognize while in Japan: we too were still dealing with harassment; we too were earning less money than men for performing the same work. My homeland did not have this completely figured out either.

Then, since I was taking my moment on the soapbox, I shared my least-favorite saying: "*Shikata ga nai.*" I said I did not believe there was nothing to be done about this situation. Surely we could do something to ensure that our students today would have better opportunities than previous generations. *After all,* I told the group, *if we see something negative in our society — something that affects approximately 50 percent of our population — it is our duty to change it. Each person should have the same chance at a good life. This is everyone's responsibility. This can be helped.*

Because I was speaking in Japanese, using vocabulary I had learned specifically for the occasion, I kept to my notes but looked up and made eye contact as often as I could, taking the temperature of my audience — ready to duck or run if need be.

What I saw, though, were heads bobbing encouragingly, eyes opened wide with interest. Now and then I heard a burst of good-natured laughter.

And when I finished, they were eager to ask questions, some intended to elicit more information about the United States, others to teach me about Japan: "Are there anti-female superstitions in America?" "Do American women study as they grow older, like Japanese women do?"

I answered as best I could, realizing how much more there was to learn about my culture and Japan's, and when our time was up, I went on with my day. I had experienced none of the negative repercussions I had feared. Nevertheless, it seemed unlikely that my preaching the gospel of equality and opportunity would catalyze any change. But maybe by advocating on behalf of my female students and colleagues, I had moved the ball a small step forward.

Even if it had made no difference to my listeners, giving that talk made a difference to me. I had put my feelings into words, translated them into the language of the culture I was critiquing and shared it with neighbors and colleagues. It was an exercise that forced me to recognize the good and the bad in both of our cultures, and the graciousness of my listeners helped me put aside some of my frustrations.

And it gave me a little holiday from my broken heart.

41

Lukewarm

WHEN the winter holidays arrived, I did not spend them with Hideo, his parents, and his sister's family up north. Instead, I retreated to Minnesota, to the snowy windswept prairie, to be with my own people, an attempt to pull head and heart back together, to begin seeking out a vision for the future, if in fact it were to lead me back to the United States. I had told the Shuho-cho Board of Education that I would be leaving when my contract ended that coming summer. I had closed my own door, and by autumn a new JET would be living in my Shuho-cho apartment and sitting at my various desks around town.

Just as when my husband and I had separated and I threw myself into my studies, teaching, and writing, when Hideo and I hit hard times, I defaulted to hyperactivity, my safe zone. When not teaching, I read books and articles about gender relations, and I wrote essays about my experiences in Shuho-cho for my master's project. I explored career options.

But as before, the flurry of activity was all about distraction. Internally, every other thought concerned what I should have done differently in the past and whether there were any signs pointing me in the right direction now. I do not recall whether I was prayerful over my situation with Hideo, but I was searching. I was anxious.

Hideo and I had already embarked on some fretful months of mostly silent, tearful phone calls mixed with a few hopeful visits. We met up in Kyoto for the fall colors and visited Kiyomizu Temple, where I had toured with my mother and Kay more than half a year previously. That earlier time, I had encountered the shrine devoted to love and had successfully made my blind love-walk, one foot in front of the other, stone to stone. This time, the maple leaves, the size and shape of babies' hands, glowed richly under gray skies as Hideo and I gazed out at the city from the temple's grand timbered balcony, that place Japanese people reference when making important decisions. We did not jump, literally or figuratively.

But I asked a stranger to take our photo there, and some days later, retrieving the envelope from the Shuho-cho photo shop, I saw in the picture's foreground someone's chubby baby, straight black hair, deep brown eyes, curious mouth. When I sent copies home, my mother wondered aloud whether that little one was a harbinger of a future with Hideo, a sneak peek at what her future grandchild might look like.

As months passed, I leaned toward being apologetic about my need for space and time; Hideo, after an initial period of almost saintly kindness — reminding me to take my vitamins, advising me to soothe myself with evening tub soaks, making himself available to talk every night — headed toward hardness of heart. En route to my Christmas in Minnesota, I stopped over in Tokyo for a night and found his eyes empty, his mouth a hard, flat line.

Despite his changing demeanor, I could not give up on us. While in St. Paul, dropping in on mentors, advisers, and dream employers, I felt compelled to call him. After one phone booth failed to connect me with him, I tried another. This time he answered, sleepy, then suddenly alert, thanking me. He had overslept and needed to race to get ready for work. Thousands of miles away, I had, it seemed, sensed his need of me. *Was this my sign? Did I need him too?*

In January we met up again in Kyoto, where I gave him a belated Christmas present, carefully selected in Minnesota, a blue silk tie printed with fish. He had nothing for me. This deviation from our usual roles — his being that of the consummate giver — felt like a blow. Unrequited gift, unrequited love. Later, as we browsed in a Kyoto shop, he secretly procured for me a pack of incense and a handkerchief, elegant but impersonal.

Our frustrations of the autumn and my professed need for space, then my choosing my family over his at the holidays, seemed to have caused us to lose the path back to each other's hearts. I recognized this geography all too well — the fruitless search for a road that seemed to have been erased from the map. I was heartbroken. When I had asked for space, I had not envisioned being left to my own universe.

At the end of our awkward weekend, as we stood on the platform at Kyoto Station, preparing to part once again, I had a revelation: if we stayed together, I would need to make tremendous sacrifices, such as giving up my country. With his current English skills, he would have few career prospects in the States, so we would have little choice but to follow his career with the company he had already married—one that would transfer him at whim for the rest of his working life. I could teach English anywhere. My American friends and family would become blurry forms, seen on rushed once-a-year visits.

Nothing specific had happened on the train platform to bring about this sense of clarity. But somehow I finally acknowledged not only the inclusion in the glass ball of our relationship but also the deeper seat of my fears: I was not ready to trade my freedom and my future for Hideo. Nor for anyone else. Not now.

The realization, which recalled similar misgivings of three years earlier, was too raw to share with him that day, when I could barely admit the truth of it to myself. If I had tried to explain it, I would probably have sounded selfish. It seemed to emerge from the same emotional palette as when I told my ex-husband that I needed out of our marriage, and soon thereafter, when I began to doubt myself, a phrase had entered my mind: "benevolent selfishness." At first I had focused on the selfishness of breaking my vows and choosing myself over couplehood. Such an act would fly in the face of how I had been raised by my family and by my church. Marriage was supposed to be forever.

But the more I thought about it, the more I realized that reclaiming my life could actually be a benevolent act. I recalled the old saw, "If Mama ain't happy, ain't nobody happy," and applied it to myself. For the previous year or more I had been so focused on my own sadness that I could not listen to anyone else's troubles. I had no energy to take on their concerns, and I struggled to share in their joys. Surely this was not the way life was meant to be, this was not what God would want for me or for those around me, even if the alternative was divorce. I determined that if I were to embrace my so-called selfishness and reclaim my single life, I would be able to move on from my heartbreak and look outward, being benevolent, helpful and useful to others.

Now with Hideo, I applied similar logic. If I made the best decision for me, it would probably also be — big picture — the best decision for Hideo and for the other people in our life.

Our lives.

Back in Shuho-cho, I waited for the universe, for circumstance, for the Power that Is, to show me that my so-called moment of clarity was simply evidence of an off day or a symptom of culture shock. I watched the want ads in the *Japan Times* for job opportunities closer to Tokyo, closer to Hideo, thinking the distance, which I once thought was saving us from moving too quickly, was now what was doing us in.

Did I pray for guidance, for help discerning my future? Certainly not in any sustained or thoughtful way. At one point I told my parents in an email that I had begun thinking I should pull out my Bible to see what guidance it might offer, but we all knew I was only joking. Our family didn't do that sort of thing, at least not that we would admit — we maintained a separation of church and fate. Sometimes, in the past, when I had asked Hideo questions, he had given me answers I did not like. When I fought his explanations, he always said, *"If you don't want to hear the answer, don't ask the question."* Maybe now I was avoiding God because I sensed that he might sort out my confusion in a way I was not ready to accept. So I kept hacking away at the unknown, struggling to figure out what was next for my relationship, my career, my life. I felt very much alone.

Finding some promising classified ads for teachers in the Kyoto area, I told Hideo I would consider moving to that halfway point between Shuho-cho and Tokyo after my JET contract ended.

There is a Japanese saying, *"Uō saō,"* which means to go this way and that, circling in search of a solution. I was like a bird with an injured wing, flying round and round over the same scenery. Hideo must have recognized this was my state and the futility of getting involved once again. When I offered to move his way, he reacted with indifference, neither encouraging nor discouraging, reminding me how much harder it is to be lonely than alone, how much more uncomfortable it is to be lukewarm than cold.

42

The Change of Seasons

MEMORIES of that winter, months during which my relationship
with Hideo unraveled, skip like a flat rock over still water:

- My fingers press pussy willows, carnations and *nanohana* into
  a *kenzan* — a pin frog — at ikebana class.
- Sasaki-*san*, his face still pale and half-slack, rings my doorbell
  with his wife, bowing and thanking me for my hospital visits.
- Mrs. Kawajiri, the Dwelling Friends *obasan*, sits at my kitchen
  table for dinner, both of us melancholy for Hideo.
- A half dozen Nice Middies sit around my *kotatsu*, giggling as we
  practice conversations in English.
- I stand in kimono and silver *geta*, hands folded primly, knees
  slightly bent, toes pointing toward each other for an *omiai*-style
  studio photograph arranged by the middle-aged friend who had
  given me the kimono. I wonder if she knows I am not so prim,
  not completely single, not seeking anyone.

My mental sightseeing feels incomplete, as if most of the slides have fallen out of the carousel, the screen dark, like a new moon. What I remember most are the feelings of that season. I clung to the hope that Hideo and I might sort out our situation and remain together on the other side.

As time passed, though, the break that I told Hideo I needed on our trip to Nagano had proved catastrophic. It had broken the spell our relationship held over him, and as winter turned toward spring, I could see that there was no going back. Our bond had been forever altered.

After limping through some more months of quiet phone calls and spending day after day trying to fill my time and avoid thinking about Hideo's and my flagging relationship, we agreed to break up completely. Hideo called our decision "divorsion," his new word taking "divorce" to a new level, adding a hint of "torsion," which perfectly described the way my heart felt twisted around itself as I envisioned the rest of my time in Japan without him, the rest of my life without him, knowing I had catalyzed this ending of something good.

Perhaps what made this breakup most poignant was that we each, in the end, agreed to it so gently.

* * *

When the wind turned warm and blew the first breaths of spring into Shuho-cho, with it came the realization that it had brought my last full season there. I would leave by mid-summer.

With that sense of finality and Hideo's palpable absence, I turned my focus to family, my host family, whom I had been visiting all along but with the casual regard young people have for people they assume to be permanent in their lives, people who it is easy to believe will always live just a quick drive away.

As a child — and as an adult as well — I had taken my own parents for granted. (Much as I was also taking God for granted.) Although their touch had registered in every area of my life, they were often all but unnoticeable, like the familiar wallpaper pattern that forms a backdrop to posters of pop stars and animals.

I had been benefitting from my host parents' and grandmother's quiet care, their comforting presence nearby. Although we had not met until I was sixteen and had long gaps in our shared history after that, I felt almost as comfortable with them as I did with my own parents, treating them similarly, going for spells without contact and then having no qualms about popping up unexpectedly, reentering their life. With my time in Shuho-cho drawing to a close, I realized they — or I — might not be around forever, and almost certainly would not be within visiting distance in my future life, wherever that might take me.

Obāchan's — my host grandmother's — eighty-fifth birthday arrived in April. I went to Hagi to spend the weekend with her and Okāsan, and baked a white birthday cake with brown-sugar frosting before we went to view cherry blossoms on Hagi's old castle grounds. Obāchan, who hardly ever left the house, was showing her age that day, moving so slowly and, giving into her aching knees, pushing a walker. Walking beside her, looking down on her tiny frame, I could see she was beyond aged. She was en route to fragile.

As we approached the castle grounds, we stopped at a pottery shop adjacent to the castle moat, and Obāchan marked her own special occasion by buying me a gift, a Hagi-yaki tea cup, its glaze the pale color of Yamaguchi soils, its face carved with a soft line reminiscent of waves moving gently across the nearby sea. It felt like farewell.

I made an increasing number of visits to Hagi that spring and summer, flowers dictating my schedule: the blooming of lavender wisteria, like sweet peas gone mad, climbing densely up and down trellises over the old castle grounds' dusty paths, cascading blooms enclosing us in flower-walled rooms; the nearby gardenia forest with its twenty-five thousand blooming trees, petals of red, pink, and white framing fringy yellow centers; a peony garden with blossoms so absurdly oversized that they dwarfed our heads.

My albums from those flower-finding expeditions are full of showy, confident blooms at the zenith of their beauty, my host parents and grandmother standing stiffly among them. Images of me show shirts and jeans hanging baggy off my hips and shoulders, which seem to sag under the weight of trying to figure out the future. My hair droops, and my mouth smiles beneath eyes that betray a rudderless uncertainty.

43

Working Out

THERE was nothing to be done about my heart, no way to dull it to my loss of Hideo, who I feared had been the love of my life, a love now apparently squandered. Neither was there a way to shield my heart from the coming pain of saying farewell to my host family, my friends, my squirrelly students, the apartment-refuge I had come to fully inhabit, the lush green rice paddies and mossy roadside statues I passed on my bicycle, the greetings at the grocery store I had come to welcome, the smoky smell of burning rubbish, my Shuho-cho life.

But I could do something about my body, the only thing I could even pretend to control, and get it in shape for whatever lay ahead. I started driving to a nearby city where another JET, a lively British woman, had discovered a beautiful swimming pool, where we began meeting up to swim laps. Our good-natured competition in the water was helping us both feel fitter by the week, and being with a fellow Westerner, I was beginning to envision reconnecting with my old life in Minnesota.

The only downside was that my neck had begun to click when I swam the backstroke, and soon it was making noises on dry land as well, giving me the sensation that there was sand in my spine. It was bearable, but before long I realized that when driving, I had all but stopped looking over my shoulder to check for traffic when changing lanes. This was untenable.

A JET friend living near the larger city of Shimonoseki, a couple of hours away, suggested I visit a doctor she knew there, a practitioner of Asian medicine who had worked on the backs of other JETs with good results. Curious, I asked her to make me an appointment and imagined myself meeting a serene man glowing with health and working in an oasis of calm. I pictured a clinic built in the traditional Japanese style, all wood and plaster, tatami-mat flooring, soft incandescent lighting and soothing sounds, sweet incense burning and haunting *shakuhachi* music playing in the background.

The only things my imagination got right were the tatami and the incense.

Yagi-*sensei* greeted us in what I recall to be an old T-shirt and athletic pants, although that part is fuzzy, because I was distracted by the absence of one of his front teeth and the presence of many crystals and gold chains hanging from his neck. He was of average height for a Japanese man but on the heavy side, and we followed him into his home where his practice was set up in a tatami room with jittery neon ceiling lamps and a television tuned to game shows.

While my friend waited in the next room, Yagi-*sensei* had me lie down on a mat on top of the tatami and gave me a once-over, quickly zeroing in on my legs, which have always been stockier than the rest of my body. "*They're always like this,*" I told him. "*This is normal, a family trait.*" "*No,*" he replied, "*you have bad kidneys.*"

He proceeded to prod at my gut, checking out each organ in turn and reporting that all of them were swollen. I tried to relax but wondered if his exertions might disconnect a critical tube. He expressed surprise that I was not in a doctor's care — for what I was not entirely sure. My neck problems (and what I regarded as the normal state of my legs) were, he insisted, related to my malfunctioning kidneys.

Diagnosis made, he set to work, beginning with my feet and ankles, using his hands to press and squeeze and knead upward, toward my kidneys. Gradually he massaged his way up to my knees and then my thighs, pushing, pushing, pushing my flesh — or was it my fluids? — northward. I wondered if he was right, whether his exertion would take the stockiness out of my legs ... whether it would simply overwhelm my poor kidneys. Was he really a doctor of anything or just some crazy guy who had hung out a shingle?

But my friend had vouched for him and told me how he helped another JET who had been having stomach pains. Yagi-*sensei* told her she had a ghost in her stomach and that he could get it to pass out like food. After he had worked on her, she woke up in the middle of the night with horrendous gas pains, pains so strong that she could not even get to the telephone to call for help. And then suddenly it was all gone — presumably with the ghost. Maybe there was something to what he was doing.

As this strange doctor worked on me, pushing and prodding away, he explained that twelve years earlier he had begun studying to be a chiropractor, but six years into training he had realized he possessed healing powers, bequeathed to him by the sun goddess, Amaterasu, whose amulet he wore on a chain around his neck, Amaterasu, whose various images hung from his walls, rays of light emanating from behind her.

Wait. He was employing the power of a *goddess* to work on my kidneys? I thought of Hideo and his certain disapproval.

In the Shinto creation myth, Amaterasu rules the heavens, and her brother rules the sea. One day, the brother tossed a flayed horse into the goddess's weaving room, desecrating her home, so she ran away and hid in a cave. The world went dark.

Something had to be done, so the other gods assembled outside her cave with a whole flock of roosters, and they hung a mirror and jewels from a tree. The noise they made caused Amaterasu to become curious, and at last she peeked out to see what was happening. When she did, she caught sight of her reflection shining in the mirror, and all the cocks crowed, heralding the dawn. According to legend, the goddess reemerged and has ruled the heavens ever since.

I did not know she also assisted in the healing arts.

After working his way up my legs, he took on the organs in my gut, saying he was pushing out excess lymph and sending it back to my kidneys for processing. This did not seem to be the best idea, if indeed I had kidney problems, but it felt impossible not to go along with his plan. He had an air of authority, perhaps magnified by his claim to be working on behalf of a goddess.

Amaterasu is immobile, Yagi-*sensei* explained, but there is a god on her right and a goddess on her left — "*like Mary,*" he added, apparently trying to connect it to a paradigm I would understand — and those gods enabled him to heal people. And because he was using their powers, he said, his pushing on my body would not result in bruises. I hoped he was right.

Not sure what to say, especially in Japanese, I offered, "*It must be fun being able to help people like this.*" He seemed to take offense. "*Fun? Fun?!*" he replied. "*It's very tiring to have a god occupy your body!*"

I would have to take his word for it, but I wondered whether he was for real or delusional. And if he was for real, what was I messing with here? In my college world religions class I had heard the story of the blind men and the elephant in which each man described the elephant a different way, one holding its trunk, saying "It's like a snake!" and another holding its tail, saying "It's like a rope!" The idea is, of course, as the blind men had various views of the elephant, we humans, blind to the broader picture of life, have various views of God. Using this paradigm, I could say Yagi-*sensei* approached God via Amaterasu while I approached him via Jesus. We were all headed in the same direction.

I liked that view and the idea that a person could tap into the power of God (a god?) to help others. My God seemed mostly unreachable, but here was Yagi-*sensei*, connecting to a source of power. Still, the question Hideo asked when I prayed at a shrine or a temple — "*Why do you pray to gods that are not yours?*" — haunted me. Maybe the answer was that I loved how close I felt to God (or was it a god?) when I entered the quiet sphere of a temple or a shrine and inhaled the scent of burning incense — any time, not just on Sunday morning. It was so much more satisfying than showing up at a specific time each week in the brightly lit churches back home, which felt as ordinary as gymnasiums and invariably smelled of coffee.

As Yagi-*sensei* worked on me, I struggled. *Was his work like the laying on of hands I had experienced in college with the charismatic group on the Mexican border? If so, if he was indeed tapping into God's power, our shared God's power, why did he not look healthier himself?*

Finally, two and a half hours into my appointment, he asked about my neck. I felt almost smug when I reported that it still hurt, that he and his kidney/leg theory had not held. He turned his focus to my neck and shoulders, noting how knotted they were, then took my head in his hands and turned it. My neck cracked so loudly that my friend heard it in the next room. It still sounded sandy, so he examined my right arm and discovered that it clunked when I moved it. He took my arm backward into an awkward pose and pushed and pushed while prodding my back until tears filled my eyes. Then he pushed some more. Little by little my neck quieted down. *Over the next few days, it will feel better*, he said.

I paid him some money and left with my friend, glad to get out of that strange place.

Yagi-*sensei* was right about two things: over the next few days, my neck did feel better, and my legs did not bruise. They did, however, maintain their sturdy silhouette.

The whole experience made me wonder what it was in me that was most bunged up: my body, my spirit, or both. Maybe this is why my homing instinct was so strong. Despite my love for Japan, the beat of my surroundings seemed not to resonate with the rhythm of my nature. Was it possible that the food did not convert properly in my body, or perhaps the different thinking and faith patterns threw off my brain and spirit? Perhaps it was that I had no one who shared the faith in which I had been raised. Now I had allowed a so-called doctor to heal me in the name of a god I had no business engaging with, unless it was true that every god is a manifestation of my own. But thanks to Hideo, the spiritual world had grown more complicated than that for me.

At the time all I knew was I was off balance, and it seemed that feeling would remain no matter how long I stayed.

44

Great Commission

M Y preparations to depart Shuho-cho gained momentum as summer neared, events and tasks increasing in velocity until days ran together in a blur of planning, purging, packing, and parties, the bobsled of my life there careening faster and faster down the track toward final farewells.

Although my spacious apartment had grown increasingly cluttered over the two years, when I began to sort items into categories — things to leave, things to purge and things to pack — I was surprised by how much I had accumulated and how many decisions I needed to make.

Paper became my number-one adversary: lesson plans, posters and props, tourist pamphlets, newspaper articles, draft essays for my master's project and correspondence. The latter was the hardest to part with, especially the notes, cards and drawings from friends, acquaintances and students of all ages. I wondered how to properly deal with all the good wishes and thank-you notes. Ship them home to Minnesota? What then? Would I dump them onto my bedroom floor and settle into them like a pile of raked leaves, reading and rereading the proof that I had established a full life in a faraway place, in this floating world?

No, they would have to go. The question was how. One day as I was sorting and packing, I smelled smoke coming from the dormitory's refuse burner in the parking lot. This simple outdoor furnace, a base of concrete blocks topped with a metal box at chest height and a chimney tube, was used to burn anything that was not recyclable or compostable.

I peeked out my window and saw the parking lot was empty, so I grabbed paper bags full of notes and cards and crept down the dormitory's stairs. I swung open the heavy metal doors to the burner and began dropping in cards, letters and notes, one by one, trying to enjoy each of them one last time, hoping no one would catch me burning these offerings as the flames licked and then gobbled up so many kind words and sweet memories.

Gray ashes drifted out of the chimney and floated in the air around me. I inhaled deeply, deciding that even if I could not carry these treasures home with me, at least my lungs could assimilate some good wishes, conveying them into my body, my bloodstream, assimilating them into my very cells.

In the midst of my sentimental reverie, a cheery tune began to play from within the fiery furnace, and as I wondered what it was, it warped into an unpleasant noise, and then a deafening BANG! split the air, my ears ringing, all other sound suddenly muffled, my spell of melancholy broken. I realized a greeting card containing a music-playing chip and battery had ended up in the flames, and its explosion put triple exclamation points on my surreptitious endeavor.

Minutes later, one of my neighbors walked into the parking lot carrying bags of groceries and wearing a quizzical look. *Did you hear a loud noise?* she asked.

I hoped she would not peer into the burner.

* * *

There were many other items I could not imagine burning or leaving behind. Most were gifts, and as I carefully packed them in boxes, I could not help but feel as if I was plundering Shuho-cho's stock of beautiful things:

- The yellow kimono from my daughterless friend, along with dozens of kimono-related accoutrements — *obi, geta*, hair pins, multi-colored ties, a soft pink under-kimono, a white undergarment, mesh storage pouches, and a *kichin* maroon bag in which to carry it all.
- Keyholders, Hagi-yaki teacups and stuffed animals — all Christmas gifts from children.
- A pair of seashells wrapped in rich brocade and decorated to look like emperor and empress dolls, from a hostess working in a Yamaguchi bar.
- Tea ceremony bowls, one from a fellow teacher and one from a student.
- A pearl bracelet, amethyst earrings and mix tapes, from Hideo.
- A vase made of Akiyoshidō limestone.
- *Furoshiki* — cloths used to wrap and carry packages — in prints appropriate to every season.
- More handkerchiefs than I could ever use, decorated with flowers, rabbits, kangaroos and goldfish; ribbons and medallions; scenes of famous places.
- A *hanten* — quilted indoor jacket — from the Board of Education, size LL (double-large), naturally.

But this was not all. As my time there drew nearer its close, the gift-giving revved up, and as I taped shut my boxes, more items arrived:

- A celadon-colored kimono with peacock motif, sleeves draping almost to the ground, from a young woman who had worn it on her Coming-of-Age day.
- Pottery plates, made by an upstairs neighbor.
- Hundreds of *origami* cranes, strung by students for good luck.
- Pencils and erasers printed with puppies and *anime* characters.
- A shimmering gold fan and music book, from a neighbor's Noh performances.
- A ceramic piggy bank shaped like a red Japanese mailbox, from the neighborhood post office.
- Pearl necklaces and earrings, from my Nice Middy conversation group, the town workers and Mrs. Santo of the culture house.
- Handmade sacks and dolls, sewn and embroidered by students.
- Several sets of *Ouchi ningyō*, the emperor and empress dolls that are said to represent happily married couples.
- A pair of Hagi-yaki mugs from the woman who had leased me my car: "*For you and your future husband,*" she smiled. (I sighed.)

I received most of these gifts on final visits to schools and farewell parties, but others came out of nowhere as I went about my daily business, visiting the post office or the store, or simply walking from point A to point B. Near South Junior High, a student's grandmother approached me and handed me a bag containing three *temari* — balls wrapped with brilliantly colored threads, designs symbolizing wishes for happiness. Another woman stopped me in my neighborhood to give me a purse, the entire accessory beaded in an exquisite rose pattern.

Then came the item I found most difficult to interpret, brought by my Board of Education friends, Sasaki-*san*, Sato-*kakarichō*, and Yamamoto-*san*, when they came to my apartment for a pasta dinner: a white T-shirt featuring Lucy, of Peanuts fame, appearing self-satisfied and standing under four answers to an implied multiple-choice question:

- ○ a. arrogant
- ○ b. domineering
- ○ c. superior
- ○ d. all of the above

The circle for option D was marked with a red X. *Were my colleagues, my friends, intending it as a commentary on my character?* Looking up, I saw their smiling, expectant faces and knew they had brought only goodwill.

*   *   *

This gift inundation reminded me of being a bride. I felt humbled that the residents of my floating world would send me off so generously. And I was baffled at how I could ever repay the kindness of these people who had integrated me into their reality, perhaps more fully than I had realized.

I could not stay forever, and neither could I bring that place and its people home with me. But, I decided, I could haul its stuff, the beauty and the weight of which would remind me of the good people I was leaving behind.

In the end, I packed a dozen large boxes full of gifts, purchases, and photo albums, and shipped them to myself in Minnesota, in care of my parents, at a cost of roughly a thousand dollars.

*   *   *

The biggest gift was still to come. One Wednesday, I climbed the steps to the second floor of the Board of Education building for my koto lesson, and my teacher greeted me with a surprise: her old koto, the one I had been using the previous two years. She had decided to give it to me.

I was astounded. I had been told that to get set up with a koto would cost roughly a thousand dollars. "*No,*" I demurred, "*I cannot take your koto.*"

"*Yes,*" she insisted, "*you will.*" Besides, she said, it was only her *old* koto.

Looking at my *sensei,* I realized I had no choice in this matter. "*Dōmo arigatō gozaimasu!*" I said, bowing low, using the most formal, deepest "thank you" I knew.

And then she set out some conditions: before sending the koto home, I would have to get it restrung and refurbished for a few hundred dollars. "*Hai, Sensei,*" I said. Then, once home in Minnesota, I must introduce the koto's music to people there. "*Hai.*" There was nothing to negotiate. It was like receiving my own Great Commission.

Not long after I had gotten drawn into her world, my *sensei* had started working on me to purchase an instrument and get my license. Much as martial artists train to attain different colored belts, koto musicians study to attain ever-higher levels of competency and then licensure for teaching.

But I had refused to engage. My intent had been to spend a discrete, delete-able year in Japan. "*What would I do with a koto in America?*" I had asked her, imagining the burden of hauling and storing a six-foot-long instrument that I would have the rarest of opportunities to perform and no one with whom to practice or consult. I was just a beginner.

Now it dawned on me that my *sensei*'s vision, perhaps from the day we first met, had been for me to introduce the koto to the uninitiated masses across the Pacific. I felt the weight of what she was asking me. *How would I share the koto with America?* I had been tossed into the middle of a musical ocean — adopted into a koto club, quickly pulled into one performance, and then another and another. I had never stopped to learn anything about this instrument's history or theory. Just as my survival-based approach to learning the Japanese language, focusing on conversation instead of reading and writing, had left me mostly illiterate, my focus with the koto, scrambling to keep up with the other students, had caused me to learn songs loosely, theory flimsily, never considering the music's pentatonic nature or how it related to or contrasted with Western music. I was treading water all around and felt unqualified to teach or explain much of anything to anyone.

I had accepted the koto as part of my life in Japan mainly because of the benefits I could reap: membership in a club and an identity beyond the designation of "foreigner." I had, during my time there, tried out the idea of a future in Japan, one with Hideo. Had that worked out, it would have made sense to dive full bore into koto. But things had changed, and I had gone back to Plan A; I would re-board my time machine imminently.

But I had failed to consider my strong-willed *sensei* and her plans. She was making sure that her sector of Japan would accompany me home. As she sent the koto to a technician for restringing, I tried to imagine hauling that cumbersome instrument — along with all my other memorabilia — from place to place to place in the as-yet-blurry future that soon would appear.

When it was time for the town's *sayōnara* party, I, almost numb with the anticipation of missing my people and my Shuho-cho life, received a special gift from a group of Shuho-cho town workers: an orange brocade koto cover, festive cranes flying across it, and a somber black case to zip over that. Obediently I double-wrapped and mailed home my refurbished koto in a long, narrow, specially made cardboard box. Box number thirteen. It went via airmail, the only way the postal service would accept such a strangely shaped object. It would beat me back to Minnesota, where my parents opened their door to accept that oversized package containing a wrapped-up wooden instrument, memories of two years lived in a small Japanese town and reminder of an old woman's wish.

45

Never Mind

ALTHOUGH my departure preparations sound like a month's-worth of Christmases, it would have been far gentler on my heart to disappear earlier. Had I gone AWOL, I could have bypassed my lame-duck tenure, when it seemed I was fighting a future JET's battle to keep the Japanese language out of the English classroom. I could have avoided weeks spent as a ghost wandering about, enduring multiple farewells, unsure whether each encounter with a friend, colleague, or neighbor might be the last; I could have skipped my speech to the students and staff of South Junior High School, which turned into a teary onstage breakdown.

But had I just disappeared, I would have missed an opportunity to make a difference. Those farewell parties were more than gift-giving extravaganzas. They also functioned as a string of speaking engagements, invitations I had received to address various town groups, ostensibly to discuss my experience in Shuho-cho, to express my appreciation, to say goodbye, to loosen, untie, and snip the many loops, bows, and knots that had formed among us during those two years.

All of the speeches were to be made in Japanese, so in the interest of efficiency I wrote a standard talk that I could adapt to each audience. This was my opportunity to fulfill the JET goal of making cross-cultural connections as well as my desire to improve the lives of women. So I adopted a platform, à la Miss America, and because I was young and bold, and possessed more moxie than sense, I resurrected my gender issues talk — memories of Minnesota, observations of Shuho-cho, concerns for my female students — the whole deal. And I gave it over and over again, all around the town.

Because I had already come through a couple of these talks unscathed, I pushed my platform one step further. At the end of the speech, I tagged on three wishes, introducing them as my dreams for Shuho-cho:

1. that women would no longer be obligated to set aside their work to serve tea,
2. that class lists and graduation ceremonies would be integrated, and
3. that girls would be encouraged to imagine big futures and to chase their dreams.

At every venue, my audiences listened attentively and applauded warmly, although looking back I imagine some were aghast at my nerve. The closest hint I got that I was treading some touchy ground came after I spoke to the town council, whose members — all men, I believe — listened politely but impassively. A regional newspaper reporter was there to cover my speech, and when his story ran, I could see he had ignored my main message, focusing instead on a crowd-pleasing section about the beauty of *botan yuki*, peony snow.

Still, I knew my message was resonating elsewhere. When I spoke to a parent–teacher association, one of my most promising students and her mother listened, eyes wide, from the edge of their seats. At the end of my talk, I watched them hug each other, smiling, tears streaming down their cheeks.

* * *

A couple of evenings before I left Shuho-cho, five of my junior high school girls visited my apartment, and as I prepared pizza, they discussed the talk I had given at their school. They confessed that they had always disliked being placed after the boys on class lists and in ceremonies but had figured *shikata ga nai* — it was something that could not be helped or changed. Now they were rethinking their assumptions. They wanted to do something.

I listened greedily, delighted that I had found some young converts, thrilled to hear them rejecting the *shikata-ga-nai* mentality, the phrase that grated on my nerves. There had been many times I had wanted to shout, "Everything can be helped!" and I had felt a growing pride in the stock phrases of my own culture, such as "Help yourself," and "The best helping hand is at the end of your own arm." I felt like living proof of this, having spent the months preceding my arrival in Shuho-cho reclaiming my single status and mending my life when I realized no one else could or would.

Marriage was the first time I had gotten into what had seemed to be an insurmountable problem, and for a while I also had fallen into *shikata-ga-nai* thinking: I was married, a decision that could not be helped or changed, and I would simply have to find a way to make it work. But when altering my own expectations and reactions failed to improve that relationship, I began to change my thinking — and then my situation, removing myself all the way to Japan.

Resettled in Shuho-cho, I was indeed able to look beyond myself and encourage my female students, speak out about gender inequities in the classrooms and spark discussion about the tea-serving tradition. I did my best to be respectful while encouraging my students and colleagues to consider a different paradigm.

Even as I struggled with it, I began gaining an appreciation of *shikata-ga-nai*. I started to wonder whether when my friends said "It can't be helped" — about gender roles or career limitations or the weather — they were speaking from some deep cultural memory of battles physical and cultural that had been fought and lost. Maybe they were acknowledging that although they wanted change, it would take longer, maybe more than their lifetimes, and they, unlike my brasher, less patient compatriots in the United States, could accept that. Maybe they were tapping into a collective patience that gave them a peace I might never know.

Besides, what would happen if non-native philosophies took root in little Shuho-cho? There is a reason customs agents demand travelers declare foreign produce and plants. If a new seed is planted or bug introduced, it might die. Or it might thrive and not only thrive but take over and squeeze out native species that have been playing their own roles, holding hillsides in place for millennia. Similar to ideas.

Even I had begun to see that accepting some things can't be changed, at least not at the moment, can be a comfort. Rather than fight my lack of transportation so I could meet up with the other JETs, I had, for a while, accepted my isolation in the countryside — *shikata ga nai* — and thereby got to know a community and date an exemplary man. Rather than fixate on practicing the piano, I had become a member of the koto club that had recruited me — *shikata ga nai* — and as a result made new friends and encountered a whole new world of music.

I must have been approaching a point in the culture shock model where, although I was not fluent in the language and would make no claims to being bicultural, I could at least see the outlines of what made my home culture and my adopted culture tick, for good and for bad.

If I were to illustrate my perspective using woodblock prints, I would point to the *nishiki-e* — "brocade pictures" — those full-colored prints popularized by Hokusai, who famously crafted the *Great Wave off Kanagawa* and whose unflinching studies of bare-chested laborers and bent travelers, wrestlers and women of the floating world reveal a documentarian's view of the place he inhabited two centuries ago. Like Hokusai and his fellow *nishiki-e* artists, I had let go of the notion of Japan being a pink and green, two-dimensional refuge, a place where real hurt could not touch me. Having encountered Japan in its many forms, both its splendor and its problems, I had come to see it in full color. It was more than an exotic escape hatch. It was a multidimensional place of competing realities. My floating world had become real.

That pizza-party evening I learned that at least some of my students had heard my messages. Now they were reflecting my sentiments back to me and recognizing that things actually can be helped. People can change. Maybe society too.

"Hold on!" I thought, replaying in my mind the optimistic tales I had spun, imagining future repercussions. But it was too late. By the time I had begun to appreciate the *shikata ga nai* philosophy, I had riled things up in the other direction. These young girls, my students, were beginning to wonder whether things they did not like could actually be helped, and whether they might in fact be the ones to catalyze change.

That is when my students announced to me that they were going to work to get the class lists at their school integrated. It was as if tides had begun running out to sea instead of in. "You're our hero," one of them declared.

Their enthusiasm knocked the breath right out of me, first for joy and then for fear as I wondered what I had done and why. It became abundantly clear that our cultures had cross-pollinated, and I hoped I had not misrepresented my own society or raised false expectations.

For an instant I wished I could take everything back. "*You know what? I was wrong,*" I could say. "*Many things can't be helped. There are limits. Change will take longer than the years you spend in junior high school, or high school. Don't waste your youth. Do something fun. Learn how to Rollerblade. Learn how to dance.*"

But I said none of those things. Instead I smiled at them and, seeing the enthusiasm and excitement in their eyes, I wished them all the luck I could muster.

"*Gambatte,*" I said, invoking a common Japanese cheer. "Good luck. Fight on."

46

Gibbous

EVENING descended as Hideo and I sat across the table from each other in a small downstairs café. Outside, the feet of salarymen and others coming off long workdays in central Tokyo hurried toward the trains, buses and taxis that would take them away to other lives: drinking parties, homes and families, clubs, tiny apartments known as "mansions."

Below all that, the sounds were muffled as if we were under water. I picked at an ice cream sundae topped with adzuki bean paste and almost flavorless, colorless cubes of seaweed-based gelatin, and Hideo ate curry rice, Japanese-style, yellow sauce poured from foil packets over steaming-hot short-grain white rice, the plate garnished with thin coral-colored pickles.

Despite our "divorsion," Hideo and I had spoken sporadically through the spring and early summer months and had seen each other once for a mostly silent, awkward visit at my apartment, when he was on a business trip to Shuho-cho. Still, he had wanted to see me one last time, to say goodbye.

I had arrived from Yamaguchi Prefecture earlier that day. My host parents, Naoko, Sasaki-*san* and dozens of colleagues and friends had waved their farewells from the observation deck of little Ube Airport, and as the airplane taxied toward the runway and the hands and faces of my people blurred and faded, I wondered what I had done, why I had not extended my JET contract another year, why I had closed off this part of my life a year earlier than necessary.

I had not entirely left Shuho-cho behind though. Seated near me were some Dwelling Friends neighbors, a couple with two young children, their family having gone through a similar set of motions, packing belongings and saying farewell to friends and colleagues. The husband had been Hideo's supervisor, the one who warned him away from me some twenty months earlier. Now he too was being transferred to the north.

Given our history and Hideo's and my current status, it would not do for this man to see Hideo meeting me in Tokyo. So his presence set in motion a final cat-and-mouse game: After landing and saying our farewells, I watched my former Dwelling Friends neighbors walk in the opposite direction until I was quite certain they would not be back. Then I put more distance between us in my search for a payphone. I called Hideo, reaching him on his recently acquired cell phone, and he appeared almost immediately with hugs and kisses, my pending departure wiping away the memories of our painful, drawn-out breakup.

By the time we sat down at the Tokyo café, Hideo and I were in a holding pattern, my time in Japan having waned to the slimmest of crescents. Several months post-breakup but only an hour since our last kiss, it seemed we had used up every last word. I was sendoff-weary, and this was the most breathtaking goodbye of all.

I was very aware that every minute ticking past brought me closer to the next morning, when my plane would depart Japan, the place that could have become my final destination had I said yes, had I not lacked a vision of my future as an expatriate, as a *salariman*'s wife, as a *gaijin*, an outside person, forever. But there Hideo and I sat, poking at our food as the air slowly seeped out of the room.

We were waiting for my host sister Miho, with whom I would spend my final night in Japan. I wanted her to appear immediately. I wanted her never to arrive. At last, Hideo's cell phone rang. He answered in his competent, efficient bass and told Miho where we were. All too soon she burst, short-skirted, into the café and hurried over to our table, ready to expedite.

Somehow Hideo and Miho were introduced, and the three of us left the rarified coolness of the café, climbed the stairs and returned to Tokyo's pulsing streets. It was dark, but outside the late-July air was warm and sticky. Hideo waved down a taxi, and Miho said goodbye to him before sliding into the cab, quickly explaining to the driver the location of the gloomy airport hotel where we would spend the night.

I lingered, standing on the street, Hideo and I looking at each other, knowing it could be for the very last time. We hugged. We kissed. "I love you," I said. "You too," he replied.

I wiped my eyes, which were almost permanently wet those days, and when I looked back at him, his gaze was already trained down the street, away from me. "Goodbye." I followed Miho into the back seat.

The door swung shut, and all at once the taxi was rolling, the space between Hideo and me yawning wider, as if my strongest line had slipped its cleat and my craft was being yawned downstream, faster and faster to unknown waters. Even as I felt the terror of losing control and heading toward an unknown future, my throat and chest filled with the awful knowledge that I was the one who had untied the knot, and it was too late to fix what had been undone.

Miho, meanwhile, was rifling through her purse and talking at me: "I don't understand you, how you can leave someone like that. That's where we're different. You're selfish and leave people, but I'm not. I stay."

I did not know what to say to this woman who sometimes dated three men at a time, this Japanese sister of mine who had left her — our — parents and grandmother in Yamaguchi, my *onēsan* in this other-side-of-the-world family with whom I had become forever connected.

The next morning, I boarded my flight, the first leg of a last-hurrah trip I had sketched out in the hopes of blunting the pain of leaving my floating world and easing myself psychologically, culturally and physically back toward my real world, my motherland, to which it had seemed predestined I would return. My journey would lead me through the glittering Grand Palace in Bangkok and the gold-domed cathedrals and musty cave-crypts of Kyiv before landing me in Paris, where I would cross the threshold of Notre Dame Cathedral, that towering stone edifice, and stand awestruck at the magnificent holiness of the space, my heart filling with an unexpected sense of familiarity, of welcome, of hope for what was to come and faith that I was not alone on my journey.

But before I traced that path, I had to rip off the bandage and make my final physical separation from the country that had been my home for the previous two years. As my airplane lifted away from Narita Airport, I watched the tarmac, then Tokyo and finally Japan disappear from view as we headed out over open water. I sunk under the weight of my sadness, cursing my independence and my selfish nature, thinking how my life in Japan did not have to end this way. It had not had to end at all.

My only consolation was an abiding sense that my heart, like the moon, was waxing gibbous. I was going home.

Epilogue

Stitches in Time

THE longer I live, the more lightly I regard farewells. Traditional Minnesota goodbyes, the ones I grew up with, involve layers of leaving: a hint that the departure time is nearing, vague movement toward a door, hugs and handshakes, the introduction of a new topic of conversation and possible full discussion, more hugs and handshakes, opening the door, possibly closing it again to finish off the conversation, reopening the door and then a slow conversational creep toward the sidewalk, bicycles or car, waves and waves and still more waves while walking or rolling down the street.

You can expect the same drama with the same people the very next week, sometimes the very next day, as if one of the parties were preparing to sail across the sea.

But in my experience, people and habits are more apt to disappear with finality while we wash the dishes, stare at a screen, or take a moment to glance at the ceiling. Grandparents pass, colleagues leave to pursue new dreams, a child slips out of bed after a morning snuggle, silently moving on to a new stage, where starting the day with mom and dad no longer holds any appeal and never will again.

These latter leavings come like sneaker waves, which warning signs admonish us to watch for on the Washington and Oregon coast, unpredictable waves that appear without warning, engulfing whole beaches and sometimes snatching beachcombers out to sea. Truly final farewells seem to stand less on ceremony than the ones we engage in daily.

The Japanese language has an old phrase, *sayo de arunaraba*, which is translated "if it be thus" or "since it must be so." Used between two other phrases, it connects how-things-have-been to how-things-will-be.

Isn't that what we do, each time we leave each other, whether for a coffeehouse meeting, a day at work, or an international flight? In such moments we split our relationships in two, into what-has-been and what-will-be when — if — we return.

During these partings, life happens. And when we are fortunate enough to reconnect with each other, we do enter a new world, even if only new by a couple of degrees, a couple of new experiences.

That phrase, *sayo de arunaraba*, evolved into *sayonara*, a Japanese word used at leave-takings, acknowledging the parting of people as well as the leaving behind of how-things-have-been. If we are fortunate enough to return, we enter the world of how-things-are-now.

* * *

In 1996, after I left Shuho-cho and parted from Hideo on that Tokyo curb, I made my way back to the States via Bangkok, Kyiv, and Paris, a slow-motion grief march away from my life in Japan, toward the new. Soon I accepted a promising position as a university science writer in Wisconsin, where for months I immersed myself in studies of zebra mussels and trout, water quality, and Great Lakes shipwrecks, absentmindedly bowing at passersby (and sometimes, strangely, even at swaying shrubs), my reverse culture shock rearing up every time I went to the grocery store, clerks carelessly dragging my apples over scales and dropping them heavily into a sack.

My restlessness there never eased, and a couple of weeks short of my one-year work anniversary, I submitted my resignation and threw my carefully accumulated credit card miles at a ticket back to Tokyo. I felt the call of my other life. Hagi, Shuho-cho, Hideo.

Fourteen months had passed since we said farewell, but Hideo agreed to meet. At lunch in the basement of Tokyo Station, I found that how-things-were-now had changed considerably from how-things-had-been. Our tiny table seemed cluttered with the remnants of every past frustration, all stacked between us, dwarfing our bowls of curried rice — or was it fried rice? — garnished with incongruously festive red *tsukemono*, pickled vegetables. We could scarcely see around the pile of disappointments, so we poked at our bowls, commuters racing past, Hideo's mouth a straight line, his eyes looking anywhere but at me.

Hideo had always been wiser than me in some ways, and I suspect he understood, as I do now, that each meeting, each interaction, stitches lives together — the pattern of my life to the pattern of yours. An introduction, a stitch. A meeting, a row of stitches. Hours in conversation, attraction and love, rows and rows of stitches, running stitches, backstitches, feather stitches, chains of lazy daisies, until our existences are so tightly connected that teasing them apart becomes a project that can last the rest of our lives.

When we try to leave, some threads get snagged, others are left hanging, the image of our own selves becoming muddled and fuzzy, like the underside of a novice embroiderer's sampler.

Months later, haunted by that taut meeting, I wrote him a card, a down-on-my-knees apology, an explanation of why I had to leave Japan, why I had to leave him, and an explanation of my deep appreciation and affection for him. I wove in my many regrets and my emerging feelings of peace. I toiled over that message, hours at my kitchen table, flipping through stacks of dictionaries and kanji workbooks, handwriting it in my juvenile Japanese, stitching my message together in characters, the entire patch of paper representing a reckless, wild foray into the challenging vocabularies of emotions and callings, apologies and hopes as I attempted to express in Japanese what I could barely identify in my mother tongue.

He did not reply.

But when I returned to Japan a year and a half later, in 1999, to visit my host family and my friends in Shuho-cho, I contacted Hideo, and he agreed, again, to meet for lunch.

Back at a shared table, I learned he was still with the cement company, still living in Tokyo, still riding his mountain bike. Hideo's life seemed the picture of stability, at least the parts he shared with me.

I told him about the long hours I spent covering meetings and breaking news, learning to write faster and faster as I honed my skills as a newspaper reporter, as I began to understand what it meant to commit to a company, to sacrifice time and relationships for a career.

This was nothing like our previous funereal meal. It felt lighter, our mood so convivial — friendly, not romantic — that I couldn't resist inviting him to the dinner party I would be attending several days later at the apartment of friends — two couples and me. *Would it be odd? Too couple-ish?* I wondered. But he agreed to join us, happy, it appeared, to be asked.

* * *

It seemed unnecessary to share with Hideo that I was seeing someone new, a man I had actually met years earlier, before I met Hideo in Shuho-cho, before I met and married my first husband. I'd encountered this Minnesota man, Jon, in 1991, just a few months after the college trip where I had fallen a second time for Ryota, my high school baseball player-turned university student, and parted from him, returning home to finish college.

The stitches Ryota had made in my young life had distracted me — in high school I had let him embroider the moon on my heart, too young to imagine how those stitches would anchor me in thoughts of him. How could I have foreseen that forever afterward the moon would be his motif, bringing him to mind whether embroidered over a vast ocean, still lake, glowing harvest fields, or through pine boughs and my bedroom window, at home, abroad, and everywhere in between?

In part due to Ryota's strange omnipresence, when I first encountered Jon, I hardly noticed the tan young man wearing a Gilligan hat and macramé necklace, despite our work teaching Japanese together at a small summer camp. During our free times, Jon sauntered off with a fishing rod — that much I did notice — while I dreamed of how I might return to Ryota in Japan.

Not long after camp ended, I met another man and fell into the type of relationship where you lean hard on your sewing machine's foot pedal, zigzagging furiously past any reasonable discernment process, which knotted us in a poorly fashioned marriage that I soon ripped seam from seam, setting my face toward Shuho-cho.

Seven years after Jon's and my paths first crossed, mutual friends introduced us, noting we shared a love for Japan, where he also had spent two years, developed a life, left a love. "I already know you," I told him at what was supposed to be our first meeting. But this time I noticed him. Some months later, we began dating, cautiously stitching our lives together with fishing trips, dinners out and jogs through my tree-lined neighborhood. Fishbone stitch, running stitch.

* * *

A happy meeting with Hideo was one of my goals for that second trip back to Japan.

Another was to track down some Hanae Mori china for my parents. Someone had given them a set of the designer's plates, decorated with butterflies on a white background, but these dishes bugged my mother because there were five of them, as that is the count by which plates are sold in Japan. Her North American sensibilities longed for six or eight or ten.

While in Japan, I called the Hanae Mori information line and learned I might find these plates at a certain department store in the Tokyo area ... the store where Ryota, the moon-man, had been working at the time of our New Year's non-meeting nearly five years earlier, when my host sister set me up for coffee with him and his pregnant wife, and they had bowed out at the last moment.

I thanked the phone rep and decided that my mother's dinnerware quandary did not merit a trip to Ryota's store, no matter how unlikely it was that he would still work there, much less frequent the china department. I had no reason to tug on that thread.

But some days later, while touring with newlywed friends in the Tokyo area, we walked past that very store, Ryota's store, the Hanae Mori store, and my gut leaped. Of all the streets and stores in Japan.

Deciding it was too much of a coincidence not to go in and inquire about those plates — just the plates — I told my friends I needed to run an errand. We entered and rambled about, and found the china department, where I asked about butterfly plates, and the woman behind the counter apologized that there were none in stock. We bowed and thanked each other anyway.

Browsing the shelves, I confided a brief version of my unlikely connection to the store. My friend's husband pressed me: *Why would you not take this opportunity to say hello to an old friend?*

I hesitated and stalled, but his question stuck. *Why would I not?* I bought a set of wind chimes, a fish swimming over a rock, for my new boyfriend. I stalled some more, picking at those moon-white stitches that had perforated my heart.

Finally, I returned to my new acquaintance at the china counter and asked her if she happened to know Ryota. She consulted her counter partner and no, they did not, *but let us look at the staff directory, oh, here, hmmm, just a moment please*, and she picked up her company phone, and as I calculated the awkwardness of what could happen next, she greeted someone on her receiver and handed it to me with a nod.

"*Moshi-moshi?*" I said.

There was the briefest of pauses.

"*Sah-lah?*"

* * *

At the dinner party a couple of hours later, Hideo and I and the two other couples crowded around a small table, eating and drinking, laughing and reminiscing in a mix of Japanese and English about times, places, and situations gone by, when five of us lived in far-away Yamaguchi.

The dinner party had begun just hours after Ryota answered his company phone and, after hearing me speak four syllables, stated my name. I told him I was going home to Minnesota the next day. He asked me to call him after work that evening.

During the dinner party, I excused myself and crept into a tiny room on the other side of the wall from Hideo and our friends, where I huddled over a phone carefully explaining to Ryota that I could not meet up with him just then.

When I returned, Hideo looked at me with mild curiosity but neither asked what I was up to nor appeared concerned. We had evolved a new sense of ourselves and were gaining strength in our relationship as two singles who had no need to discuss current statuses or whether we had new partners on opposite sides of the ocean (or old love interests right there in Tokyo). We had unknotted our love story and plucked out enough threads to loosen our bond and reclaim our initial friendship, or at least some version of it.

When Hideo left the party that night, I walked him out and down the street toward the station, where he would board a train taking him to his apartment, a building I had never seen, on the far side of the city. My heart twinged with the familiarity of yet another goodbye. Of course I too was nearly on my way, preparing to return to the far side of the world and the life-in-progress that awaited me there. Our newest version of how-things-are-now.

We paused on the empty sidewalk. We declared our everlasting friendship. (We really did.) We hugged farewell.

Absolution.

Joy.

* * *

The next morning, I saw Ryota, my moon-man, before he saw me.

He had insisted on meeting me at the station near my friends' home and riding the bus with me to the airport. I knew that seeing him, his wife unaware, put me on shaky ethical ground, but after he had chosen to marry that other woman and had stood me up in Tokyo four and a half years earlier, I wanted a chance to say hello. And goodbye. A small, ugly human part of me wanted him to wonder what he had missed.

It would have been easier had I ripped the moon out of the design of my life years earlier — snipped those threads, plucked them out, gathered them into a little pile and blown them away. But his moon had been part of my life for so long that it seemed removing those threads would leave holes, the moon's absence becoming obvious, like the new moon reminding me of that glowing sphere's next coming.

When he rushed into the waiting area, I saw he had developed the well-fed physique of a married man. A dad. But when he turned and met my gaze, he smiled from that same kind face with those enthusiastic eyes, that broad ingenuous smile, and my friend who had delivered me to the station faded away — did I even say goodbye?

Ryota and I boarded the short airport bus like a couple of high school rowdies, prowling all the way to the back seat, where we began to catch up, rapid-fire, on all that had happened to each of us in the previous eight years. He told me he was sorry about my divorce, I told him that his photo had kept my spirits up; he told me his mother still talked about me, I told him to greet her for me; he told me that he knew right away it was my voice on his work phone. I wonder if I told him that I still thought of him nearly every time I saw the blasted moon. We laughed with amazement at being together.

Before I passed through airport security that day, we shared a bowl of *an-mitsu*, cubes of seaweed gelatin, sweet bean paste and fruit, and he left me for a few interminable minutes, returning with a CD purchased from a gift shop, telling me to listen to the seventh track when I got home.

Ryota said that someday he would tell his wife about our meeting, and maybe in the future we could all get together. Perhaps if I ever had daughters, they could meet his sons. Or maybe we would see each other again when we grew old and romance would be the furthest thing from our minds. (Is it ever?) My tears flowed for whatever it was we had lost and could never regain, for what we never actually had — our time together was always so short, our stitches few but complicated, our threads knotted. He kissed my cheek, held me long and close, and we said goodbye.

Satin stitches, French knots, rosettes.

I passed through security and began making my way toward the gate, slowly, turning back to wave. Again and again.

Farewell.

* * *

The moon-man and the man who would become my second husband bookended the last flight I took home from Japan as a single
woman. One oversaw my departure, the other my arrival.

The handoff was not clean. Pieces of the moon-man stuck to my
heart like lint to black muslin. The email he sent soon afterward
showed I had stuck to him as well: After I left him at the security
gate, he had gone up to the airport roof and waited there, watching
airplanes take off, one by one, until he was sure he had seen mine
lift into the afternoon sky and head eastward. I brought my fuzzy
heart home, determining on the flight that when I reached my home
airport in Fargo, North Dakota, I would step back into what was
real: my healthy, happy life on the American Great Plains.

I would diminish Ryota-the-man into Ryota-the-memory, ripping
out some stitches, embroidering over and around others.

I had already begun creating a new design.

* * *

Less than an hour after I dragged my suitcase and my tired self
into my apartment back home, the doorbell rang with a special
delivery: an enormous fruit basket from Jon, my boyfriend of less
than two months.

I had already listened to the seventh track of Ryota's CD, the
song "Hana" ("Flowers"), which unbeknownst to him had struck a
chord in me around the time I had learned of his marriage:

Kawa wa nagarete doko doko yukuno
Hito mo nagarete doko doko yukuno
Sonna nagare ga tsuku koroni wa
Hana to shite hana to shite sakasete agetai

Naki nasai warai nasai
itsu no hi ka itsu no hi ka
hana wo sakaso yo ...

Where are the rivers flowing?
And the people, where are they headed?
When they reach their destinations,
I want them to bloom as flowers, as flowers.

Cry if you like, laugh if you like
Someday, someday
Let's bloom like flowers ...

The song pairs things that flow, rivers and people, tears and love. It tells the listener to go ahead and laugh, go ahead and cry, but know that someday, someday, our flowers will bloom.

The song played in my head as my arms cradled a basket heavy with pears, oranges, bananas, and grapes — all ripe, wholesome nutrition. The gifts, the whiplash of moving among three loves, and the jet lag made me laugh and cry all at once, telephoning my mother across town to tell her and my father hello from Hideo and to ask whether it was wrong to listen to one man's CD while eating another man's fruit and what I should do next.

* * *

He of the fruit basket steadily gained my trust and won my heart as we decorated our lives with fishing trips ... cross-country ski outings ... traveling to meet my far-flung grandparents ... long walks, flowers, and dinner dates. About a year after my return from Japan, he invited me on a quintessential Minnesota excursion, a camping trip that took us to the headwaters of the Mississippi River. There he kneeled on a sandy path, held out a glimmering ring and asked me to stay with him forever. I told him I would love to.

We married four months later, surrounded by family and hearty friends who turned out despite a storm of swirling, drifting snow, our church a sweet-scented refuge filled with pine trees and boughs installed for the coming Christmas celebrations. Late that night, we boarded a train for our honeymoon in western Montana, presaging the trajectory of our life together. Less than a year later, we retraced those steps, this time by car and moving van, to Washington State, where we furthered our education and careers, spent weekends camping and fishing, going to movies, and hiking.

Together we traveled back to Japan to visit his people and mine, including my one-time boss, Kashima-*kacho* and his koto-playing wife, Naoko's parents, who invited us to stay at their century-old farmhouse in Shuho-cho. Waking up there, in a futon laid out on the tatami-mat floor, closed off from the rest of the house by softly sliding paper doors, I looked over at my sleeping husband, blond hair tousled, skin glowing in the gathering warmth of that early summer morning, and marveled at what a difference a few years can make, how the ambiguities of life come clear, and how unexpectedly we find the places and people with whom we belong, how we create memories and motifs that creep all the way to the edge, where we reinforce them, binding the edges. Blanket stitch.

Later that day, I wandered alone, back to the Sumitomo apartment building, whose key to unit 202 used to clink against the others on my chain. I encountered the *obasan* who had been so kind to Hideo and me, she, catching sight of me, exclaiming — "*Mah!*" — and throwing aside her work to grab my hands in hers, soft and strong, rubbing my arms as I might the neck of my lost dog after he sniffed his way home. I told her about my husband. I told her I was in still in touch with Hideo. I told her that my husband's heart was similar to Hideo's.

What a strange thing to say, I thought afterward. *What a strange thing to think.*

But, at the same time, not untrue.

There is no comparing two people, two loves, but I have indeed run across a handful in this life for whom I have a special affinity, as if they have been dyed with similar patterns — they are, as we say, cut from the same cloth, one that challenges me to evolve while wrapping me in a particular brand of comfort. The pattern of Jon and Hideo includes loyalty and kindness, self-sacrifice and honesty. Connecting with each of them has made me a better human.

* * *

Jon and I were a few years married when we took a camping trip to the Upper Columbia River, in northeastern Washington. One evening, standing on shore, threading his fishing line in and out of the inky, fast-moving water, dreaming of giant sturgeon, Jon suddenly called back to where I was standing, feeling slightly suspicious of big water's power at dusk, and startled me away from noticing the moon.

It was shining particularly brightly that evening and reminded me of being seventeen and thinking myself in love, half my life and half the world away, when a different man, a boy, pointed at that very same moon and suggested we could think of one another when we looked at it, he in Japan, I in Minnesota. How-things-were-before.

"The moon!" said my husband. And I looked at him, and I looked at the moon, and I realized, *yes, there it is, and here he is, and here we are each day creating our own design with that very moon and the stars and everything else.*

How-things-are-now.

* * *

Twenty-one years have passed since the last time I went to Japan as a single woman, and twenty years since I married my fisherman.

Jon and I are settled in western Washington, where he works in management for a homebuilder and fishes for the salmon that return from the ocean and swim up the Columbia River toward the spawning grounds where they got their start. I do advocacy and public relations work — largely writing — and have collaborated with citizens groups, school districts, and businesses, exploring a wide array of topics and concerns.

When we arrived here, in 2005, I had the good fortune to find a koto *sensei* nearby, a woman from Japan who spoke little English despite living in the States for forty years, and for a decade I infiltrated her koto group, which consisted primarily of older *issei* and *nisei* women. We practiced and performed, met for lunch and visited, mostly in Japanese, and this *sensei* convinced me to work toward certification in the Seiha school of koto. I reached level four — just short of becoming a teacher — before she retired and moved away. Now I have a room that houses two koto, stacks of koto music, and my dream that I will someday return to it all again.

The biggest influence on how-things-are-now arrived in 2008, when after a good run of freedom and opportunity, Jon and I traded it all for the chance to become parents to our son, whom we adopted from India. This child presented us with an overflowing basket of opportunities to look beyond ourselves and see this world anew. Simply put, he clipped our wings, which is what it took to truly engage us in this process of parenting that is forever opening our eyes and expanding our hearts.

We live in the city, where the stars are obscured by streetlights, but the moon shines clearly enough, and it sometimes causes me to think back to the camping trip early in our marriage when Jon broke into my reverie to share the beauty of that shining orb.

All these years later, here's what I believe to be the truth: Love is like the oversized sturgeon he hooked into that night, an ancient fish threading its way just below the river's roiling surface, swallowing the bait we dangle and in an instant emptying an entire spool, your heart gone forever on a journey you never could have dreamed.

If it be thus.

Acknowledgements

From my perspective, it takes a village to write a book. Here are some of the many, many people who have helped me get this story between two covers:

- Bill Babcock, my M.A. adviser at the University of Minnesota, who suggested I turn my final project into a book.
- Nancy Roberts, another professor at the University of Minnesota, who introduced me to writing creative nonfiction/literary journalism.
- Natalie Kusz, my M.F.A. adviser at Eastern Washington University and author of *Road Song*, who pushed me to find the story within the story.
- John Sibley Williams, my indomitable and enthusiastic literary agent, and author of *As One Fire Consumes Another* and other collections.
- Zeitgeist Writers League of Portland—Teresa Coates, Michele Coppola, Carolann Curthoys, Maureen Reed, Steve Villain, and Natalie Wood—who carefully read drafts and asked insightful questions that helped this book evolve.
- Rich Skalstad of Colonus Publishing—and fellow EWU alum—who encouraged me to continue working on my stalled-out manuscript.

- David Kopp, vp, executive editor of Crown Publishing, Penguin Random House, whom I met on an airplane on the way to interview for a job I did not get. He helped me recognize how essential faith is to my story—then and now.

- Sarah Barbour, owner of Aeroplane Media, who lived part of this experience with me in Japan, where we formed the Yamaguchi Writers Group, and provided later feedback.

- Email workshopping partners Kerstin March, fellow St. Olaf College alum—Um Yah Yah!—and author of *Family Trees* and *Branching Out*, and Brenda Y. Yun, whom I met when we got locked in a stairwell at an AWP conference.

- Christi Krug and the Wildfire Writers Group of Vancouver, Washington.

- Steve Swanson, English professor at St. Olaf College, in whose creative writing class I landed in my senior year, as my path was shifting from biology to writing.

- Friends who have provided feedback and literary encouragement, including Andria Villanueva, who insisted the story deserved more romance; Karen Babine, author of *Water and What We Know* and *All the Wild Hungers*, and fellow EWU alum; Susan Parrish, who blogs at *Paddling Her Own Canoe;* Erin Hemme Froslie of Whistle Editorial; and Linda Nixon for a key assist on the cover blurb.

- Tom Hunt, my PR mentor, who offered me space and time for writing, even as we waged other battles.

- Barbara Livdahl, Joyce Wallman, and Cindy Lerfald, English teachers and encouragers at Oak Grove Lutheran High School.

- Alice Underbakke, my high school guidance counselor, who helped send me to Japan in the first place.

- Camphor Press, who found *The Same Moon* and made it shine brighter the second time around. Many, many thanks to John Ross, Michael Cannings and Mark Swofford!

My heartfelt thanks to each of you and to the many others who have helped me along the way.

I'd also like to express my deep gratitude to readers of the first edition who offered their encouragement—and some helpful suggestions—and to the special few who shared their own "same moon" stories with me. ♥

About the Author

Sarah Coomber has three hometowns: Moorhead, Minnesota—where she grew up; Vancouver, Washington—where she lives now; and Hagi-shi, Yamaguchi-ken—where at age sixteen she spent a summer with the Maeda family. They treated her like their third daughter and welcomed her into an on-again, off-again Japanese life.

That life has included summers sharing Japanese language and dance with children at an immersion camp in Minnesota, where she was known by the Japanese name "Michi"; teaching English in Yamaguchi-ken; and studying the koto—Japanese zither—in Yamaguchi and Portland, Oregon, where she achieved her level four Seiha School certification.

After working as a reporter, science writer, college English teacher and public relations professional, Sarah now works as a writing/communications consultant and teaches Holy Yoga, exploring the nexus of yoga and the Christian faith. She lives ... and tries to remember to breathe deeply ... with her family in Vancouver, where the topography, climate and people's temperaments remind her of her hometown on the other side of the ocean.

She is online at www.sarahcoomber.com.